Sport SCUBA Diving

In Depth

SECOND EDITION

Sport SCUBA Diving

In Depth
SECOND EDITION

An Introduction to Basic Scuba Instruction and Beyond

TOM GRIFFITHS, Ed.D.

Affiliate Associate Professor and Director of Aquatics
McCoy Natatorium
The Pennsylvania State University

PRINCETON BOOK COMPANY, PUBLISHERS
PRINCETON, NEW JERSEY

To Roni, Kendra, and Rachel

Princeton Book Company, Publishers
POB 57
Pennington, NJ 08534

Advisory Editor: James H. Humphrey, University of Maryland

Interior design by Anne O'Donnell after a design by
Design and Illustration
Cover design by Anne O'Donnell

Library of Congress Catalog Card Number 83-06310
ISBN 0-916622-85-1

Contents

PART III: Beyond the Basics

List of Numbered Sections

List of Figures

Acknowledgments

Many thanks to James Humphrey, Ed.D., for sowing the seed which made this book grow. Thanks also to Arthur Bachrach, Ph.D., of the Naval Research Institute, and Charles W. Schilling, M.D., of the Undersea Medical Society, both located in Bethesda, Maryland, whose works on military and commerical divers stimulated me to examine sport divers.

I would also like to thank Kevin McGettigan and Allen Mincer for their technical assistance with Part I.

Warm appreciation is extended to Rosemary Matthias of the Undersea Medical Society for providing me with countless references and additional sources.

Thanks also to Charles Woodford of Princeton Book Company for providing me with the opportunity to write this book.

Special thanks to David McCormick for his illustrations, Mike Oakes for his photographs, and Dynamo Dive Shop for providing subject matter to photograph. Paul Tzimoulis and Geri Murphy of *Skin Diver Magazine* also provided me with an abundance of great photographs.

I also wish to thank Anne R.C. Alexander, Jim Corry, Karl E. Huggins, Dennis Graver, Sid Ragona, and John Zumbado for their valuable contributions to the second edition.

Thanks to Reverend Bob Bridge for his help and expertise with the "Bubbleography" and other references.

Lastly, a special thanks to Katherine Grimes, whose meticulous editing and quick wit gave special meaning to this endeavor.

Preface

You are about to become one of the more than 250,000 people who learn how to scuba dive each year. You will be happy to discover that scuba divers come in a variety of ages, shapes, sizes, and colors. You don't have to be a gifted athlete or a great swimmer to become a diver —the proper attitude is the key ingredient. Scuba divers are not a bunch of daredevil risk takers. While as a scuba diver you may sometimes be challenged, you'll learn to avoid risky situations. Like driving a car or flying a plane, you'll find that scuba diving is fun and safe, when approached intelligently.

Why did you decide to become a scuba diver? Perhaps you heard that diving is an exciting, adventuresome, and beautiful activity. Some say that diving is the most breathtaking thing they have ever done. Whatever your reasons for choosing scuba diving, the discovery is quickly made that diving is fun. Scuba diving is a unique form of entertainment, and the common thread binding scuba divers is the thrill that they share on dive trips. While diving can be serious at times, there will no doubt be many laughter-filled moments in store. It is difficult to describe this aspect of diving, but any diver will tell you that the delight of diving cannot be described—it must be experienced.

When you enroll in a certified course of instruction, your total being must enter the class; not just your brains and your muscles but also your attitudes, expectations, and personality. For scuba instruction to be effective, it must be fun, but it must also provide you with information, develop proper attitudes, and teach you physical skins. Educators label these three general areas as learning domains (cognitive, affective, and psychomotor). While your scuba diving instructor is primarily responsible for providing you with fun and safety, this book supplements his or her efforts. Some scuba manuals are very technical and others are extremely practical; this text attempts to provide both technical and practical information while also adding the interesting psychological aspects of diving. You might say that it addresses scuba diving as both an art and a science, blending technical, psychological, and practical aspects. Although this text is designed as a serious and comprehensive treatment of the sport for college-level scuba diving courses, it should serve as an excellent resource for all.

I hope this book will help you to become a certified scuba diver. Think of your "C" card as a passport, ticket, or key to a treasure of underwater adventures. There are several different levels of certification cards available from a variety of organizations. A basic or beginning diver rating is available to students after completing approximately 30 hours of swimming pool and classroom instruction followed by at least five or six supervised open water dives. Some students may elect to enroll in a rescue diver course, which is a prerequisite for many advanced and leadership classes. This is an excellent idea. The certification progression then leads to an advanced diver rating, specialty ratings, and leadership ratings. All of these certification cards may be obtained through the following organizations: the National Association of Underwater Instructors, the national YMCA, the Professional Association of Diving Instructors, and the National Association of Skin Diving Schools. This book provides you with all the facts, figures, and theory needed to acquire any type of basic scuba or open-water certification card. It should be used in conjunction with a fully accredited course of instruction.

The diving opportunities available to a certified diver will arouse your imagination. Feeding 50-pound groupers, riding dolphins, exploring ancient shipwrecks, and relishing enchanted night dives are just a few of the wonderful experiences available to you.

Good Luck!

Tom Griffiths

PART I

The Basics

Introduction

This part of the book presents the basic information you will need to know in order to become an educated scuba diver. You might say that Part I deals with the science and "stuff" of scuba diving. You should enjoy reading about all the remarkable equipment you'll be using; how being submersed in water affects pressure, temperature, color, and buoyancy; the marine life you may encounter; how the ocean moves and works; and how your physiology is affected underwater. Just about every scuba diving course includes information from these first four chapters.

Chapter 1

~~~~~~

Equipment and Basic Skills

Your first step in becoming a proficient scuba diver is to be introduced to the equipment you will be using. It is important for you to become familiar with each item, learn how to wear it properly, and know how it works. After reading this chapter, I strongly urge you to visit your local dive shop, where an equipment specialist can give you a "hands-on" introduction to the equipment and answer all your questions regarding it.

The sport of scuba diving really began in 1943 with Emile Gagnan and Jacques Cousteau's invention of the Aqua-lung. Amazing improvements in equipment design have been made since the inception of the sport. Today's equipment and accessories take the work out of diving and ultimately make diving much easier and safer for you.

You don't have to be mechanically inclined to understand the equipment and how it works. Scuba gear is deceptively simple to understand. Moreover, the equipment you will be using is streamlined in design and quite colorful and attractive; it is not as bulky as it once was and it is no longer all silver and black.

1.1   Basic Skin Diving Equipment

Skin diving is the art of diving underwater with the aid of masks, fins, and snorkel, but without assistance of an additional air supply (in other words, while holding one's breath). Skin diving equipment should include the following items: facemask, fins, snorkel, weight belt, and *buoyancy control device (B.C.D.)*. Nearly all skin divers wear masks, fins, and snorkels, but few wear the weight belt or B.C.D. Nevertheless, the weight belt and B.C.D. are included here because they prove to be valuable in helping the skin divers to control buoyancy, rest on the surface when fatigued, and rescue themselves by providing immediate positive buoyancy in emergencies.

1.1.1 MASK

Mask Features

There are many different types, shapes, and sizes of masks on the market today. Four underlying characteristics should be kept in mind when selecting a mask: fit, safety, comfort, and vision. Too many optional features built into a mask often hinder, rather than help,

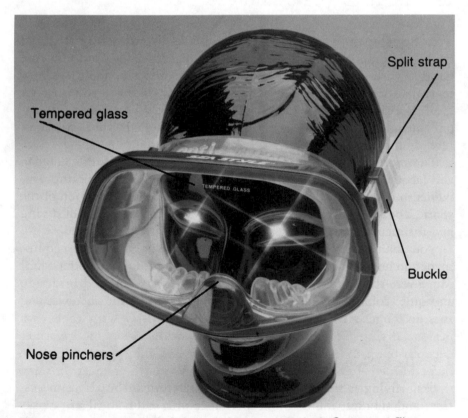

Figure 1-1. Basic mask features. (Courtesy Wenoka® SeaStyle™)

Figure 1-2. Optional mask features. (Photo by Bill Hughes)

diver performance and make selecting the right mask a perplexing challenge. However, the following features should be considered standard (see Figure 1-1): (1) tempered, hardened, or treated glass (not plastic) printed on the faceplate; (2) a firm retaining rim or band, made of metal or hardened plastic, which holds the glass securely in the rubber mask to prevent it from falling out; (3) a mask headstrap, which is divided into two separate straps where it rests on the back of the diver's head, to provide better fit and stability; and (4) strong buckles securing the straps to the mask. The buckles should allow for easy adjustment of the straps but should not slip or pull out. Most divers prefer a mask which maximizes vision and does not hold much water when flooded.

Many additional features (see Figure 1-2) may be found on masks, and divers must match the optional mask features with their own personal diving needs. Choosing the right combination of mask features depends upon individual diver preferences and the type of diving to be performed. Certain optional mask features may be a must for some divers, while other mask features may be considered totally unnecessary. A good idea would be to experiment with several different masks in the pool before deciding on one specific model.

Equalizer (Stabilizer) Masks: Many masks have either finger spaces or nose pockets to allow the diver to squeeze the nostrils shut while equalizing the pressure in the middle ear. Many divers, especially those troubled by the equalization process, require this feature to equalize easily and efficiently. A slight problem associated with this feature is that a low spot in the mask is created by the finger or nose pockets, which tends to trap small amounts of water. This can prove annoying at first, but most divers overcome this small disadvantage. When selecting an equalizer type of mask, one must be certain the pockets are large enough to allow the fingers to pinch the nose while wearing wet suit gloves.

Purge Valves: Purge valves are one-way valves located on either the lower border of the faceplate in front of the diver's nose or directly under the diver's nose mounted in the rubber mask skirt. This feature is designed to aid the diver in clearing water from the mask without using the traditional tilt method of clearing (see p. 9). The one-way valve enables the diver to push water out of the mask by simply exhaling through the nose, without allowing water to reenter the mask. With this feature, the diver is not required to manipulate the head or mask to empty water from it. The purge valve, however, may malfunction if not maintained properly. The rubber diaphragm located in the valve must be kept free of sand and salt, and must not be allowed to warp or dry out. If not cared for, the valve can easily degenerate to the point of becoming a two-way valve, allowing water to enter as well as exit the mask.

Low Volume Masks: A popular mask with today's divers, the low volume mask fits closely to the face and, as a result, holds only a small volume of air. Consequently, when the mask fills with water, little air and energy are required to remove it. This mask is particularly beneficial for diving students in that it significantly improves their ability to clear the mask, which is perhaps the most basic and important skin and scuba diving skill.

Wide Angle Masks: The wide angle or "wraparound" mask usually has two side panels or windows in addition to the frontal faceplate. This mask is designed to increase the diver's peripheral vision. Having a larger volume, this mask requires more air and energy to clear it of water. Also, a degree of visual distortion occurs when the diver's line of sight travels from one glass panel to the next. This mask is preferred by scuba divers rather than skin divers, and by experienced rather than novice divers.

Masks with Corrective Lenses: Many different options are available to the diver with poor eyesight. Prescription lenses may be ground into the faceplate, glued on the faceplate, or mounted in special frames inside the mask. Although good eyesight is restored, enhancing diving safety and pleasure, the expense of this costly mask might not be practical for those with mildly poor vision. Also, because there is a 25 percent magnification underwater, divers with slight visual problems may not need prescription lenses underwater. Divers with extremely weak eyes might, however, consider this mask a necessity. If care is taken not to lose them, contact lenses may be worn safely in the water. Wearing contact lenses is *not* recommended for students or inexperienced divers until they can clear the mask easily after unexpected flooding. If contact lenses fall out of the eyes with the mask on, chances are the lenses will either be flushed into the water when the mask is cleared or fall out of the mask when it is removed from the diver's face on land. Wearing contact lenses while performing deep diving may retard gas exchange in the eye.

Figure 1-3. Optical system mask by Mares. (Courtesy SeaQuest, Inc.)

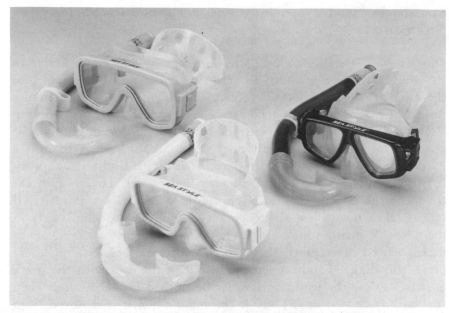

Figure 1-4. Silicone mask. (Courtesy Wenoka® SeaStyle™)

Another new mask on the market allows the diver with poor vision to purchase the basic mask and then select from many interchangeable lenses of different prescriptions to improve their vision (Figure 1-3).

Silicone Masks: Diving masks do not necessarily have to be made solely of rubber. The new, clear silicone mask (Figure 1-4) is more resistant to deterioration and also allows light to enter through the clear sides, thus aiding peripheral vision. This mask may also be worn by divers who are allergic to rubber.

Fitting the Mask

A simple technique is used to find the proper mask fit. First, the mask is placed on the face *without* the straps in place. The diver then inhales through the nose gently. If the mask makes an air-tight seal around the face, it will remain in place as long as the diver is inhaling. If the mask does not remain in place while following this procedure, it does not fit properly. Regardless of how tight the diver adjusts the straps, the mask will not keep water out, and another mask should be found.

CAUTION: If the mask, when removed, leaves a black ring around the diver's face, this means the rubber is deteriorating, and a new mask should be found.

Donning the Mask

To prevent the mask from fogging up underwater, the diver should keep the mask clean at all times. Mild liquid detergents or toothpaste may accomplish this, and antifogging solutions available in dive shops also work well. After cleaning the mask and before donning it, the diver should spit saliva on the inside of the faceplate, rub it on the glass, and then rinse the glass off. This prevents condensation from forming on the glass.

Whenever placing the mask on the face, the diver should first brush the hair back from the forehead. Wetting the hair, face, and mask before donning the faceplate helps create a better seal. After making these preparations, the mask should then be placed on the face. While the mask is held in place with one hand, the other hand may be used to pull the mask straps over the head and position them on the back of the neck. Spreading the straps apart when positioning them will help the mask to fit evenly on the face and will prevent the straps from slipping. Leaky masks are often caused by the diver hurriedly donning the mask without following the proper procedures.

Clearing the Mask

Mask clearing is a simple skill to perform, but it does require *breath control* and *relaxation*. Divers must learn to clear the mask in case it accidentally floods (fortunately, this does not happen often). The diver should follow three steps while exhaling slightly to clear the mask efficiently (see Figure 1-5):

1. Look Up—When the mask floods with water, the diver should look toward the surface at approximately a 45-degree angle, allowing the water to collect at the bottom of the mask.

2. Press the Top—While looking toward the surface, the diver gently presses the upper border of the mask against the forehead. This action strengthens the top seal and retains the air needed to displace the water.

3. Exhale—The diver, gently exhaling through the nose, fills the mask fully with air which displaces the water. As the air enters the mask, it will rise but will not escape because the top seal is pressed against the forehead.

This mask-clearing procedure, commonly referred to as the tilt method, works best when the diver is in the vertical position. If the

Figure 1-5. Tilt method of mask clearing. (Photo by Michael Oakes)

mask must be cleared while swimming in the horizontal position, the same steps are followed but the head should be rotated to the *side* in step 1, and the highest *corner* of the mask pressed firmly against the temple in step 2.

NOTE: Clearing a mask with a large purge valve necessitates that the diver look down, not up, at a 45-degree angle, with the entire mask being pressed against the face during exhalation.

1.1.2 FINS

Types of Fins

Like masks, fins are available in many varieties, but only the two major categories into which most fins fall will be discussed here. One category is the adjustable-strap or open-heel fin; the other is the full-foot or closed-heel fin. Both types of fins are illustrated in Figure 1-6.

There are advantages and disadvantages associated with each design. Of course, no one fin is perfect for all diving conditions. Again, fit and comfort, along with purpose, should be considered when selecting fins. Whenever possible, the diver should use different types of fins in the pool before making a final decision.

Adjustable-Strap/Open-Heel Fin: Divers usually refer to the adjustable-strap or open-heel fin as an all-purpose or scuba diving fin. Advantages include the following: (1) a large blade, which produces greater propulsion; (2) a flow-through design, which minimizes resistance; (3) an adjustable strap, which allows the fin to be worn on different-sized feet in a variety of conditions; and (4) the ability to easily and inexpensively replace the adjustable strap if it is broken.

Although this fin is popular, it has some disadvantages. First, the fin is large and bulky. Although most scuba divers need the extra propulsion these fins offer, they may cause fatigue and leg cramps among divers of smaller physical stature or who use an improper kick. Second, the fin may be uncomfortable for some divers. Because the fin is designed so that "one size fits all," it does not fit all divers perfectly. Third, the fin requires the diver to wear boots in order to protect the bottoms of the feet and to prevent blisters.

Full-Foot/Closed-Heel Fin: The full-foot or closed-heel fin has a smaller, more flexible blade than the open-heel fin. As a result, this fin moves less water, which in turn places less stress on the leg muscles. This type of fin is often referred to as a skin diving fin, or flipper. The full-foot fin is preferred by many small-sized divers; it provides a snug, comfortable fit. Two disadvantages are associated with the use of the full-foot fin. First, divers do not normally wear wet suit boots with the full-foot fin. If this fin is usually worn on the bare foot in warm water, it simply will not fit the same foot when wet suit boots are

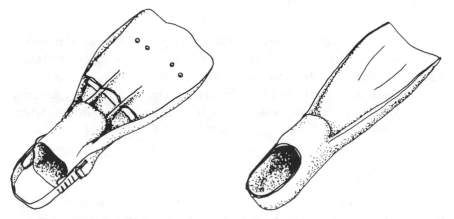

Figure 1-6. Adjustable-strap/open-heel fin (left)
and full-foot/closed-heel fin.

Figure 1-7. *How* not *to walk with fins.*

required in cold water. If this fin is desired by the diver for both warm and cold water dives, it may be advisable to wear boots under larger sized full-foot fins. In this case, boots would always be required, regardless of water temperatures. Second, if the foot pocket tears, the fin can no longer be worn and cannot be repaired. By contrast, when the adjustable strap breaks on the open-heel fin, *only* the strap need be replaced.

Donning the Fins

Whenever possible, wet suit boots should be worn with fins to prevent blisters and chafing. Placing the fins on the feet becomes easier when both boots and feet are wet. After the feet have been inserted into the foot pockets, the toes should be pushed as far forward as possible, and then the strap or heel pocket may be pulled into place.

CAUTION: Divers should not walk forward with fins; this may cause the diver to trip and fall. If fins must be worn on dry land, walking sideways or backwards is recommended, with a shuffling rather than a lifting action of the feet (see Figure 1-7).

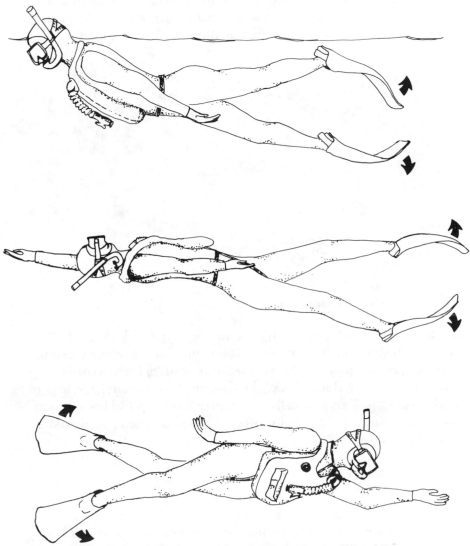

Figure 1-8. Flutter kick: (A) *on front,* (B) *on back,* (C) *on side.*

Kicking with Fins

The basic kick employed during both skin and scuba diving is the flutter kick. The main advantage gained when using this kick is constant propulsion coupled with avoidance of lags and glides. The flutter kick is an alternating leg action using the entire leg, and should be initiated at the hip. Slight bending at both the knee and ankle is necessary. A wide spread of the legs is recommended during this kick while keeping the fins under the surface of the water. The arms usually remain at the sides of the diver to minimize resistance. Another advantage of the flutter kick is that the alternating leg action may be used in the front, back, or side position as illustrated in Figure 1-8.

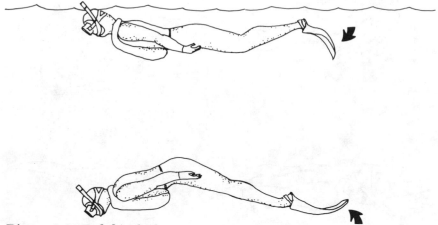

Figure 1-9. Dolphin kick.

The dolphin kick (Figure 1-9) is another type of kick used while diving. This kick offers more propulsion, but requires more coordination to learn and more exertion to perform. Unlike the alternating leg action used in the flutter kick, the dolphin kick requires the legs to work in unison. This kick calls for slightly more hip and knee flexion. Again, the fins should remain in the water, and the arms should be held at the sides.

1.1.3 SNORKELS

Snorkel Features

A snorkel allows the diver to breathe on the surface with a minimum of effort while keeping the face submerged. There are many different

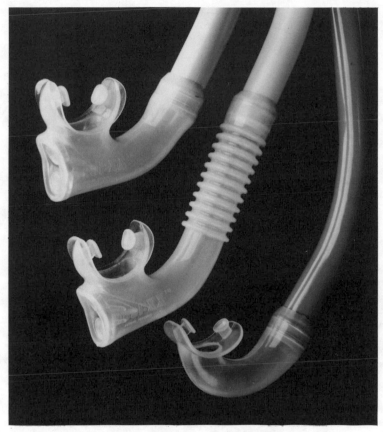

Figure 1-10. Basic snorkel. (Courtesy Wenoka® SeaStyle™)

styles of snorkel available, but one should choose a design which is smooth and simple for easy breathing. A snorkel should have the following characteristics (see Figure 1-10): (1) a smooth tube approximately 12–15 inches long, (2) a large clean bore with a diameter of approximately ¾ of an inch, (3) a subtle curve resembling the letter "L" or the letter "J," (4) a soft rubber mouthpiece to prevent chafing the gums, and (5) two prongs, or tooth-spacers, to allow the diver to hold the snorkel securely in the mouth and maintain an open airway.

Many of the optional features added to the simple design of the snorkel for diver convenience actually hinder diver performance by creating resistance and turbulence in the tube (see Figure 1-11). There are some options on snorkels which make them more comfortable to wear and easier to breathe with. Contoured snorkels, moldable mouthpieces, and silicone snorkels are just a few examples.

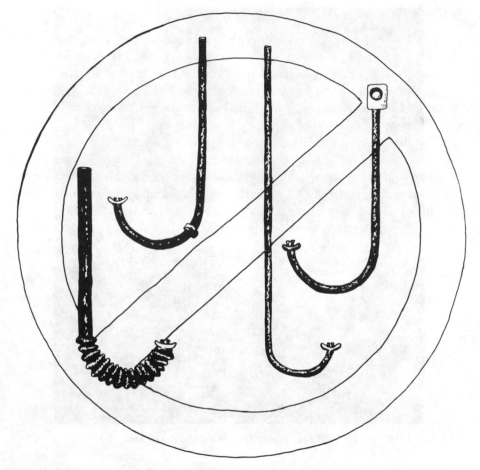

Figure 1-11. Snorkels to avoid.

The snorkel should be attached to the mask strap by a rubber snorkel tab, or keeper. This prevents loss of the snorkel by accidentally dropping it.

Donning the Snorkel

The snorkel should be worn on the left side of the diver's face to avoid entanglement with the regulator hose, which passes over the diver's right shoulder. Whether the diver is skin or scuba diving, the snorkel is a standard item which must be worn at all times, except in some specialty diving cases, such as cave diving. The snorkel should also be worn on the outside of the mask strap.

Clearing the Snorkel

The two basic methods used to clear water from the snorkel are the blast method and the tilt, or displacement, method. The blast method is easy to learn, but it demands much air and energy to remove water from the snorkel. The tilt method of snorkel clearing requires more time and coordination to learn but, once mastered, is extremely easy to perform.

The diver using the blast method requires a forceful exhalation via the mouth (Figure 1-12). This must be a ballistic type of exhalation, similar to a forceful spitting action. The snorkel must be maintained in a vertical upright position, with special care taken to keep the top of the snorkel above the surface of the water. The blast method may be difficult to perform when the diver is fatigued or short of breath.

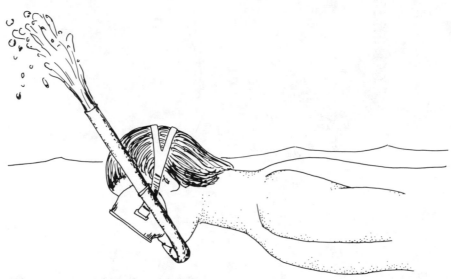

Figure 1-12. Blast clearing.

The tilt method (Figure 1-13) of snorkel clearing requires more finesse to perform, but generally makes clearing much easier to accomplish, especially when the diver is fatigued. Unlike the blast method, which is performed on the surface, the tilt technique is attempted underwater, while the diver is ascending. To prepare the snorkel for clearing, the diver must hyperextend the neck by looking at the surface, and point the snorkel tube down. As the diver ascends, the snorkel must remain inverted. The diver gently exhales a small

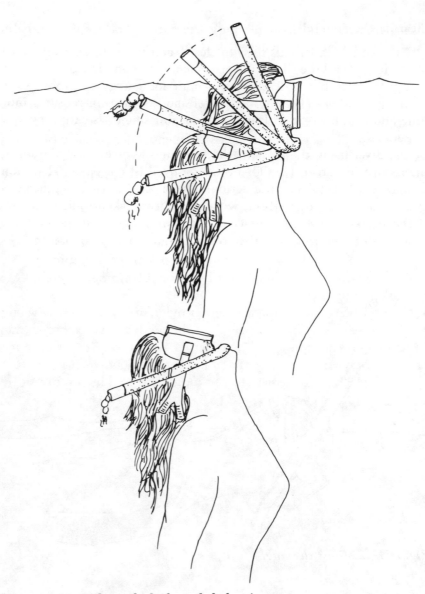

Figure 1-13. Tilt method of snorkel clearing.

amount of air into the snorkel while ascending. As long as the snorkel tube continues to point down, it will clear itself of water on the way to the surface. The snorkel may be returned to the normal upright position only when the diver's faceplate breaks the surface. Prematurely dropping the head on ascent will cause reflooding of the snorkel. If the tilt technique is performed correctly, the diver will be able to *inhale* immediately upon reaching the surface, rather than exhaling first, thus saving time, energy, and air.

1.1.4 WEIGHT BELT

Because a diver's body is positively buoyant, and even more so when wearing a wet suit, a weight belt is needed to assist the diver in descending. The weight belt helps compensate for positive buoyancy, especially when wet suits and B.C.D.s are worn. The weight belt can also be used as an emergency piece of equipment. Ditching or dropping the weight belt at the appropriate time during a crisis will help the diver to reach the surface safely. For this reason, all weight belts must come equipped with a quick-release buckle (Figure 1-14). If the weight belt must be dropped, the diver opens the quick-release buckle and pulls the belt completely away from the body before dropping it. This procedure will prevent the weight belt from becoming entangled with the other equipment.

Weight belts may be made of either nylon web or rubber. Although the nylon belts may be more durable, the rubber belts tend to be more comfortable, expanding and contracting with the diver's wet suit as depth varies. After finding the appropriate amount of weight to be worn, divers should distribute the individual weights evenly on the

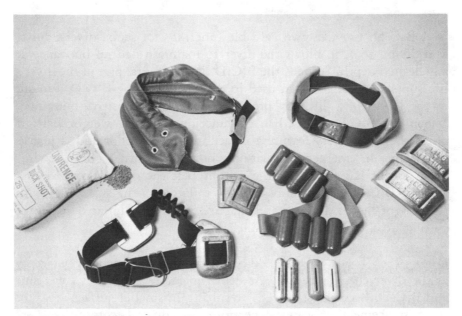

Figure 1-14. Weight belts. (© Geri Murphy, 1981)

front and back of the hips. The weights should be fastened on the belt with clips to prevent them from shifting while underwater. Taking the time to adjust the weights on the belt prior to diving increases enjoyment by providing good trim (balance) in the water. Finding the appropriate amount of weight to be worn requires careful trial and error in either shallow water or the swimming pool, first, and then again prior to each dive. The amount of lead needed will vary with the type of water (salt or fresh) and the amount of wet suit material worn. A good starting point for males is 10 percent of the body weight plus 2 pounds, while for females 15 percent plus 2 pounds might do. A practice surface dive to a depth of 10 feet should help divers in determining whether they are "light" or "heavy."

CAUTION: The weight belt should be one of the last items donned by the diver, for if it must be discarded in an emergency, it should drop freely. The weight belt *must not* be held in place by any straps or buckles other than the quick-release buckle accompanying the weight belt. The weight belt *must not* be worn underneath the B.C.D. straps or the tank straps because of possible entanglement.

1.1.5 BUOYANCY COMPENSATOR DEVICE

Functions

A B.C.D. provides two valuable functions for scuba divers. First, as a diving tool, it allows the diver to maintain neutral buoyancy at any desired depth. Second, the B.C.D. is an integral part of the diver's life support system. When used in this capacity, the B.C.D. can aid in the rescue of a diver by providing immediate positive buoyancy. When the B.C.D. is used in conjunction with the weight belt, it offers the same safety feature a parachute offers a pilot and is just as important. In emergency situations, however, when a normal swimming ascent is impossible, the weight belt should be dropped first and the B.C.D. should only be fully inflated on the surface. If both the weight belt is dropped and the B.C.D. is fully inflated at depth, an uncontrolled ascent may result.

Diving Tool: The B.C.D. should be used to maintain neutral buoyancy as the diver changes depths. As depth increases, the diver's wet suit and B.C.D. become "squeezed," resulting in smaller surface areas for the displacement of water. Therefore, the diver becomes "heavier" with depth. Rather than using the muscles and fins to overcome negative buoyancy, the diver should inflate the B.C.D. slightly to regain neutral buoyancy. On the other hand, as the diver ascends, both the wet suit and vest expand, making the diver "lighter" in water. Instead of fighting to stay down in this case, the diver should simply release some air from the B.C.D. to maintain neutral buoyancy. (Changes in buoyancy are discussed more thoroughly in Chapter 2.) The B.C.D. may also be fully inflated on the surface to permit the diver to rest.

Emergency Device: The B.C.D. also functions as an emergency apparatus when the diver is unable to regain the surface from depth. It must be remembered that, as a rescue device, the buoyancy compensator is used in conjunction with the weight belt. If the B.C.D. always has *some* air in it to make the diver neutrally buoyant, dropping the weight belt should provide immediate positive buoyancy. Again, the weight belt should be dropped first. The B.C.D. is inflated for rescue underwater only when the diver is unable to swim to the surface with or without the buddy's assistance. When the diver in trouble does reach the surface, the buoyancy compensator should then be inflated immediately.

NOTE: If a diver uses a mechanical inflator which uses air from the tank to fill the B.C.D., often the weight belt need not be dropped. The mechanical inflator enables the diver to quickly manipulate buoyancy with the press of a button. Not only does this make buoyancy control easier, but also it helps the diver immensely in getting to the surface.

B.C.D. Features

For the B.C.D. to be reliable and dependable in a variety of circumstances, the following features are highly recommended (Figure 1-15):

- 25 Pounds Minimum Lift—Every B.C.D. should provide a minimum of 25 pounds positive buoyancy to ensure that the diver will attain the surface in an emergency. The construction of the B.C.D. must enable an unconscious diver to float on the surface with the face up out of the water.

- Inflator Hose—A large-diameter inflator hose allows the diver to inflate the B.C.D. orally with a minimum of effort. This hose should originate high on the B.C.D. behind the diver's neck, but, unfortunately, some do not.

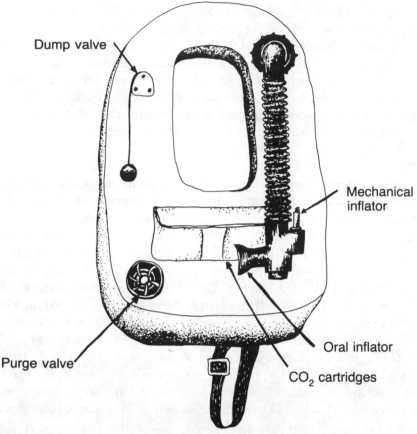

Figure 1-15. B.C.D. features.

- Overinflation Valve—This valve, located in the chest region of the B.C.D., allows overexpanding air to escape during ascent without damaging the B.C.D.

- Straps—A system of straps and buckles is required to secure the B.C.D. snugly on the diver's chest, preventing it from riding up, especially when fully inflated.

- Dump Valve—This device allows the diver to release air from the B.C.D. quickly, in case of a rapid or uncontrolled ascent.

- CO_2 Cartridge Inflator Mechanism—In emergencies, this device fills the B.C.D. automatically. The CO_2 cartridges should be a minimum of 25–38 grams. Pulling the CO_2 cords should be reserved for surface use only in order to avoid uncontrolled ascents.

    NOTE: The CO_2 cartridge-firing mechanisms have a questionable dependability record at best. This is due primarily to poor preventive maintenance by the diver/owner. (Maintenance of the B.C.D. is discussed in Chapter 12.)

- Mechanical Inflator—Once considered a luxury, the mechanical B.C.D. inflator, using tank air to fill the B.C.D., is rapidly becoming a standard feature for scuba divers. With the press of a button, the diver controls changes in buoyancy in a variety of situations.

Several B.C.D. designs are now available, but no agreement exists on which type is most desirable. When selecting a B.C.D., a diver should consult a dive shop for advantages and disadvantages associated with each model. Figure 1-16 shows just a few of the B.C.D.

Fitting the B.C.D.

As with the diving mask, fit and comfort are important criteria for selecting a B.C.D. A relatively new design in B.C.D.s is the jacket type, which is almost like a sports coat (Figure 1-17). It fits extremely well, provides excellent buoyancy, and incorporates right into the

Figure 1-16. Various B.C.D.s. (Photo by Bill Hughes)

Figure 1-17. *Jacket-type B.C.D. (© Geri Murphy, 1981)*

backpacks. Now, for the first time, the backpack and B.C.D. are one, thus eliminating many straps and buckles and thereby making the B.C.D. easier and more comfortable to use. This "wraparound" style also offers better balance in the water.

Using the B.C.D.

While the B.C.D. is perhaps the most important scuba diving tool and rescue device worn in the water, proper use requires much training and practice in a variety of situations. Accordingly, the diver should be introduced to it as early as possible. The B.C.D. must be worn and used in conjunction with the weight belt to ensure that the diver can become positively buoyant when necessary.

Donning the B.C.D.: The B.C.D. must be donned prior to putting the weight belt in place around the diver's waist. B.C.D. straps must be adjusted to fit the diver snugly. When the B.C.D. is fully inflated, the straps must prevent it from floating or rising away from the diver's body. B.C.D. straps (and tank straps) must not inhibit the dropping of the weight belt in emergency situations.

Inflating the B.C.D.: To inflate the B.C.D., the diver takes a breath of air into the lungs and exhales through the oral inflator. The inflator button on the mouthpiece must be depressed while inflating the B.C.D. orally. The diver should stop swimming and rest in a vertical position to inflate the B.C.D. efficiently. Of course, breath control and relaxation make this skill much easier to perform.

Deflating the B.C.D.: The removal of air from the B.C.D. is best achieved while the diver is in the vertical position (Figure 1-18). The oral inflator hose must first be extended fully, over and behind the diver's head. After the inflator hose is properly positioned, the diver then depresses the button or the mouthpiece at the end of the hose to allow the air to rise and escape from the B.C.D. The diver's free arm may be used to squeeze the B.C.D. to aid deflation.

1.2 Basic Scuba Diving Equipment

SCUBA is an acronym which stands for Self-Contained Underwater Breathing Apparatus. The scuba tank is a steel or aluminum cylinder which holds compressed air *(not oxygen)* at high pressure. The regulator is a simple yet remarkable device which controls the flow of high-pressure air from the tank to the diver. Gauges, such as the submersible air pressure gauge, depth gauge, underwater timer, and compass, are also necessary to make the scuba diver's journey through the underwater environment safe and enjoyable. These gauges are discussed in the Accessories section.

Figure 1-18. Deflating the B.C.D. (© Geri Murphy, 1981)

1.2.1 TANK

Tank Features

Scuba tanks are structurally sound, durable containers made of either steel or aluminum. Although the first scuba tanks manufactured were steel, aluminum tanks are more popular with divers today. Tanks are constructed well and will last indefinitely if properly maintained. If misused, scuba cylinders can, but don't often, explode. The fact that the Bureau of Explosives within the U.S. Department of Transportation regulates the use of scuba tanks should indicate the potential danger that could result from their misuse.

Scuba tanks are available in a variety of sizes (Figure 1-19). The

Figure 1-19. Various scuba tanks. (Courtesy Parkway)

tank size determines the air capacity of the tank. Some of the more common scuba tank sizes are as follows; 50 cubic feet, 71.2 cubic feet, 80 cubic feet, 90 cubic feet. The 71.2 and the 80 are the most popular sizes.

The standard working pressures of tanks also vary with tank size. The recommended pressure for each tank is stamped on the neck of the tank. The range of tank pressures is listed as follows in pounds per square inch (psi): 1,800 psi; 2,250 psi; 2,475 psi; 3,000 psi. The 2,250 and the 3,000 psi are the most popular pressures.

Most divers prefer either a steel 71.2-cubic-foot tank rated at 2,250 psi or an aluminum 80-cubic-foot tank rated at 3,000 psi. The larger the tank, the greater its air capacity. Unfortunately, tanks holding more air are heavier and more cumbersome. The average scuba cylinder weighs between 28 and 35 pounds. Some divers should probably consider aluminum 50-cubic-foot tanks, which are smaller and lighter, but obviously hold less air. These tanks are apparently ideal for divers of smaller physical stature or ones who have a slower breathing rate.

NOTE: Many consumers purchase steel tanks assuming that they will be able to begin a dive with 71.2 cubic feet of air. This, however, is the case for *new* tanks only. Although the standard steel tanks are commonly referred to as 72's, they only have an air capacity of 71.2 cubic feet when the tank is overfilled by 10 percent (2,475 psi). When the tank is filled to its normal standard working pressure of 2,250 psi (which is more often the case), only 64.5 cubic feet of air is available.

How long will a tank last underwater? The answer to this question depends on many factors, including breathing rate, swimming speed, water conditions, depth, physical size, and stress. Therefore, a diver must consider his/her personal experience to determine how long a tank will last underwater.

The following scuba tank accessories should be purchased along with the tank: tank boot, backpack with straps and buckles, and valves. These items are essential for proper tank use and vary in construction, design, and cost. Visiting a dive shop can help divers decide which combination of tank accessories is most suitable for their particular diving needs.

Tank Markings

Much can be learned about a scuba tank by examining the information stamped on the neck of the tank (Figure 1-20). All divers should

Figure 1-20. Markings on aluminum tank (left) *and steel tank.*

be able to recognize and understand the information marked on the tank, in order to maintain the tank properly.

The *first line* stamped on the neck of the tank indicates three separate items of information: the regulatory agency for scuba tanks, the material of which the tank is made, and the standard working pressure of the tank. The regulatory agency may be DOT (U.S. Department of Transportation), CTC (Canadian Transportation Commission), or ICC (U.S. Interstate Commerce Commission; this agency was responsible for U.S. tanks manufactured prior to January 1970). The material may be 3AA, which is a type of steel alloy (chrome molybdenum steel), SP6498, or E6498. The last two numbers indicate a special aluminum alloy used in aluminum tanks. The standard working pressure is either 2,250 psi (for most steel tanks) or 3,000 psi (for most aluminum tanks).

The *second line* stamped on the scuba tank neck refers to the individual serial number (e.g., HJ 287027) of that particular tank. It may also indicate the purchaser of the cylinder; for example, a tank bearing the marking "P 137725 USD" was purchased by the U.S. Divers Company.

The *third and subsequent lines* provide timely information that is extremely important to diver safety. These lines indicate when the tank was last hydrostatically tested (see p. 30), by whom, and the name of the manufacturer (Figure 1-21).

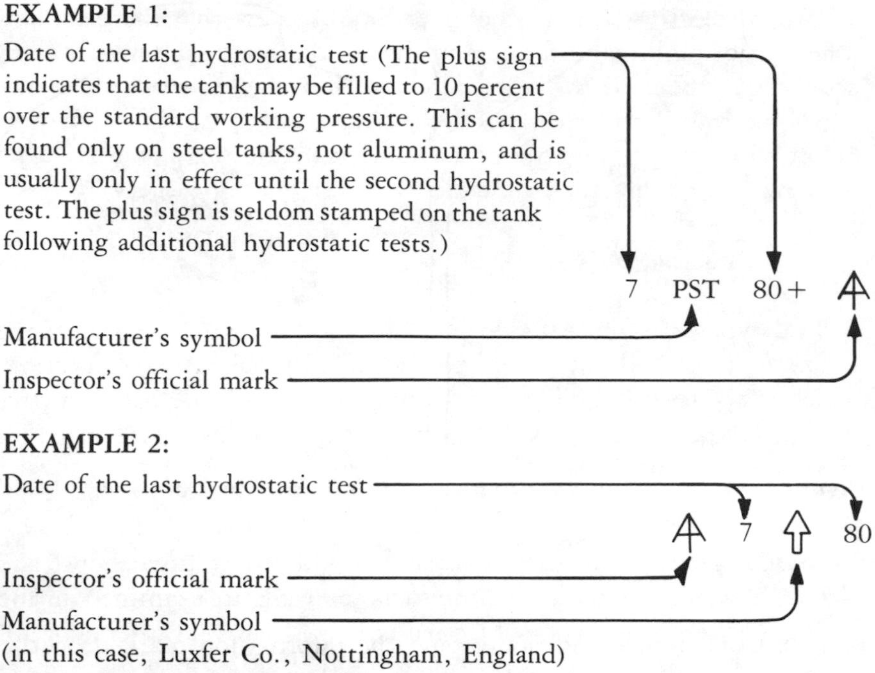

EXAMPLE 1:

Date of the last hydrostatic test (The plus sign
indicates that the tank may be filled to 10 percent
over the standard working pressure. This can be
found only on steel tanks, not aluminum, and is
usually only in effect until the second hydrostatic
test. The plus sign is seldom stamped on the tank
following additional hydrostatic tests.)

7   PST   80 +   ⍓

Manufacturer's symbol

Inspector's official mark

EXAMPLE 2:

Date of the last hydrostatic test

⍓   7   ⇧   80

Inspector's official mark

Manufacturer's symbol
(in this case, Luxfer Co., Nottingham, England)

*Figure 1-21. Examples of information provided on
third line of tank markings.*

TABLE 1-1

INTERPRETATION OF TANK MARKINGS

Manufacturer	Manufacturer's symbol	Inspector's official mark	Inspector's name
Alcan Aluminum	ALCAN	⍓	Industrial Analysts
Norris Industry	⟨N⟩	⍓	Industrial Analysts
Pressed Steel	PST	⍟	T.H. Cochrane Lab
Walter Kidde	⟨K⟩, WK, WK&Co.	⬭	Arrow Head Industrial Service

SOURCE: R. Gonsett, *Scuba Tanks* (Colton, Calif.: National Association of Underwater
Instructors, 1973), p. 31.

When selecting a tank, the diver should know that there are only a few major tank manufacturers in the United States. However, many scuba equipment distributors purchase these tanks, place their own labels on them, and then resell them to divers. Table 1-1 may be helpful in interpreting the scuba tank markings in regard to who manufactured and tested the tank.

Tank Inspections

Two types of scuba tank inspections are conducted to protect the scuba cylinder and the diver. One is an internal visual inspection, which is not required by law but is highly recommended at least once a year. The other is a pressure hydrostatic test, which is required for all scuba tanks once every 5 years.

Visual Inspection: This test is usually conducted at dive shops, and although both the external and internal tank walls are examined during this inspection, the major objective is to evaluate the internal walls of the tank. The steps included in an internal visual inspection are as follows:

1. The high-pressure air is slowly drained from the tank. When it is empty, the tank valve is carefully removed.

2. The interior walls of the cylinder are inspected with the aid of a special light. The examiner checks for any signs of contamination or corrosion, particularly rust.

3. If corrosion does exist, it is usually removed by a process called *tumbling*, which also polishes the walls of the tank by spinning the tank along its long axis at a high rate of speed, while abrasives like carbide or aluminum oxide chips tumble inside the cylinder.

4. If the tank strength is still in question after tumbling, it is sent out for a hydrostatic test.

5. When the tank does pass the internal visual inspection, a waterproof decal (Figure 1-22) is usually placed on the outside of the tank indicating that the cylinder is free of corrosion. The month and year of the inspection are clearly marked on the decal, which becomes invalid after a year.

Figure 1-22. Visual inspection decal on tank. (© Geri Murphy, 1981)

Hydrostatic Test: The hydrostatic test, required by U.S. DOT is a stringent stress test of the scuba cylinder. Hydrostatic testers must be licensed by the DOT Bureau of Explosives. The steps involved in this test are as follows:

1. The high-pressure scuba air is slowly released from the tank, the tank valve is removed, and a special test fitting is inserted into the neck of the tank.

2. The cylinder is placed in water and injected with water pressure (water is used instead of air to prevent an explosion in case of a rupture). The tank is overpressurized by five thirds the standard working pressure of the tank, which would be equal to 3,600 psi for a standard 71.2-cubic-foot tank rated at 2,250 psi.

3. When the tank pressure reaches five thirds the standard working pressure, it is held for 30 seconds, total tank expansion is measured by water displacement, and then the pressure is slowly released.

4. The permanent expansion of the tank is measured and cannot exceed more than 10 percent of the total rate of expansion.

Both steel and aluminum tanks are subjected to the same test. When the cylinder passes the hydro exam, the date and tester's symbol are stamped high on the outside tank wall (Figure 1-23).

Figure 1-23. Hydro exam stamp. (© Geri Murphy, 1981)

Safety Rules for the Use of Scuba Tanks

When using scuba diving tanks, the diver must adhere to the following safety points:

1. Whenever possible, do not leave the scuba tank standing alone, unattended. It could fall or be damaged and may even cause injury.

2. Whenever possible, do not completely empty the tank of air pressure. Always leave approximately 100 psi in the tank to prevent moisture from seeping into the tank, which could cause internal corrosion (rust).

3. Whenever possible, do not don the scuba cylinder or remove it by yourself. Allow your dive partner to assist you; it is much easier and safer.

4. Whenever possible, store the tank by securing it with straps or buckles while standing the cylinder in the vertical position.

5. Always have the tank internally inspected once a year.

6. Always have the tank hydrostatically inspected every 5 years.

7. Always block your tank to prevent it from rolling and to protect the valve from damage when you transport the tank by automobile.

8. Never empty or fill the tank rapidly. This practice may create condensation inside the tank which may, in turn, produce rust.

9. Keep tanks away from heat and *do not* bake the tank when repainting.

Tank Valves and Related Parts

J-valves and K-valves: There are two different types of valves which are located on the neck of the tank: the J-valve (reserve) and the K-valve (nonreserve). Figure 1-24 illustrates both valves.

The major difference between the two valves is that the J-valve prevents the diver from accidentally running out of air by warning him or her when the air is running low. It must be noted that the J-valve system provides a warning, not additional air that has been saved to increase time underwater. The warning provided by the J-valve is increased breathing resistance with each inhalation. When the J-lever is activated by pulling it down, the diver must proceed directly to the surface. J-valves have been known to malfunction, however, and may even be bumped down accidentally.

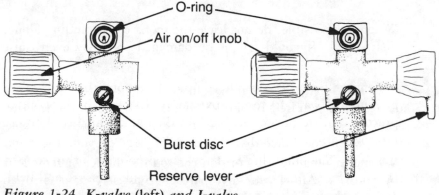

Figure 1-24. K-valve (left) and J-valve.

The J-valve uses a spring which is calibrated at approximately 300 psi. The spring allows air to flow through the valve until the tank pressure drops to roughly the same pressure as the spring. At this point, the spring becomes relatively stronger with each inhalation by the diver, thus gradually reducing the flow of air from the tank. The J-valve was designed to be pulled down in this situation by the diver, to ensure a safer ascent by temporarily ending the breathing resistance which the valve creates. At first glance, many divers find the safety feature of the J-valve appealing. J-valves were developed before the use of submersible air pressure gauges, so the use of a J-valve as a low-air warning was important for diver safety. Today's divers, however, dive with submersible air pressure gauges which constantly monitor scuba tank pressure. A conscientious diver will always swim to the surface to end a dive with 500 psi remaining in the tank, making it extremely difficult to run out of air unexpectedly. Therefore, many instructors believe that diving with the J-valve in the up position is an obsolete practice.

The K-valve, unlike the J-valve, is a simple on-off valve similar to a water faucet and does not provide a low-air warning system. Use of a K-valve in conjunction with a submersible pressure gauge is perfectly safe and is rapidly replacing the need for the J-valve. Problems associated with the J-valve include wear and malfunction of the spring and the accidental bumping down of the J-lever during the dive, thus leaving divers without reserve air on which they may be depending. This is not to say that J-valves are no longer useful, but rather that J-valves provided a more valuable service in the past.

O-ring: The O-ring, a black rubber washer located on the tank valve, provides an airtight seal between the regulator and the valve. The O-ring should be kept round and moist, not flat and dry. It may fall out of the tank valve periodically, so divers should have extra O-rings on hand. Many divers carry spare O-rings on their key chains or on the regulator yoke screw.

Burst Disc: The burst disc assembly, another safety feature found on the tank valve, is required by law. This disc will rupture when the tank is subjected to excessive pressure and/or heat. Although the tank will empty when the burst disc ruptures, it does prevent the tank from exploding. The burst disc assembly is composed of a thin copper or metal disc which is exposed to the internal tank pressure and held in place by a screw. After rupturing, the burst disc is very easily

TABLE 1-2

BURST DISC RANGE

Standard working pressure (psi)	Burst disc range (psi)
1,800	2,400–2,700
2,015	2,700–3,000
2,250	2,850–3,375
3,000	3,960–4,400

NOTE: Placing two burst discs in one tank valve ("double discing") is a dangerous practice and must be avoided.

SOURCE: M.B. Farley and C. Royer, *Scuba Equipment Care and Maintenance* (Port Hueneme, Calif.: Marcor Publishing, 1980), p. 50.

Figure 1-25. Donning the tank. (© Geri Murphy, 1981)

replaced. The approximate tank pressures which may cause the burst disc to rupture are listed in Table 1-2.

Donning the Scuba Tank

Whenever possible, the tank should be placed on the diver's back with assistance from the diving partner (Figure 1-25). This practice makes donning the tank much easier and safer. The B.C.D. should be put in place before the tank except, of course, with the jacket-type vest, which is already attached to the tank's backpack. When the diver is ready to don the scuba tank, the shoulder straps should be adjusted to the proper length. The waist strap should remain open. The diver's partner should then hold the tank behind the diver while he/she slips the arms through the shoulder loops much like the way a sports coat is put on. When the tank is in place, the diver should then bend over at the waist to allow the weight of the tank to rest on the back. While the tank rests on the back, the diver can pull on the waist straps to tighten the shoulder loops. The waist strap is then buckled, and the weight belt may then be put in place.

1.2.2 REGULATOR

Although salvage and military divers had been using various types of breathing apparatus throughout the nineteenth and early twentieth centuries, sport scuba diving was not available to the general public until the introduction of the Aqua-lung. Drawing on the ideas of several earlier prototypes, Gagnan and Cousteau invented the first true SCUBA, which combined a fully automatic regulator with a high-pressure air cylinder.

The demand regulator is a vital component of the open-circuit scuba system used by sport divers. Open-circuit scuba means that the breathing system is open to the environment. More specifically, air is inhaled from a high-pressure tank, used for respiration, and then exhaled into the environment. In closed-circuit scuba, which is still used in commercial, scientific, and military diving, the diver rebreathes the same air in a closed-loop fashion.

Basic Regulator Features

Many makes and models of scuba regulators are available on the market, but all regulators function similarly. The first regulators produced were double hose regulators (Figure 1-26).

Figure 1-26. Double hose regulator. (Photo by Michael Oakes)

There are some advantages associated with the double hose model. For example, the double hose model has a lightweight mouthpiece, releases exhaled bubbles behind the head rather than alongside the face, and is less likely to freeze up in frigid waters. However, the single hose regulators (Figure 1-27) are generally more efficient and economical for today's sport divers. The single hose regulator costs less than the double hose version; is easier to operate, maintain, and adjust; simplifies emergency buddy breathing; offers more efficient underwater breathing; creates less drag in the water; and is easier to purge and clear of water in the mouthpiece.

Because single hose regulators are more widely accepted and double hose regulators are quickly becoming things of the past, only single hose regulators will be discussed in detail here.

The basic function of the regulator is to regulate the flow of high-pressure air in the tank and reduce it to ambient pressure, permitting the diver to breathe on demand. The scuba regulator provides the diver with air upon demand and automatically controls the flow of air to the diver. The air pressure supplied to the diver must be equal to the surrounding water pressure, making for easy breathing.

Most regulators perform this air pressure reduction process in two steps or stages. Each stage contains an automatic air valve which opens and closes as the diver inhales and exhales. When the diver inhales, high-pressure air quickly travels from the tank into the first stage of the regulator. The first stage then reduces this high-pressure air to an intermediate pressure of approximately 100-150 psi. The intermediate-pressure air quickly passes through the hose of the regulator into the second stage located behind the mouthpiece, where it is further reduced to ambient (breathing) pressure. This two-step process takes place instantaneously during inhalation. Upon exhalation, the "used" air is

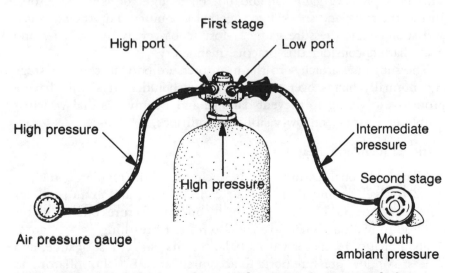

Figure 1-27. Single hose regulator with pressure gauge attached.

forced out into the water via the exhaust ports located below the mouthpiece.

There are many different valves which can be used in the regulator's first stage to reduce high-pressure air. The two major categories of valves are *unbalanced* and *balanced*. Unbalanced valves, which are becoming outdated, fluctuate with changing tank pressures. As a result, a regulator with an unbalanced first stage has a breathing performance which varies with tank pressure—an undesirable trait.

The balanced valve in the first stage keeps hose pressure consistent regardless of changes in tank pressure. The preferred regulators today usually combine a balanced first stage with some type of downstream second stage, whereby hose air pressure assists opening the valve at the mouthpiece. If the first stage does malfunction, permitting excessive pressure to enter the hose, neither the hose nor the second stage would be damaged. In this case, the regulator would "freeflow" by allowing excess air to escape from the mouthpiece. Although this wastes air, the diver may continue breathing while the regulator is malfunctioning, thus allowing a safe return to the surface.

Submersible Pressure Gauge

The *subgauge* or *seaview* gauge constantly monitors available tank pressure and must be considered a vital part of the open-circuit scuba system. It is similar to a fuel gauge in a car but much more important. When you run out of "fuel" underwater, it becomes more complicated. This tank pressure gauge should not be thought of as an accessory. Just as the mask and snorkel go together as a unit, so do the regulator and submersible pressure gauge. Most scuba certifying agencies and boat charters consider this practice mandatory.

The subgauge attaches to the high-pressure port on the first stage and normally hangs over the diver's left shoulder. It should have a protective covering to prevent damage and a luminous dial which is visible in a variety of low-visibility conditions.

Optional Regulator Features

Many additional features may be included on the regulator, including a J-valve, a sonic alarm, an air control knob, and extra ports for other attachments. However, too many optional features on a regulator can lead to malfunctions and may also restrict breathing performance. A good quality regulator with a balanced first stage, a subgauge, and at least two low-pressure ports to accommodate a B.C.D. inflator and an auxiliary second stage is more than adequate for most divers.

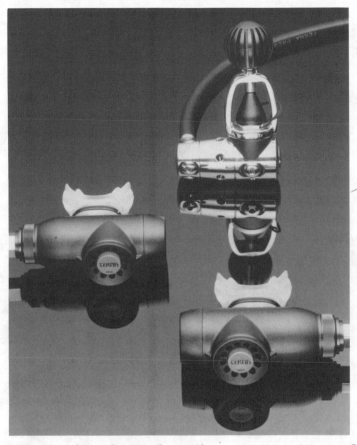

Figure 1-28. Regulator first and second stages. (Courtesy Tekna®)

1.2.3 ALTERNATE AIR SOURCES

In the past, buddy breathing was thought to be the only acceptable method of getting an "out-of-air" diver safely to the surface. Of course, proper dive planning prevents a diver from running out of air. Fortunately for today's divers, the scuba industry has developed a variety of Alternate Air Sources (A.A.S.) for dealing with out-of-air emergencies resulting from poor dive planning.

The Alternate Air Source may be any type of scuba regulator with an additional second stage. This includes miniature, independent air units such as Spare Air.™ The major advantage of modern A.A.S. is that both rescuer and victim may share air without passing a regulator back and forth.

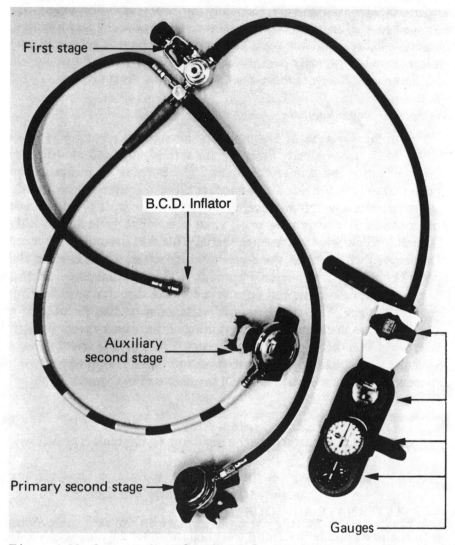

First stage

B.C.D. Inflator

Auxiliary
second stage

Primary second stage

Gauges

Figure 1-29. Octopus rig. (Photo by Michael Oakes)

The A.A.S. should be located in the chest area and be freed for use with a single action. The A.A.S. must be clearly visible. Because there are many different types of A.A.S. now available, pre-dive rehearsals of air-sharing procedures are required prior to each dive.

Some of the Alternate Air Sources available include:

Auxiliary (Octopus) Regulator

The unique feature of the auxiliary or octopus regulator (Figure

1-29) is that a completely independent second stage and mouthpiece are attached to the primary regulator. The purpose of this auxiliary second stage is to provide air to another diver in an emergency. Buddy breathing with just one mouthpiece, while relatively simple to perform in the safe confines of a swimming pool, is a difficult and awkward skill to perform in the open water. This skill becomes even more complicated when one of the divers is under stress, which is often the case. The octopus regulator improves a shared emergency ascent, making it more efficient and safer because each diver has an independent mouthpiece. The auxiliary second stage may also be used for self-rescue as a backup air source in case of a malfunctioning of the primary second stage.

Octopus regulators should have longer hoses (at least four feet) to facilitate reaching a dive buddy in need of air.

A major disadvantage of the octopus regulator is that there is no standardized placement or procedure for using the extra second stage. This may lead to a frantic search when faced with a real out-of-air emergency. Also, octopus regulators not secured properly become easily entangled. Most diving instructors urge securing the octopus in the chest area and also recommend a pre-dive rehearsal using the octopus.

Pony Bottle

A pony bottle is a smaller, additional tank complete with an extra regulator. It is a completely separate scuba system and is usually attached directly to the primary scuba system. Pony bottles are popular with cave, ice, and wreck divers. One advantage of this system is that the diver has a completely separate system with abundant air to back up the primary system. The system is particularly beneficial in case of a primary regulator malfunction. The pony bottle is approximately the size of a household fire extinguisher. The pony bottle regulator should also have an extra long hose to facilitate air sharing. Disadvantages of the pony bottle system include size, weight, and cost. See Chapter 7 for further discussion and picture of the pony bottle.

Spare Air

An exciting new development in A.A.S. is the Spare Air™ cannister manufactured by Submersible Systems. This miniature and completely independent scuba bottle is approximately the size of a flashlight. The major advantage of Spare Air™ is that it has no air hose; the regulator sits on top of the bottle without any hose, thus no entanglements. It is small, light, and simple to use. The Spare Air™ unit may be either used by its owner or passed to an out-of-air victim. The beauty of passing the Spare Air™ unit to a victim is that the donor is not tethered to a panicky diver. One disadvantage of the Spare Air™ unit is that its air supply is more limited than larger devices.

Other A.A.S. are available, some of which are incorporated into the Buoyancy Compensator.

Procedures for using the A.A.S. are discussed in Chapter 9. Although running out of air is not probable for the well-trained diver, it is a *remote* possibility. For this reason, the A.A.S. comes highly recommended for novice and experienced divers alike.

Regulator Hook-up

The procedure for attaching the regulator to the tank is as follows:

1. Open the air knob on the tank valve slightly to blow off any water or dirt which might enter the regulator's first stage.
2. Check to see that the O-ring is in place on the tank valve.
3. Remove the dust cover and place the first stage over the tank valve with the raised "O" part of the first stage over the circular screen and the regulator hose situated so that it will fall over the right shoulder. Attach the first stage to the tank valve by gently tightening the yoke screw with the thumb and index finger. (*Do not* use excessive force.)
4. Slowly turn the air on and check the subgauge for tank pressure.
5. Test the regulator by inhaling and exhaling through the mouthpiece.

Regulator Removal

The procedure for removing the regulator from the tank is as follows:

1. Turn the tank air off by closing the on-off knob.
2. Relieve the regulator hose of high-pressure air by depressing the purge button.
3. Detach the regulator from the tank valve by loosening the yoke screw.
4. Towel dry both the air screen on the first stage and the dust cap; then secure the dust cap in place.

Figure 1-30. Spare Air™.

For preventive maintenance of the regulator, see Chapter 12. Regulators should be cleaned and overhauled annually by a trained equipment specialist.

Recovering the Regulator

If the regulator should ever fall from the mouth or become lost underwater, the diver should remain calm and think about where the regulator attaches to the tank *before* attempting to recover it. Realizing that the regulator comes over the right shoulder, the diver should simply reach the right hand up and back behind the neck to find the regulator hose attached to the tank valve. With the hose in hand, the diver then straightens the right arm by extending the hand in front of the face. When the right arm is fully extended, the hand will join the mouthpiece. The regulator must first be cleared of water before a breath may be taken from it. Another method of recovering the regulator is to simply lean forward; the second stage should drop in front of the diver's face.

Clearing the Regulator

Whenever the regulator leaves the mouth, it must be cleared of water before breathing is resumed. This is usually accomplished by simply exhaling into the mouthpiece, or, if the diver doesn't have sufficient air to exhale, by depressing the purge button. The regulator must never be placed into the diver's mouth upside down because it is impossible to clear in this position.

Correcting Temporary Freeflow

The second stage will often freeflow when the purge button faces down in the water and the mouthpiece points up. This occurs frequently during buddy breathing. To prevent this type of freeflow, the mouthpiece should be pointing down with the purge button up whenever the regulator is not in the diver's mouth.

1.3 Other Diving Equipment

1.3.1 UNDERWATER GAUGES

Gauges (diving watch, bottom timer, depth gauge, and compass) are necessary to monitor the diver's depth, time, and direction. These items may be considered as defensive diving tools because they help the diver to avoid pressure-related problems.

Timepieces

Watch: Time underwater must be recorded for any dive performed at a depth greater than 33 feet in order to avoid decompression sickness (discussed in Chapter 3). A water-resistant watch (Figure 1-31) is commonly used to monitor bottom time. Although dive watches vary widely, some features should be kept in mind. A diving watch should be pressure tested to a minimum of 220 feet. A movable bezel on the perimeter of the watch helps greatly to mark time underwater. The dial should be luminous so that it can be read during night dives. The dive watch must be secured either on the diver or on other equipment and placed so that it can be easily viewed. There are now some very reliable and inexpensive underwater digital watches available. Regardless of the type of watch purchased, a guarantee is an important factor to consider.

Figure 1-31. Diver's watch. (© Geri Murphy, 1981)

Digital Dive Timer: This is a convenient timing device designed for divers. This device also records depth and dive number.

Depth Gauge

The depth gauge is worn by the diver to monitor depth. Accurate and reliable depth readings are essential to diver safety.

There are three basic types of depth gauges: the capillary depth gauge, the open bourdon tube, and the oil-filled gauge (Figure 1-33). Both the capillary tube and the bourdon tube function by allowing water at ambient pressure to enter the gauge in order to indicate depth. As water pressure increases with depth, more water is forced

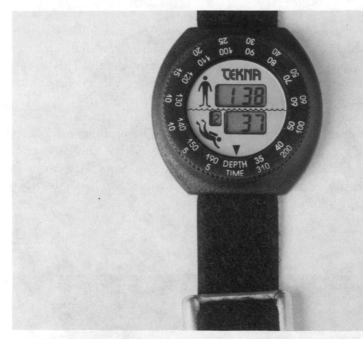

Figure 1-32. Digital dive timer. (Courtesy Tekna®)

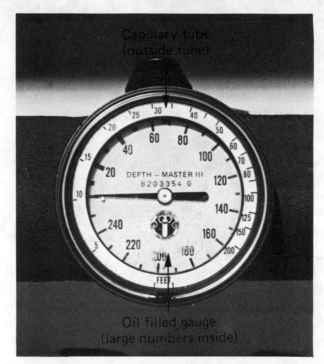

Figure 1-33. Capillary tube and oil-filled gauge. (Photo by Michael Oakes)

into the tube of the depth gauge. In the case of the capillary depth gauge, the tube is located on the outside border of the dial, and the diver actually reads the water column to determine depth. This gauge is very accurate in water not deeper than 35 feet but becomes less accurate as depth increases. This gauge is very inexpensive.

The open bourdon tube works similarly, but water enters the gauge forcing a pointer around the face of the gauge. The problem associated with any depth gauge utilizing an open tube is that the tube may become clogged, thus rendering the gauge useless. Sand, silt, and salt deposits can easily become lodged in these tubes. Probably for this reason, the open bourdon tube is becoming obsolete.

Figure 1-34. Dive computer. (Courtesy Orca Industries)

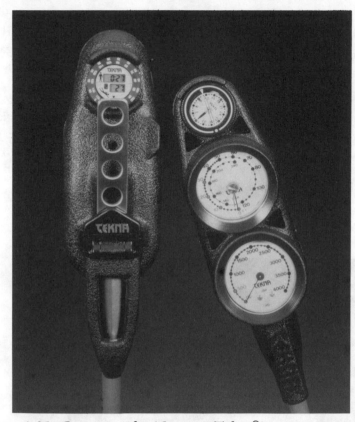

Figure 1-35. Gauge console. (Courtesy Tekna®)

The depth gauge preferred by most sport divers is the oil-filled depth gauge. This gauge is very accurate and reliable and is almost maintenance free because the completely sealed unit does not allow water or other contaminants to enter the gauge. The oil-filled depth gauges are also more shock resistant than the other gauges.

Dive Computers (Decompression Meters)

These very accurate but expensive computers monitor depth, bottom time, residual nitrogen, surface intervals, and many other important factors all on one gauge. The primary purpose of the dive computer is to help the diver avoid decompression sickness, although it performs many additional functions. The dive computer is becoming very popular; a detailed discussion of dive computers can be found in Chapter 11.

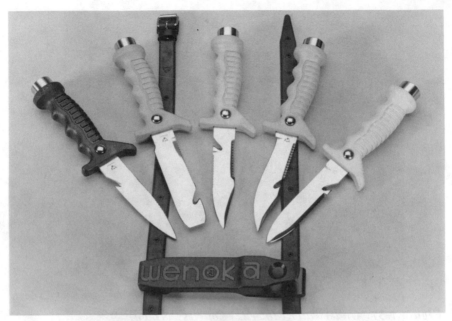

Figure 1-36. Dive knives. (Courtesy Wenoka®)

Gauge Consoles

Consoles resemble dashboards in a car on a smaller scale. They hold all types of gauges, meters, and knives and eliminate the need for strapping all these items on the diver's limbs.

1.3.2 KNIVES

Dive knives are needed tools, not weapons, and must be carried appropriately with care by the serious diver.

1.3.3 UNDERWATER PHOTOGRAPHY EQUIPMENT

Cameras, Strobes, and underwater housings are available to divers interested in photography. While this equipment tends to be expensive, priceless pictures may be obtained with a little bit of training and practice.

1.3.4 DIVE GEAR BAGS

Because scuba diving is such an equipment-oriented sport, gear bags are highly recommended to store, transport, and protect your diving equipment. They come in a variety of shapes, sizes and colors.

Figure 1-37. Underwater camera. (Courtesy Nikon)

1.3.5 WET SUITS

Although many divers select a wet suit (Figure 1-39) solely for its thermal protection, the wet suit is much more versatile than one might expect. In addition to preventing heat loss, the wet suit also provides protection against abrasions and stinging marine life, and it produces positive buoyancy during emergencies. Therefore, wet suits are not reserved for cold waters only and are worn by most sport divers.

Wet suits are composed of foam neoprene rubber and are often lined with a nylon fabric and come in a variety of colors. *Nylon-Two* refers to nylon lining both inside and outside the suit. This lining improves durability and ease of entry, but does not enhance the warmth of the suit. Recently, a new type of wet suit material has emerged on the market. These suits are made to stretch by using a material called Lycra. As a result, these suits are much easier to put on, more comfortable to wear, and extremely attractive.

The warmth of the wet suit is determined by its thickness and fit. Exposure suits vary in thickness from ⅛ to ⅜ inch, with the ³⁄₁₆ and ¼ inch being most popular. A snug fit is preferred, but a suit which is too tight can cause discomfort and cramps. A loose-fitting wet suit

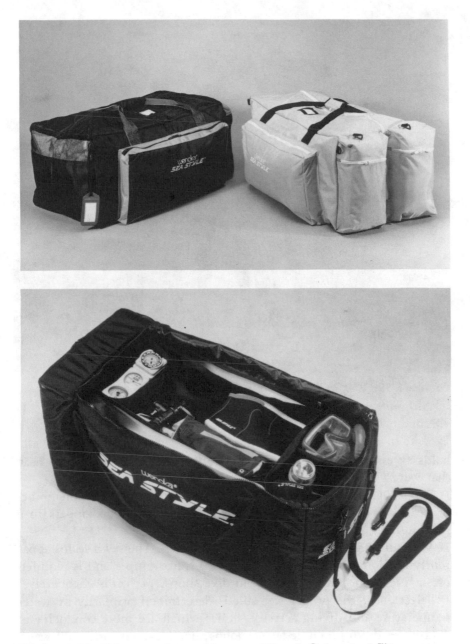

Figure 1-38. Dive gear bags. (Courtesy Wenoka® Sea Style™)

Figure 1-39. Wet suits. (Courtesy Skin Diver Wet Suits Co.)

holds excessive water, causing the diver to exert more energy to heat that water; thus the diver gets cold more quickly.

Zippers aid the diver in donning the suit, but often become points of heat loss and malfunctions. Cold-water divers keep zippers to a minimum.

Wet suit seams may be either glued or sewn. The sewn seams apparently last longer. Repairing wet suits is quite simple and is required often. Neoprene glue, available in dive shops, performs adequately.

Selection of the proper wet suit is determined primarily by water temperature and diving activity. Styles which are more conducive to cold-water diving include farmer johns, hooded vests, and cold-water hoods. Cold-water suits should be at least ¼-inch thick. Wet suits which are 3/16-inch thick or less are preferred in warmer waters. "Shorty" wet suits are also popular in these waters.

Since the head, hands, and feet are more susceptible to heat loss and abrasions, hoods, gloves, and boots should be selected carefully. Gloves are available in three-finger or five-finger models, but some

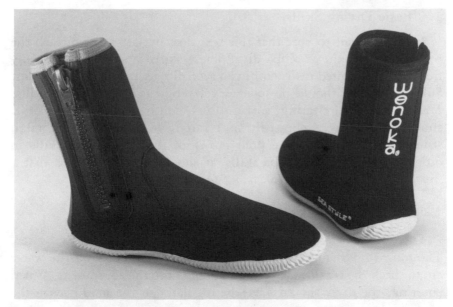

Figure 1-40. Dive boots. (Courtesy Wenoka® SeaStyle™)

divers prefer mitts. Hard-soled boots provide foot protection both on land and in the water.

The buoyancy produced by the wet suit varies with thickness, suit size, and number of items worn. Depth will also affect the suit-induced buoyancy by compressing the gas-filled suit.

1.3.6 DIVER FLAG

The sport diver flag (Figure 1-41) should be flown by all divers in the United States at a sufficient height so that it is clearly visible by approaching boats. The flag indicates that divers are below and all boats should stay at least 100 feet away. The international diver flag (Figure 1-41) may also be seen flying from diving vessels throughout the world.

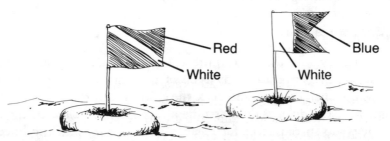

Figure 1-41. U.S. sport diver flag (left) and international diver flag.

1.4 Basic Diving Skills

It is important to note that this text does not attempt to teach the reader how to skin or scuba dive. These skills must be learned only from a fully certified instructor in an accredited scuba diving program. Substantial time should be spent developing basic skin diving skills. Mask and snorkel clearing, surface dives, and buoyancy control skills should be practiced repeatedly in a variety of situations. Although students and teachers alike prefer to skim the skin diving skills in order to rush into the scuba skills, it should be remembered that *a strong skin diver usually evolves into a safe scuba diver*.

1.4.1 SCUBA ENTRIES

There are two popular entries used by divers to enter the water. The most important things to remember prior to entering the water are to check the conditions below and hold onto the equipment, When entering, the diver should have the regulator in the mouth with the air turned on.

Giant Stride

The giant stride entry (Figure 1-42) is easy to learn and safe to perform. The diver prepares for this entry by first standing close to the edge of the deck or dock. The mask should be pressed firmly against the face and the regulator held in the mouth with one hand, while the other hand is used to hold the tank in place. Just prior to performing the giant stride, the diver must check the point of entry on the surface. The entry is initiated by extending one leg forward, up and over the surface of the water, while the trailing leg pushes the body away from land. The legs should be kept wide apart, one forward and one back, as the diver enters the water. As the diver penetrates the surface, both legs are forcefully kicked together to support the diver on top of the water. Both hands should be used to secure the equipment during the entry.

Backward Roll

The backward roll entry (Figure 1-43) is especially useful from small boats. When performing any type of roll into the water, the diver must keep the body low and tuck the chin toward the chest. To begin this entry, the diver should assume a tuck position close to the edge. The legs are spread apart for balance and stability and the knees are

Figure 1-42. Giant stride entry.

bent to keep the diver close to the water. The chin is tucked into the chest to protect the face. When ready to enter, the diver must check the area immediately behind and below. The diver then simply falls back into the water, attempting to land on the surface with the buttocks and the lower back. Again, both hands should be used to prevent the equipment from dislodging on impact.

1.4.2 DESCENT TECHNIQUES

Surface dives, which enable the diver to descend underwater quickly and efficiently, should be mastered to reduce diver energy and air consumption. Two basic surface dives are recommended for both skin and scuba diving: head-first and feet-first.

Figure 1-43. Backward roll entry.

Head-first Surface Dive

The head-first surface dive (Figure 1-44) must be initiated while the diver is swimming on the surface in the horizontal position. This dive is best performed in the pike position, which means the body bends at the waist while the legs are held straight. When the diver wishes to descend, two quick moves are initiated. First, the diver bends vigorously at the waist. When the upper body points down and forms a 90-degree angle with the legs, the fins are then quickly kicked up out of the water, with toes pointed toward the sky. In this manner, the forward horizontal swimming momentum on the surface is transferred directly into a downward, vertical direction, thereby eliminating the need to swim down. The head-first dive is preferred by skin divers.

Feet-first Surface Dive

The feet-first dive is perhaps the best way to submerge, and some diving experts emphasize that it is the *only* way to descend while scuba diving. This dive aids the diver in equalizing the ears, because the head is the last body part submerged. To perform the feet-first surface dive, the diver must begin in the vertical position. The preparatory

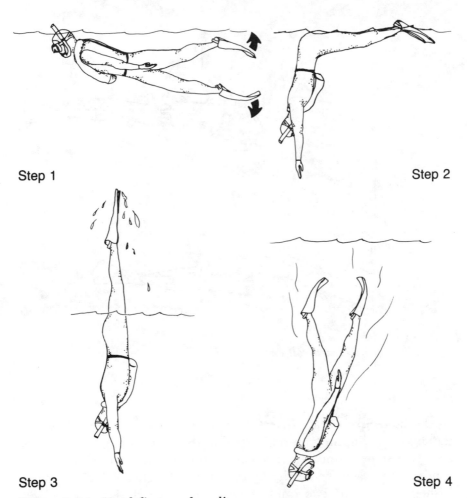

Step 1

Step 2

Step 3

Step 4

Figure 1-44. Head-first surface dive.

position requires the diver to spread both arms and legs, with the arms extended sideways at shoulder level and the legs extended with one leg in front of the body and the other leg behind the body.

When ready to submerge, the diver simultaneously pushes the hands down to the side and kicks the fins together forcefully. This action results in pushing the diver above the surface. When the diver reaches the apex of the upward lift, the diver must stretch and streamline the body with toes pointed to eliminate resistance, thus improving the descent. A streamlined body position is imperative for a deep and quick descent. As the diver's descent slows, the palms of the hands may be thrust upward for additional downward propulsion. Figure 1-45 illustrates the feet-first dive.

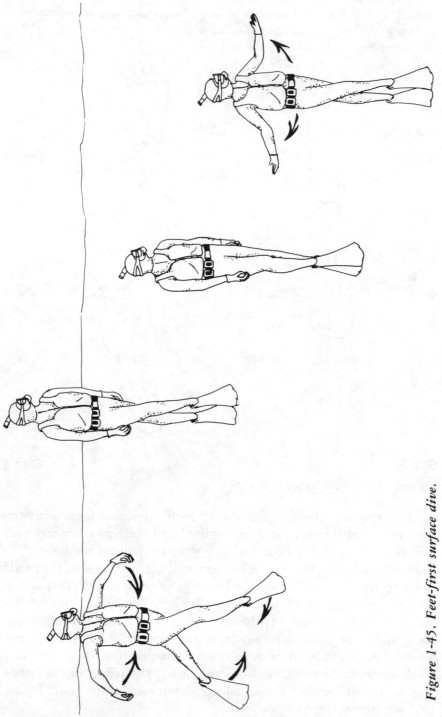

Figure 1-45. Feet-first surface dive.

CAUTION: Great pressure is placed on the ears and sinuses during surface dives. Descents should not be attempted without equalizing the internal pressure of the ears and sinuses *before and during* the surface dive. Diving with head colds, allergies, or sinus infections must be restricted. (An in-depth discussion of the equalization process is found in Chapter 3.)

1.4.3 ASCENT TECHNIQUES

Returning to the surface following a surface dive also requires some safety procedures. These surfacing techniques (Figure 1-46) should be adhered to in all diving situations, but especially in conditions with limited visibility.

Figure 1-46. Ascent technique.

1. Look Up—The diver should always look directly up at the surface to detect obstructions, boats, or other divers.

2. Hand-Up—Extending one hand high over the head serves as protection and is particularly beneficial in murky waters or while diving at night. The extended hand should also hold the B.C.D. hose to control the ascent.

3. Rotate—While surfacing, the diver should rotate around the long axis of the body to achieve a complete view of the area above.

CAUTION: *Never* hold your breath on a scuba ascent. *Always* breathe normally while using scuba gear.

Selected References

Gonsett, R. *Scuba Regulators*. Colton, Calif.: National Association of Underwater Instructors, 1975.

Chapter 1 Review

The instructor should correct the student's answers, record the results, and return them to the student. Both teacher and student should sign after the last question.

REVIEW QUESTIONS	ANSWERS
1. List three important factors to consider when selecting a mask.	1. _____ _____ _____
2. List two advantages of using (a) full-foot fins and (b) open-heel fins.	2. (a) full-foot fins: _____ _____ (b) open-heel fins: _____ _____
3. List four important features to consider when selecting a B.C.D.	3. _____ _____ _____ _____
4. Identify and interpret the scuba tank symbols listed.	4. 3AA _____ DOT _____ E6498 _____ 3,000 _____
5. How often *must* scuba tanks be hydrostatically tested?	5. _____
6. How often should a visual inspection be made of the inside of a scuba tank?	6. _____
7. What is a J-valve?	7. _____

REVIEW QUESTIONS	ANSWERS

8. What is a K-valve?

8. _____

9. Where is the burst disc located and what is its function?

9. _____

_____

_____

10. Draw the sport diver flag and mention the colors.

10. _____

_____

_____

11. What gauge must always be attached to the high pressure port on the first stage of the regulator?

11. _____

12. Which scuba surface dive is usually the preferred method of descending in the water and why?

12. _____

_____

_____

13. List three things divers should do while ascending to the surface.

13. _____

_____

_____

_____

14. What is the purpose of finger pockets in a diving mask?

14. _____

_____

_____

15. The snorkel should be worn on which side of the face?

15. _____

16. Why should the scuba tank be emptied or filled slowly?

16. _____

_____

_____

REVIEW QUESTIONS	ANSWERS
17. How does a capillary tube depth gauge work?	17. _____ _____
18. What is an Alternate Air Source (A.A.S.)?	18. _____ _____ _____
19. List three different types of A.A.S.	19. _____ _____ _____
20. Where is the first stage of the regulator located?	20. _____ _____ _____
21. Where is the second stage of the regulator located?	21. _____ _____
22. When wearing fins, how should a diver walk?	22. _____ _____
23. What features produce easy breathing in a snorkel?	23. _____ _____ _____
24. What is a dive computer?	24. _____ _____ _____
25. What is the function of a burst disc on a tank?	25. _____ _____

REVIEW QUESTIONS	ANSWERS
I have graded, recorded, and returned this student's responses.	Instructor's Signature:
	Date:
I have seen my corrected review questions and now know the appropriate answers. Note: The answer sheet may either be taken out or retained with this book.	Student's Signature:
	Date:

Chapter 2

Underwater Physics

Like most people, you are probably very comfortable when surrounded by air at normal atmospheric pressure. When you venture into the underwater world, you will experience a drastic change in environment. One of the most pleasurable sensations that you will experience underwater is that of weightlessness. By understanding the principles of buoyancy, you will be able to suspend yourself peacefully in the water. This unique feeling of weightlessness can only be experienced by astronauts and aquanauts like yourself!

The physical laws of nature, particularly the properties of light, sound, temperature, and pressure, which are taken for granted on land, are significantly modified underwater. Your diving pleasure and safety depends on how well you understand and adapt to the changes explained by underwater physics.

Water is, quite obviously, a much denser medium than air. You will discover that, because of the higher density of water, light travels slower and sound travels faster (Figure 2-1); the transfer of heat away from the body is accelerated; and pressure, measured in pounds per square inch, increases proportionally with depth. But you are taking a scuba course, not Physics 202, so the discussion of the properties of light, sound, temperature, buoyancy, and pressure will be kept on a practical level.

2.1 Light

Light has deceptive characteristics underwater. Light travels at three quarters the speed it travels through air. Water also serves to reduce

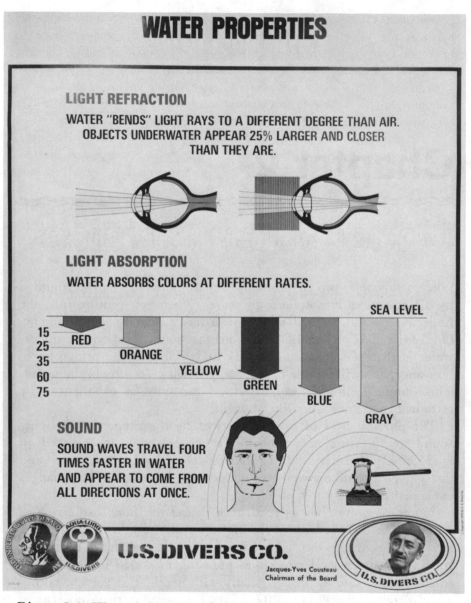

Figure 2-1. Water properties. (© U.S. Divers Co.)

the intensity of light due to the bouncing of light off suspended particles in water.

When light travels from air to water, it undergoes a change in direction, or bending, known as refraction. This bending of light rays also has an effect on what divers see through their masks underwater. As a result, all objects viewed by a diver underwater appear to be 25 percent larger, thus improving a diver's vision considerably. It may be said that a diver with 20-40 vision in air will experience close to 20-20 vision capability underwater. (An example which illustrates this phenomenon is the placement of a teaspoon in a glass of water: a significant magnification can be readily detected below the water line in the glass.) However, slight problems may arise for divers from this magnification factor. For instance, a diver who attempts to grab an anchor line which appears to be an arm's length away will be quite surprised to discover that the line is well out of reach.

The filtering and absorbing effects the water and suspended particles have on light also affect the colors perceived by the diver. The intensity of light and the degree to which colors can be distinguished both diminish with depth. The warmer colors (red, yellow, orange) disappear first, and at a depth of about 100 feet only the cooler colors are visible (blue, indigo, violet). Specifically, red is visible at 10 feet, orange at 20, yellow at 30, green at 75, and blue, indigo, and violet at 100–150 feet. These depths are approximate and vary with water clarity, available sunlight, and other conditions. Fortunately for underwater photographers and night divers, colors are restored with the use of artificial lighting.

2.2 Sound

Unlike the hindered transmission of light, sound travels more efficiently in water due to the relative density of water as a medium. Sound waves travel approximately 4 times faster underwater than in air: 4,800 feet per second versus 1,100 feet per second.

Although sounds may be detected more easily underwater, it does not necessarily follow that a diver's hearing is improved. Rather, hearing can be said to be qualitatively impaired because of the difficulty in determining the origin of underwater sounds. The time delay between when a sound hits one ear and when it hits the other is the most important factor in one's ability to determine the source of that sound. The increased speed of sound reduces that time delay to such an extent that the brain centers for hearing cannot react quickly enough; the brain becomes "confused" because it reacts as if the sound hits both ears simultaneously. Therefore, the time delay makes the determination of sound origin and direction underwater virtually impossible.

2.3 Temperature

Heat is transferred through water in two ways: conduction and convection. *Conduction* is a type of heat transfer occurring when heat passes from the molecules of one temperature to the molecules of a different temperature. In the case of conduction, the molecules of varying temperatures must be immediately adjacent to each other. As a conductor, the water touching the warm skin of the diver transmits the heat from the body to the water. Water is an excellent conductor of heat; water absorbs heat from the diver's body at a rate 25 times faster than in air. Thus, although water temperature may be equal to air temperature, the water *feels* colder to the diver who experiences both. *Convection* utilizes the circulatory motion that occurs in fluids due to the variation in water densities. During convection, warmer molecules circulate and mix with colder molecules, eventually warming them.

Both conduction and convection contribute to the diver's heat loss in water, which is significant. Divers become cold underwater quickly because the body cannot produce heat as fast as conduction and convection deprive them of it. Whether diving in a warm swimming pool, in the tropics, or in a cold-water lake, divers must contend with this rapid heat loss.

Divers maintain body heat by wearing a neoprene rubber wet suit. While wearing a wet suit, the diver actually gets wet, but only a small film of water surrounds the body. Conduction and convection allow the diver to warm the water inside the suit, but the wet suit prevents the transmission of heat from the warmed water inside the suit to the colder water outside the suit. However, the major source of thermal protection is the thickness of the suit, which insulates the diver from the colder surrounding water. The wet suit works well even in extremely cold water, although it would be more accurate to say that the wet suit keeps the diver functional, rather than comfortable, in such conditions.

NOTE: Hypothermia is a malady especially threatening to outdoor sports participants who get wet either intentionally or by accident. Hypothermia is caused by a rapid loss of body heat and is usually enhanced by being wet. It is a serious threat and, in some cases, may be fatal. Hypothermia is discussed more thoroughly in Chapter 3.

2.4 Buoyancy

Positive buoyancy refers to the diver's ability to maintain a lighter-than-water (floating) state. *Negative buoyancy* is the state experienced when a diver cannot float and is sinking. *Neutral buoyancy*, which is the objective of most divers, is a suspended state allowing the diver to rise and fall in the water with ease. Neutral buoyancy means that the diver has balance and control in the water, thus eliminating unnecessary work and making diving more enjoyable.

The Archimedes Principle explains why objects float. This principle, simply stated, says that an object will float when it displaces an amount of water which weighs more than the object itself. For example, a scuba diver weighing 190 pounds when fully equipped might displace 210 pounds of water. That diver would be positively buoyant by 20 pounds, and then would be required to wear 20 pounds on the weight belt to achieve neutral buoyancy.

Density, or weight per unit volume, plays an important role in determining buoyancy. For example, salt water weighs 64 pounds per cubic foot, whereas fresh water weighs only 62.4 pounds per cubic foot. The same diver in these two differing densities of water would displace the same *amount* of water, but would displace more weight in salt water than in fresh; therefore, the diver would be relatively more buoyant in salt water. A diver must be cognizant of the density of water in which the diving activity will take place in order to be in control of buoyancy. Using the previous example of our 190-pound diver, 4–6 additional pounds of lead may be needed to make this diver neutrally buoyant in salt water.

Specific gravity is the ratio between the weight of an object and the weight of an equal volume of water. It follows that the specific gravity of water is a constant, defined as 1.0. When the average specific gravity of a submerged object is greater than 1.0, the object weighs more than the water it displaces and will sink. Conversely, when the average specific gravity is less than 1.0, the object will float. However, different body components and tissues have different specific gravities. Therefore, the personal specific gravity of divers depends on their individual body structure and the proportion of different tissues. The specific gravities of the major body parts are as follows: bone, 1.90; muscle, 1.08; adipose tissue (fat), 0.7–0.9. Compare these numbers to the specific gravities of fresh water (1.00) and salt water (1.02).[1]

The percentage of bone, muscle, and adipose tissue vary immensely from person to person. Large-boned and muscular people do not float as well as would people with an average build and a more equal

1. Charles Silvia, *Manual and Lesson Plans for Basic Swimming* (Springfield, Mass.: published privately by the author, 1970), p. 63.

proportion of fat to muscle. Also, women tend to float more easily than men because of an additional layer of adipose tissue. Consequently, women divers and those with a higher proportion of adipose tissue require more lead on the weight belt to attain neutral buoyancy than would a large-boned, muscular diver. An accurate assessment and understanding of one's own personal specific gravity will aid the diver in controlling buoyancy. Basically, as the percentage of adipose tissue increases, so will buoyancy.

Other factors also affect buoyancy in water. For example, when divers are wearing wet suits, the surface area is increased with volume, but no appreciable change in weight takes place. Therefore, wet suits require divers to add more lead weight in order to reestablish neutral buoyancy. The amount of lead needed will also vary with the thickness of the wet suit and the number of items worn, such as hood, boots, gloves, jacket, and pants.

The B.C.D., which holds air, will also increase buoyancy in the same manner as a wet suit, but with varying effects. The volume of air in the B.C.D. changes with depth, thus changing the diver's buoyancy. Imperative to controlling buoyancy is the diver's ability to regulate the amount of air in the B.C.D. through careful inflation and deflation. This point cannot be overemphasized.

The lungs hold a large amount of air and, consequently, have a significant impact on buoyancy. The difference in buoyancy between a full lung and a nearly empty lung can be as much as 8 pounds. Therefore, conscious breath control and relaxation while in the water are perhaps the two most important prerequisite skills for developing buoyancy control. This comes with practice and experience. Experienced divers, particularly underwater photographers, learn to manipulate breathing in pursuit of varying buoyancy and control of movement in the water.

The most practical way to obtain the proper weight to maintain neutral buoyancy is to experiment and practice with different amounts of lead. Overweighting must be avoided at all times.

2.5 Pressure

The most sensational physical change experienced by the scuba diver is the increase in pressure exerted on the body. Most people are not even aware of the atmospheric pressure which is experienced at all times. However, this pressure is greatly amplified in the medium of water. The pressure changes encountered underwater are significant and vitally relevant to all diving activities.

2.5.1 DEFINITIONS

When discussing pressure in the context of scuba diving, two terms are commonly used: atmospheres (atm) and pounds per square inch (psi). One atm is equal to 14.7 psi, or the atmospheric pressure of air at sea level. Pressure is referred to as being *absolute*, or *total*, when it is the sum of air and water pressure. This absolute, or total, pressure is abbreviated as psia. Pressure may also be expressed as *gauge* pressure, which is 1 atm or 14.7 less than the total pressure. This value is read from the zero level, indicating no pressure whatsoever, and is abbreviated as psig.

A helpful way to conceive of atmospheric pressure at sea level would be to consider the weight which a 1-by-1-inch column of air 60 miles high exerts on the surface of the earth. This equals 14.7 psi. One can think of water (hydrostatic) pressure in much the same way. This hydrostatic pressure increases proportionally with depth. For every 33 feet of water depth, 1 additional atm (14.7 psi) is accumulated. In salt water, this increase in pressure occurs at a rate of 0.445 psi per foot of descent. Again, one must remember that absolute pressure (psia) is the combination of hydrostatic and atmospheric pressure. Therefore, at sea level 14.7 psia is experienced, while at a depth of 33 feet, 29.4 psia is experienced. Table 2-1 lists absolute pressure for various depths.

TABLE 2-1

ABSOLUTE PRESSURE AT VARIOUS DEPTHS

Depth (feet)	atm	psia
18,000 above sea level	½	7.35
Sea level	1	14.7
33	2	29.4
66	3	44.1
99	4	58.8
132	5	73.5

Absolute pressure (also referred to as ambient, or surrounding, pressure) is easily contrasted with gauge pressure. For example, when a diver's tank is empty, the pressure gauge will read 0 psig, which is 14.7 psi less than the absolute pressure. In the theoretical discussion of underwater physics which follows, pressure will be described in terms of absolute pressure.

2.5.2 THE GAS LAWS

The gases breathed by humans under normal atmospheric conditions react differently under pressure. The individual components of air each have a different effect on the human body when breathed at depth, and are more pronounced as the diver descends deeper. The gas laws offer an explanation of how the gases breathed by the diver react to increased pressure. Understanding these laws will enable the diver to avoid complications due to breathing compressed air at depth.

Boyle's Law

More than any other gas law, *Boyle's Law* can be labeled as *The Scuba Diver's Law* because the application of Boyle's Law affects the diver constantly. This law states that with temperature constant, a given volume of gas will vary inversely with the absolute pressure. Simply stated, as a diver descends and pressure increases, the pockets of air both inside and outside the body decrease in size. It follows that as the diver ascends toward the surface and the surrounding pressure decreases, the different volumes of air will increase in size.

The air volumes listed in Table 2-2 are subject to significant changes with changing water depths. The air in the scuba tank, however, is *not* affected by the pressure volume changes dictated by Boyle's Law because the scuba cylinder is a rigid container capable of withstanding great increases in pressure.

Numerous air receptacles are influenced by Boyle's Law. Internally, these include lungs, sinuses, middle ear spaces, intestines, stomach, and throat. The external receptacles include mask, wet suit, B.C.D., and any additional air pockets trapped on the body. According to Boyle's Law, all air cavities (except for the air in the scuba tank) will

TABLE 2-2

PRESSURE/VOLUME CHANGES
AT DEPTH

Depth (feet)	atm	Air volume
Sea level	1	1 or 100%
33	2	½ or 50%
66	3	⅓ or 33%
99	4	¼ or 25%
132	5	⅕ or 20%

tend to shrink or become squeezed while descending and expand while ascending. If these air spaces are not equalized so that the internal air pressure is equal to the external air pressure, serious injury and/or uncontrolled buoyancy could result. (The physiology associated with Boyle's Law is discussed at length in Chapter 3.)

Not only does Boyle's Law create physical concerns for divers, but it also can lead to problems with equipment use. A diver consumes more air at depth because more air is required to fill the lungs in order to equalize for the increased water pressure. In addition, whenever changing depths, the diver's buoyancy changes accordingly. As a diver descends, the B.C.D. and the wet suit will be compressed. This causes the diver to displace less water, thereby raising the specific gravity. As the diver progresses to the surface, water pressure decreases, causing the air in the B.C.D. and wet suit to expand, thereby making the diver more buoyant. As the diver changes depths, variations in buoyancy must be anticipated and controlled.

Dalton's Law

Dalton's Law explains how the partial pressures of a gas function. Partial pressures may be defined as the portion of the total pressure contributed by the individual gases in a mixture. Under normal atmospheric pressure, nitrogen exerts roughly 80 percent of the total air pressure and oxygen exerts approximately 20 percent. Dalton's Law states that each gas in a mixture of gases exerts individual pressure according to its percentage in the mixture and that the total pressure of a gas is equal to the sum of the partial pressures. Therefore, at the surface, nitrogen has a partial pressure (pN_2) of 0.8 atm and oxygen has a partial pressure (pO_2) of 0.2 atm. As the diver's air supply is subjected to greater water pressure, there is a resulting increase in the partial pressures of both nitrogen and oxygen as shown in Table 2-3.

Physiological changes occur as the partial pressures of nitrogen and oxygen increase with depth. For example, oxygen may become toxic to the diver if the partial pressure becomes great (usually 2.0 atm pO_2 or 297 feet), but, fortunately, sport divers don't dive that deep. In addition, nitrogen becomes narcotic as its partial pressure increases with depth. The effect of high pN_2 is similar to alcohol intoxication and is normally experienced around 100 feet, although the narcotic effects of nitrogen vary widely among divers. These and other physical concerns associated with high partial pressures are more thoroughly discussed in Chapter 3.

TABLE 2-3

RELATIONSHIP BETWEEN WATER
PRESSURE AND PARTIAL PRESSURES
OF NITROGEN AND OXYGEN

Pressure	Depth (feet)	pN_2	pO_2
atm			
1	Surface	0.8	0.2
2	33	1.6	0.4
3	66	2.4	0.6
4	99	3.2	0.8
psia			
14.7	Surface	11.76	2.94
29.4	33	23.52	5.88
44.1	66	35.28	8.82
58.8	99	47.04	11.76

Henry's Law

Henry's Law states that the amount of any given gas that will dissolve in a liquid at a given temperature is proportional to the partial pressure of that particular gas. This law is significant for divers because most of the human body is composed of water. As the diver descends, the partial pressures of the gases breathed, namely nitrogen and oxygen, increase (Dalton's Law). As the partial pressures increase, so does the ability of these gases to become soluble in the tissues of the body (Henry's Law).

Nitrogen in the breathing air presents a particular problem to scuba divers. Nitrogen is an inert gas which is not normally utilized by the diver, but under pressure, this gas is forced into solution. As the diver's depth and bottom time increase, the amount of nitrogen absorbed by the diver's body also increases. If sufficient nitrogen has been picked up by the tissues and the diver then ascends quickly to the surface, the nitrogen forced into the body may "bubble out" of solution as the pressure decreases. This diving phenomenon is known as decompression sickness, which is discussed in Chapter 3.

Charles' Law

Charles' Law explains the effect that temperature has on pressure and volume. It states that, for any gas at a constant pressure, the volume of gas will vary directly with the absolute temperature. Because sport divers carry a constant volume of air in the scuba tank which does not change when the tank pressure does, Charles' Law by itself is not applicable to diver safety. However, when Charles' Law is combined with Boyle's Law to form the General Gas Law, it becomes more meaningful. The General Gas Law explains how pressure and temperature are directly proportional when the volume is constant. For example, when a rigid scuba tank is warmed, its volume will not change because the walls of the cylinder are too strong. As a result, the pressure will increase. Divers often refer to the combined effect of Charles' and Boyle's Laws as the Scuba Tank Filling Law.

When a scuba tank is filled rapidly with high-pressure air, the tank becomes quite hot. Conversely, when this tank is placed in cold water for a dive, the pressure will drop significantly. In this situation, the diver usually feels cheated after paying full price for an air fill. To prevent this problem, scuba tanks should be placed in an ice bath to reduce heat buildup while they are being filled.

Scuba tanks should also be kept away from excessive heat because an increase in temperature will cause an increase in pressure, which could lead to an explosion if the burst disc should fail to function.

Selected References

Miller, J.W. (Ed.). *NOAA Diving Manual*. Washington, D.C.: U.S. Government Printing Office, 1979, 1.1–1.15.

Somers, L. H. *Research Divers Manual*. The University of Michigan Sea Grant Program, August 1972, 2:1–2:6.

Chapter 2 Review

The instructor should correct the student's answers, record the results, and return them to the student. Both teacher and student should sign after the last question.

REVIEW QUESTIONS	ANSWERS
1. Does light travel faster or slower underwater than it does through air?	1. _____
2. Which colors disappear first with increasing water depth?	2. _____
3. Does sound travel faster or slower underwater than it does through air?	3. _____
4. Which is a better conductor of heat, air or water?	4. _____
5. Which is the most desirable state of buoyancy for most occasions underwater: positive, negative, or neutral?	5. _____
6. What does the Archimedes Principle deal with?	6. _____
7. List three factors that affect a diver's buoyancy.	7. _____ _____ _____
8. Fill in the chart.	8.

Feet	ATM	PSIA
Sea Level	___	14.7
___	2	___
66	___	___
___	___	58.8

REVIEW QUESTIONS	ANSWERS

9. Boyle's Law specifically deals with what physical fact?

9. _____

10. Dalton's Law explains which physical principle?

10. _____

11. Henry's Law deals with the _____ of gases.

11. _____

12. Water absorbs body heat approximately _____ times faster than air.

12. _____

13. List three different functions provided by a wet suit.

13. _____
_____
_____

14. Will a diver be more buoyant in fresh or salt water?

14. _____

15. When you look through a mask underwater how much are objects magnified?

15. _____

16. What percentage of air is composed of nitrogen?

16. _____% ____

17. What percentage of air is composed of oxygen?

17. _____% ____

18. Do people with a larger percentage of body fat tend to sink or float?

18. _____

19. Do lean individuals tend to sink or float?

19. _____

20. What is a "partial pressure"?

20. _____

REVIEW QUESTIONS	ANSWERS
I have graded, recorded, and returned this student's responses.	Instructor's Signature:
	Date:
I have seen my corrected review questions and now know the appropriate answers. Note: The answer sheet may either be taken out or retained with this book.	Student's Signature:
	Date:

Chapter 3

Physiological Aspects of Diving

Perhaps you've heard that scuba diving is a dangerous sport. Not true! Scuba accidents have occurred, but usually only to uneducated or untrained divers.

The primary objective of any scuba course and of this chapter is to avoid careless accidents. By understanding the causes and symptoms of possible physiological problems, you will learn the importance of taking preventive measures prior to your dives, thus avoiding mishaps. In the event that a careless, uneducated, or untrained diver gets injured, this chapter provides treatments, enabling you to be of assistance to the victim.

The physiological concerns of scuba divers are discussed in six categories: descent, ascent, miscellaneous concerns, the female diver, drugs, and panic/drowning.

3.1 Descent

When the diver begins to descend in the water, Boyle's Law goes to work immediately on the various air pockets which the diver possesses. As the water pressure surrounding the diver increases, the volumes of air both inside and outside of the body decrease in size. This pressure imbalance creates a compressing effect on the body that can result in injuries referred to as *barotrauma*. However, all forms of barotrauma may be avoided by equalizing the pressure in the body air spaces with the outside water pressure. The two major forms of baro-trauma on descent are internal squeeze and external squeeze.

3.1.1 INTERNAL SQUEEZE

Internal squeezes consist of barotrauma located inside the body. The sites of internal squeeze include the middle ear, the sinuses, and, occasionally, the teeth and intestines.

Middle-Ear Squeeze

The middle ear is an air-filled compartment separated from the outer ear by the eardrum and connected to the throat by air passages known as eustachian tubes.

Cause: As water pressure increases on descent, the air space in the middle ear is reduced, causing a vacuum, with the outside water forcing the flexible eardrum inward (Figure 3-1). If the internal air pressure in the middle ear is not increased (equalized) to compensate for the increasing water pressure, the eardrum may become perforated. Fortunately, equalizing the pressure in the middle ear is a simple process.

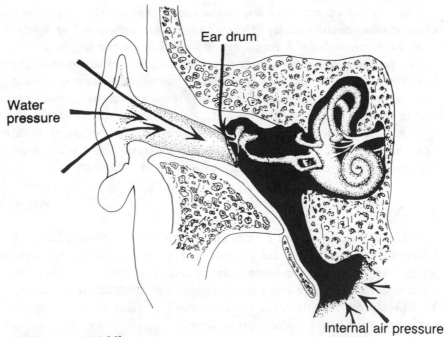

Figure 3-1. Middle-ear squeeze.

Symptoms: Pressure felt on the eardrum warns the diver that equalization is necessary, and pain indicates that trauma already exists. Divers must equalize pressure in the ears *before* experiencing pain. If the water pressure continues to increase without equalizing the pressure in the ears, the eardrum may rupture, allowing cold water to enter the middle ear. Because the centers for balance cannot function properly when flooded with cold water, the diver will experience an unpleasant state called vertigo. This is characterized by a sudden loss of equilibrium, which may be accompanied by dizziness, nausea, and vomiting. Fortunately, as the water in the ear warms, balance and equilibrium are restored.

Treatment: The treatment for middle-ear squeeze requires the attention of a physician. Antibiotics are usually prescribed to thwart infection. The eardrum heals rapidly, and diving may often be resumed within 6 weeks.

Prevention (Equalization): Prevention calls for equalizing whenever changing depths. Diving with head colds and congestion prevents equalization and therefore should be avoided. While ascending, expanding air in the middle ear usually escapes through the nose and mouth. If, however, a nasal spray was used prior to the dive, and the medication wears off during the dive, the expanding air may not be able to escape, thus causing a reverse block or squeeze.

Some divers experience more difficulty than others when attempting to "clear" the ears. Equalization problems may be associated with the physical structure of the air passages of the ears. In any event, several methods may be attempted to facilitate middle-ear equalization. One of the best ways to encourage the ears to clear is to "warm up" the ears before the dive by going through facial gymnastics, such as swallowing and yawning. In addition, the eustachian tubes may be stretched and the head can be cleared of congestion before the diver enters the water by chewing gum or using a nasal spray or decongestant tablet. However, chewing gum underwater is extremely dangerous, because of the possibility of choking, and must be avoided. Nasal sprays, such as Afrin, and decongestant tablets, such as Sudafed,[1] may be used as a last resort, 20–30 minutes before the dive. However, many diving physicians discourage their use because of potential side effects, such

1. L. Somers, *Research Divers Manual* (University of Michigan Sea Grant Program, 1972) 3:2.

Figure 3-2. Valsalva maneuver.

as drowsiness and dizziness. Therefore, both nasal sprays and decongestant tables should be taken on a trial basis well before the day of the
dive to test for adverse reactions.

As the diver descends, several actions may be taken to aid middle-ear
equalization, but controlling the rate of descent is most important.

1. Descend slowly—Equalizing the ears is a continual process which
   becomes much easier if the diver descends as slowly as possible.
   Some instructors tell their students to descend in "slow motion."

2. Use a down line—Holding on to a line (anchor line, for example)
   while descending helps to control the rate of descent. Some divers
   hold the down line with one hand and their nose with the other.

3. Descend feet first—This procedure gives the diver additional

time to clear because the head is the last body part subjected to the increasing pressure.

4. Yawn and swallow—Yawning, swallowing, or any combination of facial gymnastics will help to open the airways and increase internal pressure.

5. Perform the Valsalva maneuver—The Valsalva maneuver may be used to increase internal middle-ear pressure. To perform this technique, the diver closes the mouth, pinches the nostrils shut with the thumb and index finger, and blows *gently* against the closed nostrils without letting any air escape. This creates a back pressure which forces air into the middle ear. Unfortunately, this popular method of clearing may cause complications. A forceful or prolonged Valsalva maneuver may not only damage the eardrum but can also cause vertigo, hearing loss, and unconsciousness (Figure 3-2).

If the five steps listed here do not produce equalization, the diver must stop descending immediately. The diver may want to ascend slightly and repeat the clearing steps while at a lesser depth or even go to the surface to start the process again. The diver should not descend further if pain is experienced.

Sinus Squeeze

The human skull contains four sinuses which are filled with air. They are the frontal, ethmoidal, maxillary, and sphenoidal, all of which come in pairs (Figure 3-3). The sinuses must be equalized just like the middle-ear space. The sinus ostia are the passageways through which internal pressure travels to equalize the sinuses.

Cause: Whenever the sinus ostia become blocked, which may be due to head colds, allergies, sinusitis, or smog, a sinus squeeze may result.

Symptoms: The most prevalent symptom of a sinus squeeze is a mild to strong pain or headache occurring wherever the affected sinus is located. This may vary from mild pressure to sharp pains in the forehead, the cheekbones, or even the teeth in the case of a maxillary sinus squeeze. Any tightness or pain in the facial region should be considered a sinus squeeze and treated accordingly. When a sinus membrane ruptures, a slight, bloody nasal discharge usually follows. This may, on occasion, occur without any pain or discomfort to the

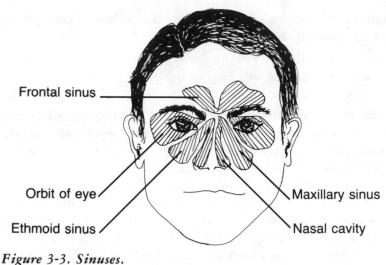

Frontal sinus

Orbit of eye

Ethmoid sinus

Maxillary sinus

Nasal cavity

Figure 3-3. Sinuses.

diver. It must be emphasized that this is a slight impairment and will not end one's diving career.

Treatment: Damaged sinuses can become infected. If pain and tenderness persist after a sinus squeeze, a physician should be consulted. Antibiotics which promote healing and prevent infection are usually prescribed. The sinuses are quick to heal, and diving may often be resumed in a matter of weeks.

Prevention: The ear, nasal, and sinus passages are interconnected, so the methods used to equalize the ears may also be used for the sinuses. Diving with head colds, allergies, or any other conditions which might impair clearing must be avoided.

Miscellaneous Squeezes

The teeth and intestines may, on rare occasions, be affected by barotrauma. Many diving authorities, however, are skeptical of the validity of the tooth squeeze. Maxillary sinus squeeze, which affects the nerve endings of the teeth, may be mistaken for tooth squeeze. Slight discomfort is the only symptom of intestinal squeeze.

3.1.2 EXTERNAL SQUEEZE

External squeezes are induced by air pockets located on the surface of the diver's body which cannot be equalized. These air pockets are usually produced by the diver's equipment. When an equipment squeeze occurs, body tissues are pulled out and away from divers, rather than pushed into them.

Mask Squeeze

Cause: The mask squeeze, which may be the most common external squeeze, is caused by the inability to equalize the air pressure between the mask and the face on the diver's descent.

Figure 3-4. Earplug squeeze.

Symptoms: Suction felt on the face, especially around the eyes, is the prominent symptom of mask squeeze. Bloodshot eyes or a bloody nose may, on some occasions, be the result of a severe mask squeeze.

Treatment: A physician should be consulted following a serious mask squeeze to determine if eyesight has been impaired.

Prevention: Preventing a mask squeeze is simple, requiring that the diver exhale through the nose when suction is experienced on the face. A slow descent also helps the diver avoid this problem.

   CAUTION: Sport divers should never wear earplugs or goggles. These devices create air pockets over the ears and eyes which cannot be equalized and therefore may cause serious injury (Figure 3-4).

Suit Squeeze

   The occurrence of the suit squeeze is not probable because wet suits seldom trap air on the body. However, if air pockets form between the suit and the skin, blood vessels on the surface of the skin could rupture. Suit squeezes are prevented by venting the suit of air and filling the former air pockets with water.

3.2 Ascent

   The problems related to descent are forms of barotrauma caused by increased water pressure accompanied by a decrease in air volumes. The problems related to ascent are also caused by an application of Boyle's Law, but in this case surrounding pressure decreases, causing air pockets in the diver to increase in size. The two most notorious types of ascent problems are lung overexpansion with its associated embolisms and emphysemas and decompression sickness (bends).

3.2.1 LUNG OVEREXPANSION

Cause: When a diver breathing compressed air returns to the surface, air in the lungs will expand due to the decreasing water pressure. Divers must allow this reexpanding air to vent itself normally by breathing regularly on ascent. Breath holding, uncontrolled ascents, or airway blockage could cause the expanding air to rupture the alveoli (air sacs) in the lungs, allowing air bubbles to enter the body and resulting in tissue damage, blood circulation blockage, or both.

   Although many divers fear the perils of deep diving, the greatest chance for the occurrence of lung overexpansion lies near the surface. This is because the greatest pressure/volume change occurs between 33 feet and the surface. A fully inflated lung could overexpand in just a few feet of water when the breath is held.

Symptoms

Overexpansion of the lungs (Figure 3-5) may result in as many as four separate subailments. All are associated with lung rupture, although the symptoms of each vary. The symptoms depend on the exact location of the escaped air bubbles.

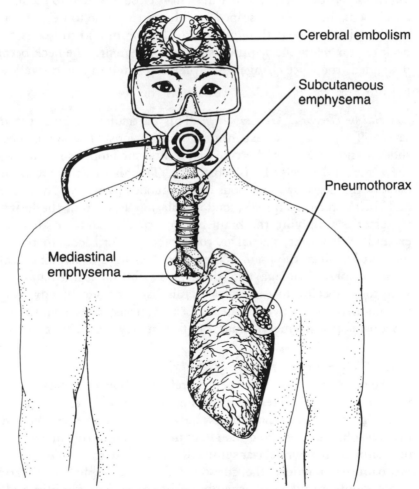

Cerebral embolism

Subcutaneous emphysema

Pneumothorax

Mediastinal emphysema

Figure 3-5. Lung overexpansion.

Pneumothorax: When air escapes the lung via the alveoli, it may become lodged between the lung lining and chest wall. This accumulation outside the lung may cause the lung to collapse, placing pressure on the heart. Chest pain and breathing difficulties indicate a pneumothorax.

Mediastinal Emphysema: The symptoms of mediastinal emphysema are evidenced in the mediastinum, which is located in the chest under the sternum (breastbone) between the lungs. Air may lodge in this area after leaving the lungs and rising along the bronchi. Tightness and/or severe pain, along with a shortness of breath and cyanosis (bluish color) will accompany a mediastinal emphysema.

Subcutaneous Emphysema: This ailment is closely related to mediastinal emphysema because the escaped air follows the same route, but in this case continues to rise through the mediastinum and migrates to the neck region. Here the symptoms become apparent. The neck becomes distended, the voice changes, and breathing, talking, and swallowing become impaired.

Arterial or Cerebral Air Embolism: This particular injury is the most severe of the lung overexpansion complications. The symptoms are sudden and severe. In the case of cerebral air embolism, air escapes the lungs and enters the bloodstream. The air bubbles are pumped back to the heart by the venous flow of blood, pass through the heart, and then enter the arterial blood circulation away from the heart. As the arteries supplying the brain become smaller and the air bubbles expand with ascent, partial or total blockage of blood to the brain may occur. Since the brain is extremely sensitive to hypoxia (lack of oxygen), brain damage and death may follow immediately. The symptoms specific to cerebral air embolism include bloody froth at the mouth, impaired vision, headaches, cyanosis, and convulsions. Air embolisms are extremely serious, but fortunately they are not common.

Treatment

The prescribed treatment for cerebral air embolism and its associated problems is immediate recompression in a recompression chamber. Under pressure, the air bubbles are forced back to a smaller, more manageable size, restoring blood circulation. Pure oxygen should also be administered while transporting the victim to a chamber. This procedure will reduce the chance of further bubble complications. When the victim is in the chamber, pure oxygen is administered and the chamber is pressurized to an equivalent of 165 feet of salt water. Underwater recompression (i.e., taking the victim underwater rather than to a chamber) is not recommended.[2]

Prevention

Lung overexpansion can be avoided simply through self-control. Regardless of the circumstance, divers should be able to perform a controlled ascent at a moment's notice, breathing normally or exhaling slowly along the way. Scuba divers must never hold their breath while ascending. Good breath control and relaxation make emergency ascents much easier, although emergency ascents should never be necessary for the well-trained diver. The "blow and go" emergency technique, which stresses a rapid, full exhalation on ascent, should be avoided. This practice may collapse small airways in the lungs, making the areas of the lungs which they supply more susceptible to overexpansion. Continual breathing or normal exhalation is preferred to forced exhalation during ascents.

Research studies suggest that cigarette smoking causes lung irritability and an increase in bronchial mucus. Chronic smoking weakens the lungs and creates blockage of the airways. This condition increases the chance of lung overexpansion; therefore, scuba divers should abstain from smoking.[3]

3.2.2 DECOMPRESSION SICKNESS

Decompression sickness, also known as the bends, is one of the most feared diving maladies, but it is also one of the least understood. Although it receives much adverse publicity, in reality the bends rarely occurs among sport divers, according to studies at the University of Rhode Island.[4]

Cause

A combination of Dalton's, Henry's, and Boyle's Laws explains how divers may contract the bends. With increasing depth, the partial pressure of nitrogen also increases (Dalton's Law). As the partial pres-

---

2. *Ibid.*, 3:44.

3. T. Mount and A.J. Ikehara, *The New Practical Diving* (Coral Gables, Fla.: University of Miami Press, 1979), pp. 76–78.

4. H.V. Schenck and J.J. McAniff, *U.S. Underwater Diving Fatality Statistics, 1976*, Report No. URI-SSR-78-12 and Report NOAA Grant No. 4-3-158-31 (Rockville, Md.: U.S. Department of Transportation and U.S. Department of Commerce, 1978), pp. 3–19.

sure of nitrogen elevates, it accordingly becomes more soluble in the tissues of the body (Henry's Law). At depth, the diver with nitrogen dissolved in the tissues and bloodstream experiences no apparent problems. On ascent, however, significant pressure/volume changes occur (Boyle's Law). If the rate of ascent is faster than the ability of the body to vent nitrogen through normal respiration, the nitrogen gas will expand and "bubble out" of solution.[5]

Several conditions predispose a diver to decompression sickness. In general, any physical features that restrict circulation or respiration allow the body to absorb more nitrogen, thus enhancing bubble formation. Specific factors contributing to the likelihood of the bends include: excess adipose tissue (fat), alcohol consumption prior to diving, smoking, physiological aging, excessive fatigue, poor physical condition, and extremely cold water. The ratio of fat to total body weight may be the most important factor increasing susceptibility to the bends because nitrogen is much more soluble in fat than in the other tissues of the body.[6]

Symptoms

Specific symptoms of the bends depend upon the location of the expanding nitrogen bubbles. Bubbles forming in the blood may restrict circulation; those collecting in joints, muscles, bones, or nerves may cause paralysis. The two most frequent symptoms are localized pain, especially in the joints of the arms and legs, and skin rash with itching, usually found on the thighs, stomach, and upper back. The symptoms are often delayed. However, in severe cases of neurological decompression sickness (affecting the brain and spinal cord), the diver may immediately lose control of the bladder, bowels, and balance. Table 3-1 summarizes how often, when, and in what combinations symptoms occur.

Treatment

The recommended treatment for serious cases of the bends is immediate recompression in a recompression chamber. While in the chamber, the victim is pressurized until the nitrogen bubbles are forced back into solution; this is followed by a slow and gradual decompression. Central nervous system and brain bends require immediate recompression. Mild skin and limb bends may not require recompression,

5. *Practical Diving*, p. 96.
6. *Ibid.*, p. 98.

TABLE 3-1

SYMPTOMS OF THE BENDS

Symptoms	Number of divers (%)

Local pain
   Lower extremity (70%)
   Upper extremity (30%)
	89.0

Skin rash with itching	11.0
Visual disturbances	6.0
Motor paralysis or weakness	5.5
Vertigo	5.0
Numbness	4.8
Respiratory distresss ("chokes")	2.4
Headache	1.9
Unconsciousness	1.5
Aphasia	1.2
Nausea	0.9

How symptoms occur	
Single symptom only	70.0
Two symptoms	25.6
More than two symptoms	4.4
Pain as only symptom	68.0
Localized pain not symptom	5.3

When symptoms occur (interval after surfacing)	Occurrence of initial symptoms (%)
Within 30 minutes	50
Within 1 hour	85
Within 3 hours	95
Within 6 hours	99
Delayed more than 6 hours	1

SOURCE: L. Somers, *Research Divers Manual* (University of Michigan Sea Grant Program, 1972), 3:31.

but a diving physician should be consulted. Again, while transporting the victim to the chamber, pure oxygen should be administered.

Prevention

The best way to avoid decompression sickness is to dive well within the limits of the U.S. Navy No-Decompression Tables (discussed in Chapter 10). Careful monitoring of conditions of both the dive and the diver are highly recommended. This monitoring includes the following steps:

The Dive

1. Restrict depth.
2. Monitor bottom time.
3. Control rate of ascent.
4. Use reliable gauges.

The Diver

1. Refrain from alcohol within 12 hours of a dive.
2. Keep body fat to a minimum.
3. Stay physically fit.
4. Avoid smoking.
5. Avoid excessive fatigue, cold water, and overexertion.

Flying after a scuba dive is not advisable because less than atmospheric pressure is present to hold nitrogen in solution. Diving at high altitudes also presents specific problems with decompression; therefore, high-altitude diving tables must be consulted. Interestingly, bends victims are usually experienced rather than novice divers. Additionally, decompression "hits" occur most often on repetitive rather than initial dives. These facts are easily explained. Many experienced divers become overconfident and are not so concerned with depth and bottom time. In repetitive dives (performed within 24 hours of a previous dive), residual or excess nitrogen absorbed by a dive made earlier in the day can add to the nitrogen collected recently. This residual nitrogen must be accounted for in order to avoid the bends.

3.3 Miscellaneous Concerns

Relaxation and conscious breath control are essential to safe diving. When the diver becomes physically or psychologically stressed, the slow, easy, rhythmic breathing pattern may be disturbed. Rapid, forced respiration rate may cause complications. Interruptions in the normal breathing pattern can lead to air exchange difficulties, such as hyperventilation and carbon dioxide (CO_2) buildup.

3.3.1 HYPERVENTILATION

Hyperventilation, or shallow water blackout, has more potential to occur on skin, rather than scuba, dives, but may occur on both. Whether it is voluntary or involuntary, hyperventilation results when rapid, forced exhalations significantly lower the levels of both oxygen (O_2) and CO_2 in the bloodstream, which may lead to unconsciousness.

Cause

Some skin divers hyperventilate (inhale and exhale forcefully) intentionally in order to increase breath-holding time underwater. This practice does in fact help one's breath-holding ability, but it is a dangerous practice. CO_2 is the stimulus that triggers the brain centers for respiration. Intentionally hyperventilating prior to a breath-holding dive rids the bloodstream of much of the breathing stimulus. During the breath-holding dive that follows, O_2 is used by the diver. Swimming to the surface reduces the oxygen partial pressure (pO_2) and carbon dioxide partial pressure (pCO_2) because of decreasing water pressure, thus complicating the problem. The combination of low levels of CO_2 and O_2 may cause unconsciousness, often without warning.

Rapid respiration is a sign of stress which may go unnoticed. Involuntary hyperventilation may be caused by the extremely nervous diver who cannot control the respiration rate prior to the dive. Any breathing irregularity prior to a dive must be corrected before the diver enters the water. The physiology of involuntary hyperventilation is the same as that of voluntary hyperventilation.

Symptoms

Often the symptoms are unnoticed. If any symptoms are detected, usually the urge to breathe or "breakpoint" is experienced. Frequently this urge to breathe is suppressed by the diver attempting to increase time underwater. This is sometimes followed by faintness, headaches, and dizziness.

Treatment

If unconscious, the diver should be removed from the water and laid on the back. The airway should be opened by hyperextending the neck. Mouth-to-mouth artificial respiration may not be necessary if the CO_2 level builds up and triggers the breathing mechanisms, which happens quite often.

Prevention

Divers should refrain from excessive hyperventilation to increase breath-holding time. When rapid respiration occurs due to stress (physical or psychological), the diver should stop, rest, and concentrate on a slow, controlled breathing pattern. If in the water, the diver should inflate the B.C.D. and rest on the surface. A continuous, slow, rhythmic breathing pattern will prevent hyperventilation and shallow water blackout.

3.3.2 HYPERCAPNIA

Hypercapnia, or CO_2 excess, is similar to hyperventilation in that it is caused by an interruption of the normal respiration rate. As in hyperventilation, CO_2 is the gas creating the problem, but in this case the CO_2 is not sufficiently purged from the body.

Cause

Excessive CO_2 in the tissues is caused primarily by interference in the normal breathing process, such as fatigue, stress, or deliberate breath restriction (skip breathing). Additionally, poorly designed or faulty equipment may have dead spaces which trap air along with CO_2. In short, anything that interferes with ventilation and CO_2 elimination will cause a CO_2 buildup.

Symptoms

The symptoms are usually quite subtle and may go unnoticed. Breathing difficulties like breathlessness or feeling starved for air may be experienced. As the CO_2 levels increase, drowsiness and mental confusion arise, followed by headache, dizziness, nausea, and muscle spasms. Unconsciousness occurs only when the CO_2 level is equivalent to 10 percent of the breathing mixture.

Treatment

Treating a CO_2 buildup requires a slow, deep ventilation of fresh air. Mouth-to-mouth artificial respiration may be needed if consciousness is lost.

Prevention

Normal ventilation will in most cases be sufficient to prevent CO_2 buildup. Deliberate respiration reduction to conserve air must be avoided because CO_2 will not be removed from the lungs properly. Good equipment will reduce breathing resistance. Physical exertion and stress must also be avoided. Once again, it is important to remember that relaxation coupled with a slow, deep rhythmic breathing pattern is all that is needed to avoid respiratory problems while diving.

3.3.3 HYPOXIA

Hypoxia is an affliction caused by a lack of oxygen. This problem is rare among scuba divers because sport divers breathe normal air containing 20 percent oxygen with a pO_2 equal to 0.2 atm at sea level. The brain is extremely susceptible to low partial pressures of oxygen. If the pO_2 in the air supply fell below 0.10 atm, unconsciousness and brain damage could occur.

Cause

It is not likely that a sport diver would suffer from insufficient oxygen, especially at depths where pO_2 increases. Hypoxia is more likely to affect a skin diver and may be promoted by hyperventilation. If a diver suppresses the urge to breathe during a breath-holding dive and then ascends at the last possible moment, the decreasing pO_2 experienced while surfacing may cause unconsciousness. The combination of oxygen utilization on the bottom and decreasing pO_2 on ascent can be disastrous.

A neglected scuba tank, on rare occasion, may not have sufficient oxygen to support life. This could only happen if a tank was stored for a long time with moist air in it. Rusting is an oxidation process which utilizes oxygen. A severely rusted tank may contain high-pressure air with virtually no oxygen content because the oxygen was used to produce rust.

Symptoms

As hypoxia develops, headache, mental confusion, and a loss of coordination may result. Sudden unconsciousness may occur.

Treatment

The diver should be removed from the water, and mouth-to-mouth artificial respiration must be administered in the case of respiratory arrest. When conscious, the victim should be encouraged to ventilate fully with fresh air; a physician may treat with pure oxygen.

Prevention

Repetitive breath-holding dives without rest periods should be avoided. Normal breathing should be restored between skin dives. Divers must never suppress the urge to breathe, which warns the diver that oxygen is needed.

Scuba tanks must be filled with clean, *dry* air only to avoid internal rusting, and they should be internally inspected once a year.

3.3.4 CARBON MONOXIDE POISONING

Traces of carbon monoxide (CO) in the breathing air can cause serious physiological problems. This ailment is not reserved for scuba divers, but may affect anyone at any time.

Cause

Hemoglobin is the substance in blood that transports oxygen to the tissues in the body. When CO is present in the breathing air, hemoglobin combines with it almost 200 times faster than with oxygen, thereby leaving the body without sufficient oxygen (hypoxia).

CO is commonly produced by combustion engines. The two major potential contributors of CO in the scuba diver's air supply are (1) gasoline-driven air compressors with the air intake in the vicinity of the engine's exhaust and (2) an improperly lubricated compressor causing impartial combustion, which produces CO.

Symptoms

The symptoms of CO poisoning are subtle and unreliable. Underwater, these symptoms are even less noticeable. Symptoms include cherry red lips and fingernails (which, of course, are not perceived at depth), headache, dizziness, nausea, and drowsiness.

Treatment

The afflicted diver should be removed from the contaminated air supply. If the victim is not breathing, mouth-to-mouth resuscitation must commence immediately. Pure oxygen may be administered.

Prevention

Scuba diving cylinders must be filled with clean, dry air. All air compressors should be maintained properly and should be equipped with a filtration system. Compressed air should be obtained only from reputable dive shops.

3.3.5 NITROGEN NARCOSIS

Nitrogen (N_2) narcosis, or "rapture of the deep," is a disorder caused by high pN_2 produced by deep diving. A "narced" diver may experience a pleasurable, euphoric state which leaves him unable to attend to important details, such as depth and time. Tricked into a state of well-being by nitrogen narcosis, the diver may not be able to ascertain when all is *not* well. Other divers, instead of feeling euphoric, may become paranoid or "jumpy." The inability to cope with emergencies is perhaps the major hazard associated with nitrogen narcosis.

Cause

Nitrogen is an inert gas under normal pressure, but it becomes intoxicating when breathed at high pressures. As the diver descends, the pN_2 increases with depth as does its ability to intoxicate the diver. Although the susceptibility of nitrogen narcosis varies among individuals, most novice divers become quite "high" at 100 feet. Factors predisposing divers to nitrogen narcosis include inexperience, psychological stress, fatigue, and alcohol consumption.

Symptoms

The severity of the symptoms increases with depth, but the onset of narcosis may be sudden. The correlation of depth and symptoms is as follows:[7]

30–100 feet—mild impairment; mild euphoria

100 feet—reasoning and memory affected; delayed response to visual and auditory stimuli

100–165 feet—idea fixation; overconfidence; calculation errors

---

7. J.W. Miller (Ed.), *NOAA Diving Manual* (Washington, D.C.: U.S. Government Printing Office, 1979), 2:21.

165–230 feet—talkative, uncontrolled laughter; terror reaction in some

230 feet—severe impairment of intellectual performance

These symptoms vary widely among individuals.

Treatment

Simply ascending to a shallow depth to reduce the pN_2 will quickly remedy the situation.

Prevention

Sport divers should refrain from diving deeper than 90 feet or should take advanced training in order to dive up to 130 feet. Keeping a watchful eye on depth at all times is important, especially when underwater pleasure increases substantially.

3.3.6 OXYGEN TOXICITY

Becoming poisoned by O_2 underwater is a real possibility only while breathing pure O_2, as some military and commercial divers do. Fortunately, sport scuba divers breathe normal air containing only 20 percent O_2, making oxygen toxicity a very remote threat. Therefore, no further discussion of this problem will be included here.

3.3.7 HYPOTHERMIA

A rapid loss of body heat (hypothermia) can be life threatening. Divers must be aware of the dangers of overexposure to cold temperatures because they are susceptible to hypothermia both while in the water and out of it between dives.

Cause

Body heat is lost 25 times faster in water than in air because water is a better heat conductor. If heat from the body core is lost rapidly, physical performance underwater may be hindered and health endangered. Proper insulation must be worn in cold water, with particular attention given to the head, hands, and feet. The diver must also be wary of hypothermia after emerging from the water, especially when a wet diver is exposed to cold and wind. Much body heat is lost through an uncovered head, so it must be well protected in both environments.

Symptoms

The symptoms include cold feet and hands, shivering, loss of hand control, drowsiness, slurring of speech, and the inability to think clearly. These symptoms sometimes are mistaken for alcohol intoxication.

Treatment

A diver exhibiting symptoms of hypothermia while diving should be removed immediately from the water, and measures should be taken to warm the victim up. First, the victim should be brought into a warm, dry enclosure, stripped of wet clothing, and dried. Dry clothes should then be worn. Wrapping the victim in blankets is also suggested. If conscious, the victim should be given hot liquids, such as soup and coffee, but *not alcohol*.

Prevention

An insulated wet suit must be worn to prevent heat loss. The thickness of the suit will vary with the water and air temperatures. To be effective the suit must fit properly and have a minimum of zippers. The head, hands, and feet especially must be protected both in and out of the water. The diver should refrain from alcohol consumption because it accelerates heat loss, although the diver may actually feel warmer while drinking.

3.4 The Female Diver

Today approximately 25 percent of all divers are women. In general, women make better divers than men if for no other reason than women breathe less air than men. Because much of the equipment and many of the safe-diving principles were developed by males for a male diving population, it would be prudent for the female diver to consider some areas of concern.

While women can, without a doubt, handle the physical stresses of diving, there are some very definite physiological differences between male and female divers. It must be emphasized that most female divers never experience problems while diving. Because of the scarcity of data concerning the physiology of the female diver, however, this discussion of the female diver is more speculative than definitive.

In some sports, physiological differences often favor the female participant. In endurance events, such as marathon running, the extra adipose tissue (fat) that women have provides an additional source of energy.

Perhaps the greatest difference between males and females concerning the effects on diving is this greater amount of adipose tissue females possess. The average lean female has approximately 24 percent body fat while the average lean male has 17 percent body fat.[8] This extra adipose may present minor problems to some female divers. They include:

1. Buoyancy—Females tend to be more buoyant in the water than males because of the additional layer of adipose tissue. Therefore, women typically require relatively more lead weight than males to achieve neutral buoyancy. When one considers that women in general have significantly less upper-arm strength than males, carrying, wearing and removing weights could physically tax some women more than their male diving counterparts.

2. Thermal Balance—Adipose tissue can serve as an insulator to keep the body warm. Female divers, however, become chilled faster in water than most males because they have a greater body surface area to body mass/area ratio; therefore they lose heat to the water at a faster rate.[9]

   Conversely, because women have fewer sweat glands than men (evaporation of perspiration is a cooling mechanism), they tend to overheat faster than males, especially when suiting up. In a co-ed diving situation, it may be best to suit up at the female diver's pace.

3. Decompression Sickness—Because nitrogen is five times more soluble in adipose tissue than in lean tissue it has been hypothesized for many years that women are more susceptible to the bends than men. Some research studies have also noted this tendency while other studies have found no significant differences between male and female divers and the incidence of the bends. While it may be true that women might absorb more nitrogen than men while diving, some recompression chamber operators claim they treat relatively fewer females because they dive more carefully. Women should also be aware that while diving during the menstrual cycle is acceptable, blood circulation may be impaired at this time, thus slowing nitrogen elimination.

8. K.W. Kizer, "Women and Diving." *The Physician and Sportsmedicine* 9 (February 1981):86.

9. *Ibid.*, p. 87.

While this aspect of diving physiology may be debated for some time to come, women are urged to dive conservatively and stay well within the limits of the no-decompression limits.

Other concerns for the female diver include menstruation, birth control, and pregnancy.

3.4.1 MENSTRUATION

Contrary to popular belief, diving during menstruation is not a problem for the vast majority of female divers. The basic question which each woman must ask herself is, "How do I feel?" Women who experience severe premenstrual syndrome (PMS) might want to reevaluate the dive plan. PMS is characterized by severe cramping, irritability, depression, and slowed mental alertness and physical reaction time. Dr. Ken Kizer cites research studies which suggest that some women with PMS experience significant performance decrements just prior to their periods.[10] Fortunately, PMS occurs in only a very small percentage of women, but one who experiences it should avoid diving or take precautions, such as planning the dive more carefully and conservatively and informing her dive partner of her condition.[11] It has been suggested that a high-protein diet may reduce the psychological symptoms of PMS.[12]

While PMS might make women more accident prone, this syndrome only affects a very small number of women. In fact, many female athletes experience improved physical performance just prior to and during their period. However, an accurate assessment of the female diver's reaction to her cyclical hormonal changes is imperative for diving safety.

Blood loss during menstruation will not attract sharks for the following reasons:

1. Blood loss during menstruation is almost insignificant (1–3 ounces).

2. Blood loss is spread out over several days. As a result, little blood will escape into the water during a 45-minute dive.

10. *Ibid.*

11.   B.E. Bassett, "Safe Diving Equals Fun Diving: Prescriptions for Diving Women," Proceedings of the Tenth Conference on Underwater Education, Anaheim, Calif., November 9–12, 1978 (Montclair, Calif.: National Association of Underwater Instructors, 1979), p. 46.

12. *Ibid.*

3. Tampons or other internal protectors will stop nearly all discharge.

4. Sharks are not attracted to the old, hemolyzed blood released during menstruation.

3.4.2 BIRTH CONTROL

All means of birth control that are acceptable on land are also acceptable underwater. At one time it was thought that oral contraceptives might make women more susceptible to the bends but this theory has not proved to be true. Some women wearing diaphragms while diving have complained of mild discomfort and pain but apparently no further complications were evidenced. Practicing birth control and scuba diving are compatible.

3.4.3 PREGNANCY

Although there is conflicting evidence regarding the effects of diving on the pregnant woman and the unborn fetus, most diving physicians today agree that pregnant women should abstain from scuba diving.

The pregnant diver *and* the unborn child (Figure 3-6) could be more susceptible to decompression sickness. The fetus may also be more

Figure 3-6. Pregnant diver. (Illustration by Katherine Flood)

sensitive to high partial pressures of oxygen encountered at depth and also in the recompression chamber if the mother is being treated for decompression sickness.

Additionally, every fetus has a *patent foramen ovale*, which is a hole in the wall (septum) of the heart. This hole, or "flap-valve," closes at birth or very shortly thereafter. If the fetus is subjected to scuba diving and bubbles do form, the *patent foramen ovale* may allow these bubbles to "shunt" from right to left and enter the systemic circulation, where they could easily find their way to the brain of the fetus, resulting in a cerebral air embolism. The existence of the *patent foramen ovale* in the fetus alone should preclude females from diving while pregnant.

Because a fetus is surrounded by amniotic fluid there is no chance for any type of barotrauma. Many women have dived through term without incident to themselves or child. However, because so little is known in this area of diving physiology and the *patent foramen ovale* appears a definite threat, women are urged to refrain from diving while pregnant.

The psychological aspects of sport diving could be more pertinent to some women than the physiological concerns. In the past, scuba diving was reserved for young, adventuresome, healthy males. Fortunately, today's divers come from all ages and both sexes. Unfortunately, much of the advertisements and diving media still depict diving as a macho sport and rely on sexist advertising to sell diving equipment. Women must realize that they can and will excel in sport diving provided they ignore some of the sexist vintages of the sport. In fact, scuba diving is rapidly becoming a very popular family sport.

3.5 Drugs

This section does not deal with the moral and legal ramifications of drug use; rather, the effects of drugs on underwater performance are identified. For the purposes of this discussion, a drug will be defined as any chemical substance that affects a biological system.[13] Thus, cigarettes and alcohol are included here and given as much attention as the illegal drugs.

The use of drugs before, during, and after the dive is becoming a major problem in the sport because drug use in our society is widespread. Additionally, sport diving is a form of recreation which takes place in a social atmosphere that lends itself to parties. While the effects of drugs on the body under normal atmospheric conditions are

13. J.M. Walsh, "Drug Abuse and Diving," *Skin Diver* 24 (August 1975):55.

known, when the body is subjected to pressure, drugs react differently and are, for the most part, unpredictable. Under pressure, the effects of a drug may become more potent or be reversed.[14]

3.5.1 CIGARETTES

While the health hazards of smoking are known to most people, further complications are risked by the smoking diver. Smoking causes an increase in carbon monoxide in the respiratory system, leading to impaired oxygen transport and susceptibility to both hypoxia and hyperventilation. Smoking, which constricts the vessels, also promotes loss of body heat. More importantly, because cigarette smoke is a lung irritant, the smoking diver is more prone to embolisms. Smoking causes stickiness of the blood platelets, increasing the chances of the bends.[15] Because smoking so adversely affects underwater respiration, divers should abstain from smoking. If total abstinence is not possible, however, smoking should be strongly curtailed as the day of the dive approaches.

3.5.2 ALCOHOL

Several studies reveal that alcohol plays a leading role in drownings.[16] The diver who consumes alcohol prior to or immediately following a dive becomes prone to diving ailments.

The diver's body normally vasoconstricts to preserve body heat, but alcohol consumption inhibits this process. Alcohol is a central nervous system depressant and peripheral vasodilator, which hastens body heat loss in water. Drinking before the dive causes blood to move toward the diver's extremities when submerged in cold water. While the diver feels warmer, the body core and vital organs are deprived of needed heat, thus making the diver susceptible to hypothermia.[17]

As a skin vasodilator, alcohol consumption also encourages nitrogen absorption by the subcutaneous skin, thus predisposing the diver to decompression sickness. Overindulging in alcohol also causes fluid loss, increasing the likelihood of the bends for those who dive with hangovers.[18] Drinking following the dive likewise promotes a rapid

---

14. C. Brown, "Drugs and Diving: Part II," *NAUI News* (April 1976):13.

15. V. Barber, "Getting It Straight about the Bends," *Diver* 23 (September 1978):445.

16. A.L. Thygerson, *Accidents and Disasters* (Englewood Cliffs, N.J.: Prentice-Hall, 1977), pp. 187–188.

17. J. Betts, "It All Depends on What You Mean by Drink," *Diver* 23 (August 1978), p. 373.

18. "Getting It Straight," p. 145.

release of nitrogen, amplifying the symptoms of the bends.

Knowing the effects of alcohol, divers can reasonably assume that drinking and diving don't mix. Therefore, abstaining from spirits 24 hours prior to and immediately following the dive is good advice.

3.5.3 MARIJUANA

Diving while under the influence of marijuana may render the diver less capable of recognizing problems underwater and reacting to underwater emergencies. Underwater, the effects of marijuana include impairment of memory and motor performance, lethargy, rapid loss of body heat due to vasodilation, and a decrease in breath-holding ability.[19] In addition, heavy users of marijuana risk the same lung problems as cigarette smokers.

"Getting high" before a dive is a dangerous practice. Diving under the influence impairs the ability to make correct decisions underwater in emergency situations and also prevents an accurate assessment of depth, bottom time, and rate of ascent.

3.5.4 AMPHETAMINES

Amphetamines are stimulants which often reduce mental activity and emotional stability.[20] Most stimulants interfere with the body's heat-conserving mechanisms, contributing to hypothermia. Stimulants plus diving stress may cause heart dysrhythmias.[21]

3.5.5 NONPRESCRIPTION DRUGS

Divers literally gobble up many types of over-the-counter drugs in order to be able to make a dive. Medications consumed to assist middle-ear and sinus equalization, decongestants (stimulants), and antihistamines (depressants) are particularly abused. Decongestants may cause serious dysrhythmias of the heart, and antihistamines can cause dry mouth and blurred vision. Antinausea drugs, especially motion sickness remedies, inhibit skin vasoconstriction, allowing blood and heat to leave the body core and exit via the skin, thus producing chilling.[22]

19. W. Groner-Strauss and M.B. Strauss, "Divers Face Special Peril in Use/Abuse of Drugs," *The Physician and Sportsmedicine* 4 (August 1976), p. 33.

20. "Drugs and Diving II," p. 13.

21. "Divers Face Special Peril," p. 32.

22. C. Brown, "Drugs and Diving," Proceedings of the Seventh Conference on Underwater Education, Miami Beach, Fla., September 26–28, 1976 (National Association of Underwater Instructors), p. 62.

3.5.6 SUMMARY

Some experts believe that any diver suffering from an ailment requiring treatment by drugs should refrain from diving. Not only do drugs cause complications underwater, but they also mask the reason for which they were taken. If divers believe they must take drugs for medicinal purposes prior to a dive, they should first test the effects of the drug in nondiving situations. Then the divers can use the drug in the safe environs of a swimming pool and later in the open water. However, the dive master and dive partner should always be alerted to the diver's use of medication.

The following drugs should never be used when diving because of their potentially dangerous effects: alcohol, antiasthmatics, anticonvulsants, cardiovascular medications, depressants (for example, barbiturates), LSD, marijuana, narcotics, steroids, and stimulants. Drugs that may have adverse effects and should be used with caution when diving (if they can't be avoided) include analgesics, antibiotics, antidiarrheal agents, antiemetics, antihistamines, antitussives, aspirin, cigarettes, insulin, relaxants, thyroid medications, and vasoconstrictors. Drugs that are not known to have any adverse effect on diving include antacids, laxatives, mouthwash, vitamins, and external agents, such as lotions, salves, and oils.[23]

3.6 Panic/Drowning

Scuba diving accidents are becoming more remote with new advances in diving equipment and upgraded instruction. If and when a diving accident does occur, the cause usually centers around the panic/ drowning syndrome, rather than faulty equipment or dangerous marine life. Scuba diving drownings usually take place in a specific aquatic environment for which the diver was unprepared or untrained. Diving in rough waves or strong currents, diving in caves, and diving too deep are just a few situations which could lead to panic/drowning for the untrained diver.

Drowning may occur in two ways, physiologically. *Dry drowning* is due to asphyxia without water being inhaled. This is usually precipitated by a laryngospasm, a spasm of the larynx which stops all water from entering the lungs and occurs when cold water floods the larynx. Dry drownings have the highest recovery rate for victims.[24] *Wet drown-*

23. "Divers Face Special Peril," p. 34.
24. *Accidents and Disasters*, p. 181.

ing occurs when asphyxia causes the laryngospasm to relax, allowing water to enter the lungs. Water in the lungs inhibits oxygen absorption by the lungs and encourages the loss of blood protein. When water is aspirated into the lungs, the physiological response of the body differs between fresh water and salt water. After fresh water enters the lungs, it is absorbed by the bloodstream, dilutes it, and destroys red blood cells. With salt water in the lungs, additional fluids are drawn from the bloodstream to the lungs, causing a drop in blood pressure and promoting shock.[25]

Regardless of the type of water aspirated, much lung irritation accompanies near drowning. Near-drowning victims must be treated by a physician immediately following the rescue. Specific scuba lifesaving techniques are discussed in Chapter 6.

While the physiological causes of drowning are easy to understand, the psychological causes of panic and drowning are more difficult to comprehend. Usually a chain of events, including a host of additive factors, leads to panic. Diver panic is often preceded by poor judgment. Panicky divers are usually found in rough, dangerous waters, overweighted, inadequately equipped, and poorly trained. Good judgment, common sense, and proper training prevent panic, thus reducing drownings. If panic-induced drownings could be eliminated as a cause of scuba diving fatalities, there probably wouldn't be any! Panic is specifically discussed in Chapter 9.

Since 1970, while the diving population grows by thousands, annual scuba fatalities remain at approximately 100. This indicates that scuba diving is surprisingly safe and is much less dangerous than many other sports.

25. *Ibid.* p. 182.

Chapter 3 Review

The instructor should correct the student's answers, record the results, and return them to the student. Both teacher and student should sign after the last question.

REVIEW QUESTIONS	ANSWERS
1. What is barotrauma?	1. _____
2. How does a diver prevent middle-ear squeeze and sinus squeeze?	2. _____
3. List three practices which promote middle-ear and sinus equalization.	3. _____ _____ _____
4. How is mask squeeze prevented?	4. _____
5. Immediate recompression in a chamber is required by which underwater physiological problems?	5. _____ _____ _____
6. Where in the body do the following specific lung over-expansion problems occur: • pneumothorax • mediastinal emphysema • subcutaneous emphysema • arterial air embolism	6. _____ _____ _____ _____ _____
7. What physiological factors predispose a diver to getting the bends?	7. _____ _____ _____

REVIEW QUESTIONS	ANSWERS
8. What is the treatment for decompression sickness?	8. _____
9. What is the prevention for decompression sickness?	9. _____
10. What is hypercapnia?	10. _____
11. What is hypoxia?	11. _____
12. How does a diver prevent nitrogen narcosis?	12. _____
13. List three symptoms of hypothermia.	13. _____ _____ _____
14. How does a woman's thermal balance differ from a man's?	14. _____
15. May a woman dive during menstruation? Why or why not?	15. _____ _____
16. Should a woman dive while pregnant?	16. _____
17. How does smoking affect underwater performance?	17. _____ _____
18. List three disadvantages of drinking alcoholic beverages prior to diving.	18. _____ _____ _____
19. List three drugs that absolutely should be avoided prior to diving.	19. _____ _____ _____

REVIEW QUESTIONS	ANSWERS
I have graded, recorded, and returned this student's responses.	Instructor's Signature: _____ Date: _____
I have seen my corrected review questions and now know the appropriate answers. Note: The answer sheet may either be taken out or retained with this book.	Student's Signature: _____ Date: _____

Chapter 4

Diving Environment

You, like most divers, will undoubtedly be fascinated with the wonders of the underwater world. Especially in tropical waters, you'll see more shades of blue on the water's surface than you knew existed. Underwater, you'll become engulfed in a kaleidoscope of colors and a smorgasbord of marine life forms.

In this chapter, the new world you will be exploring is divided into two major areas: basic oceanography and marine life. While there is an abundance of fascinating information available to you concerning the oceans and their teeming wildlife, only facts pertaining to your diving safety are presented here. Please remember that the diving environment only presents hazards to the careless, unknowing diver, which of course excludes you! In addition to being familiar with the information provided in this chapter, you should also consult local authorities, such as dive shops, dive clubs, and the Coast Guard, prior to diving in unfamiliar environments.

4.1 The Oceans

Approximately 72 percent of the earth's surface is covered by water. The deepest point found in the ocean to date is approximately 36,000 feet. By comparison, Mount Everest is 29,000 feet, illustrating that if it were possible to place Mount Everest in the deepest trench in the ocean, the mountain top would still be about 1 mile beneath the surface. The average depth of the ocean is 12,000 feet. Considering the sport diving limit of 100 feet, much of the ocean remains unseen and unexplored by divers. The limit is set at 100 feet to avoid the physiological effects that high partial pressures will cause beyond that depth.

4.1.1 TIDES

The daily vertical rise and fall of water caused by the gravitational pull of the moon, and to a lesser extent the sun, is known as the tide. When the pull of the moon is greatest, high tides occur, and low tides occur when the moon's pull is negligible. Most seashores on the globe experience two tidal changes daily. The tidal range (the difference between high tide and low tide) can be as great as 50 feet, as in the Bay of Fundy, or as little as a few inches in the Mediterranean. Divers must consider tidal changes when planning dives, because water conditions, such as visibility and currents, will be affected.

A *tidal current* accompanies the rise and fall of the tides. This current is a periodic horizontal flow of water. The *flood tide* is a term used to describe the tide's coming in, while *ebb tide* refers to the outgoing tide. Tidal currents can be hazardous to divers, especially in bays, channels, or inlets. When one dives in an enclosed body of water with a restricted opening or mouth, *slack tide*, which comes before high tide, is usually most suitable for diving. Slack tide occurs between flood tide and ebb tide and is accompanied by relatively still water with little or no current. The tide tables furnished by the U.S. Coast Guard should always be consulted when diving in coastal waters.

4.1.2 OCEAN CURRENTS

The oceans contain six major ocean currents, which are continuously flowing streams. These ocean currents are found in the Atlantic, Pacific, and Indian Oceans. Two well-known currents are the Gulf Stream in the Atlantic and the Japan current in the Pacific. Sometimes referred to as gyres, large ocean currents travel clockwise in the Northern Hemisphere and counterclockwise in the Southern Hemisphere. A combination of factors, including the earth's rotation, large wind patterns, and centrifugal force, help to explain this phenomenon.

When diving in ocean currents, divers must remain in the immediate vicinity of the boat. Even the strongest of swimmers cannot compete with a large ocean current. When large ocean currents are encountered the following precautions should be taken:

1. A trail line, at least 200 feet long with a float, should be attached to the boat.

2. Lines attached to the boat and the bottom should be used for ascents and descents.

3. Divers should always dive into or against the current, not with it, at the beginning of the dive.

4. The B.C.D. should be inflated and assistance summoned by whistle if the boat cannot be reached upon surfacing.

4.1.3 WAVES

For the most part, waves are generated by the wind. At sea, waves transmit energy through the water, but the water in the wave does not actually move. Waves only move water when they enter the surf zone, that is, when the wave breaks close to the shoreline. Breaking waves are a considerable hazard to divers entering the surf and must be understood in order to ensure safe beach entries.

As waves approach land and water depth becomes shallow, the speed of the wave decreases, while the height increases dramatically. As the lower portion of the wave "feels bottom," it slows down, while the top, or crest, of the wave continues forward. No longer able to support itself, the crest falls over, or breaks. Waves generally break when the depth of water is approximately 1.3 times the height of the waves. Knowing this, a diver observing small waves breaking away from shore can predict a shallow depth of water, indicating sand bars or coral heads.

Combating a *plunging wave* (Figure 4-1) during a beach entry can be tricky and dangerous. The plunging wave is characterized by great

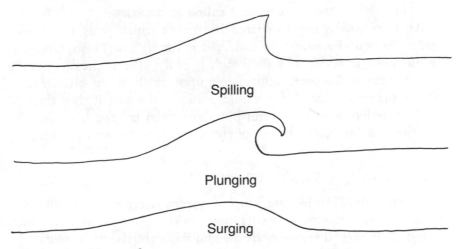

Spilling

Plunging

Surging

Figure 4-1. Types of waves.

force and velocity. Strong winds from the sea and a sharply inclined beach affect the magnitude of this wave. When breaking, the crest of the wave curls over and falls to the base without touching the face of the wave.

Occurring with little wind behind it and approaching flat shores, the *spilling wave* (Figure 4-1) is less imposing than the plunging wave and more suitable for beach entries. When a spilling wave breaks, the crest of the wave rolls or tumbles down the face.

Sport divers are often deceived by the action of the *surging wave* (Figure 4-1) because it does not truly curl or break. Rather, it abruptly rises around rocky coastlines, piers, pilings, jetties, and some steep beaches. The surge is characterized by a sudden rise and fall of a large mass of foaming aerated water. The power of the surging wave is often underestimated by divers.

4.1.4 SURF ZONE

Scuba divers entering and exiting the ocean from the beach should know how surf operates in this area. Surf entry and exits are tricky at best, and not knowing how the water works in this region may cause problems to the diver. The surf zone refers to the wave activity between the shoreline and the breakers farthest from it. When a wave breaks, water moves up the beach and is referred to as the *uprush*, *swash*, or *wash*. After being deposited on the beach, the water rolls back down the beach to seek its own level. This is called the *backrush* or *backwash*. When the waves are tall and the beach is severely sloped, the backrush can be powerful and is sometimes called an *undertow*.

An undertow is not a mysterious current which pulls a swimmer out to sea or under waves. An undertow is simply a backrush. Granted, if the wash is severe and the beach is steep, the backrush may be intense, but it dissipates immediately upon reaching the breaker line. Fewer swimmers and divers would panic in the surf if they realized that an undertow is a powerful but short-lived backwash affected by the slope of the beach, height of the waves, and bottom conditions.

4.1.5 NEARSHORE CURRENT SYSTEM

The nearshore, or inshore, current system is generated by the wave action in the surf zone. Currents found in the nearshore system which particularly affect diver safety are the longshore and the rip currents.

Longshore Current

A longshore current, produced by waves breaking at an angle to the shoreline, runs roughly parallel to the beach. The longshore velocity depends mostly on the intensity of the surf. Although not overly hazardous, the longshore current may affect the diver's entry and exit point. The longshore current can either offer a free ride down the beach or inconvenience the divers by depositing them far down the beach after the dive. When obstructions, such as pilings or jetties, cross the path of a powerful longshore current, the diver must confront the current with caution.

Rip Current

The inshore condition causing consternation to swimmers, divers, and lifeguards is the rip current. Rips are strong, yet narrow, currents flowing perpendicular from shore through the surf line. Whenever waves or longshore currents pile up water on shore, the rip current develops to allow this excess water to escape and return to its own level. Rip currents often flow between two sandbars or where two opposing longshore currents meet (Figure 4-2).

Problems are created by rips when unsuspecting swimmers or divers find themselves in the grasp of the current and believe they are being pulled out to sea. The immediate—but wrong—response of many is to swim directly back to shore, *against the current*. In this case, the rip wins as the swimmer often fatigues, then panics. Understanding the

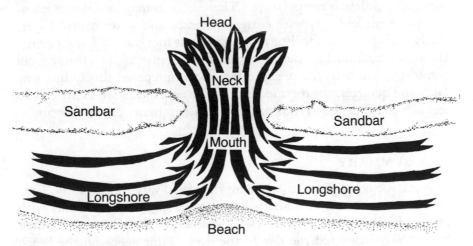

Figure 4-2. Rip current.

principles of the rip current, the swimmer or diver needs only to swim parallel to shore across the narrow current, ride the current out beyond the surf line where it quickly dissipates, or choose a new exit route.

Rip currents may be easily detected by observing the following surface conditions from the beach: discolored water in the neck region, white water or foam in the neck, and small choppy waves heading out through the neck, with larger waves breaking on either side.

4.1.6 ROCKY SHORELINES

Diving in and around rocky coastlines and pilings can be treacherous. Slipping on rocks while attempting to make an entry occurs frequently. Surf may also knock divers off balance and onto the rocks if they are not careful. Scuba entries and exits made through a rocky shoreline require prudence and patience. Protective wet suits, particularly hard-soled boots, are a must.

4.1.7 WATER TEMPERATURE

Although surface waters can rise above 85°F, most scuba divers experience temperatures ranging from 45° to 75°F, regardless of season or location. Because body heat is lost rapidly when submerged, exposure (wet or dry) suits are recommended for all diving.

Thermocline refers to the transitional layer between two layers of drastically different temperatures. Thermoclines may be either seasonal or permanent and vary with currents, winds, and water depth. Layers sandwiching the thermocline may differ by as much as 20°F and passing through a thermocline can be traumatic (because of the change from comfort to cold) to the unexpecting and unprepared diver. In many lakes and quarries, the thermocline may be experienced in as little as 25 feet of water, but there is no standard depth for thermoclines to occur.

4.1.8 SUMMARY

Aquatic environments throughout the world vary significantly. Currents, waves, coastlines, and other conditions change dramatically with geographical regions. Waves, wind, weather, currents, and tides must be carefully inspected the day of the dive. Time spent on the beach examining these conditions prior to the dive provides valuable information, promotes relaxation, and, most important, aids diver safety.

4.2 Marine Life

The beauty of the underwater world cannot be described by words or pictures; it must be experienced. Splendid colors, exotic shapes and forms, and unique relationships are all found on each dive. Fish guides, available in dive shops, offer a quick and enlightening introduction to the underwater world.

Few underwater organisms threaten divers. The organisms discussed in this section are categorized by the manner in which they *might* inflict injury to the diver. It must be emphasized that large creatures with notorious reputations, while potentially dangerous, rarely pose a real threat to divers. On the other hand, small, apparently innocuous organisms often injure the diver who fails to attend to them. Ironically, many novice divers bump into these small creatures while on the lookout for sharks and barracuda.

4.2.1 ORGANISMS THAT ABRADE, LACERATE, OR PUNCTURE

Types of Organisms

Barnacles: Barnacles are crustaceans that literally cement themselves on ship hulls, rocks, piers, pilings, and other shoreline structures. Although they are nonpoisonous, barnacles are extremely sharp and can easily cut an unwary diver. Divers entering, exiting, and working in the presence of barnacles must be alert and wear protective clothing, especially in surging water.

Hard Corals: Most hard (stony) corals are characterized by sharp limestone skeletons capable of inflicting scrapes and abrasions and are found in almost all warm waters throughout the world. Coral cuts are a nuisance because they are slow to heal and are therefore prone to infection. However, coral cuts are nonpoisonous. Protective clothing, particularly gloves, is sufficient to prevent coral scrapes. In warm tropical waters, jeans, long-sleeved shirts, and cotton gloves may suffice.

Sea Urchins: The sea urchin (Figure 4-3), found in most oceans around the world, is perhaps the most common marine-life hazard. Although most urchins are nonpoisonous, their spines inflict painful puncture wounds which are slow to heal and susceptible to infection. Being bottom feeders, urchins are not very mobile, and divers have an apparent knack for sitting, stepping, or placing a hand on them. A watchful eye is all that is necessary to avoid the sea urchin.

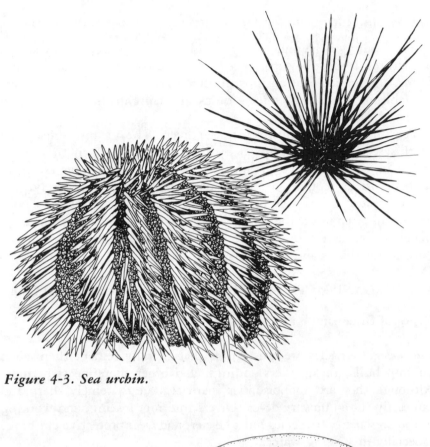

Figure 4-3. Sea urchin.

Figure 4-4. Stingray.

Stingrays: Although stingrays (Figure 4-4) have a notorious reputation, divers should not fear them because it is actually difficult to be injured by one. Stingrays do not attack or bite. They are cartilaginous, bottom-feeding fish, often found buried in the bottom with only their eyes exposed. The long tail of the stingray presents a possible, but not probable, hazard to divers. However, when a stingray is stepped on, the tail snaps up rapidly. One or more serrated and dirty barbs located on the tail may inflict a puncture wound. Rarely do stingrays inject toxin, but when they do it travels through the barb on their tail.

Many different types of stingrays present the same hazard to those wading through shallow waters. Bathers are more likely to provoke the stingray than divers. Encounters with stingrays can be avoided by keeping the feet off the bottom whenever possible or shuffling the fins when walking in shallow water.

Cone Shells: Cone shells (Figure 4-5) are perhaps the only shelled mollusks in the sea capable of harming divers. They are relatively small, cone-shaped shells. Found especially in tropical waters, cone shells are extremely colorful, making prized trophies for avid shell collectors. The potential hazard lies in the barbed tongue which quickly darts out of the narrow end of the shell. If the cone shell must be touched, only the widest portion should be handled.

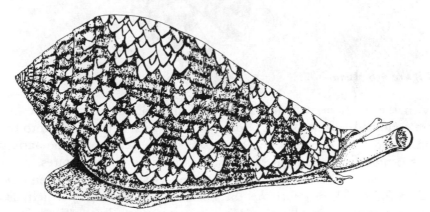

Figure 4-5. Cone shell.

Venomous Fish: Some species of fish are venomous, but many poisonous fish are only found in remote, tropical waters, particularly in the Indo-Pacific region. The venomous fish fall into one of two categories: (1) well-camouflaged but unattractive fish or (2) beautiful, highly colored, and decorative fish. When provoked, many venomous fish defend themselves by injecting toxin through spines, particularly the dorsal spines. Generally, they are slow to move and are found lying about, rather than swimming freely. Venomous fish do not attack or bite; they cause injury only when divers accidentally come in contact with them.

The *scorpion fish* family is perhaps more widespread than the other venomous fish. Scorpion fish usually lie on the bottom, blending in

Figure 4-6. Lionfish.

with the sea floor, which makes them difficult to detect. These fish are equipped with poisonous dorsal spines which inject toxin into the unwary diver who grabs one by mistake. The sculpin is one variety of scorpion fish found on the West Coast of the United States.

The *stonefish* is so well camouflaged underwater that it is often mistaken for a rock or debris on the bottom. The stonefish, which also injects toxin from the dorsal spines, is found in the Indo-Pacific region.

The venomous *zebrafish* and *lionfish* (turkeyfish) (Figure 4-6) are highly ornate and considered by many among the most beautiful fish in the sea. Fortunately, because of their attractiveness, these fish are easily detected. Poisonous spines again are responsible for their ability to injure.

Unlike other venomous species, the *weever fish* is aggressive. Weevers enjoy burying themselves in sandy or muddy bottoms with only their heads exposed. They have been known to attack divers. The weever fish possesses poisonous dorsal and cheek spines and is found in the Eastern Atlantic Ocean, the North Sea, and the Mediterranean.

Treatment of Wounds

When bleeding occurs with a nonpoisonous abrasion or puncture, the diver should apply direct pressure. The wound should be cleaned thoroughly with an antiseptic solution. All spines or other particles should be removed when possible. A sterile dressing should then be applied, and additional medical attention should be sought.

The laceration inflicted by the stingray is often accompanied by pain, swelling, and nausea. First aid should include soaking the wound in very hot water to break down the toxin. A physician should be consulted immediately.

The venom injected by the barbed tongue of the cone shell is powerful, causing severe pain, numbness, paralysis, and sometimes cardiac arrest. First aid includes soaking the wound in hot water to neutralize the toxin, immobilizing the victim, treating the shock, and summoning a physician.

Symptoms of venomous fish punctures include intense pain, redness, swelling, paralysis, and convulsions. Treatment should be immediate. The wound should be thoroughly washed, then soaked in extremely hot water. Antibiotics should be prescribed to thwart infection.

4.2.2 ORGANISMS THAT STING

Organisms from the phylum Coelenterata frequently sting swimmers and divers. Luckily, most stings are annoying rather than debilitating. The coelenterates are characterized by spring-loaded stinging mechanisms called *nematocysts*, which fire out reflexively. Wet suits and other protective garments protect the diver from these stinging organisms.

Types of Organisms

Jellyfish: While many jellyfish inflict bothersome stings, few are considered dangerous. A variety of jellyfish exists in waters throughout the world. They travel by drifting with the wind or current, or pulsate their bodies to propel themselves. The stinging jellyfish have long tentacles which house the nematocysts. Contact with jellyfish should be avoided. Tentacles remaining on gloves or wet suits may still sting when contact is made with the skin, even though the organism is dead.

Sea wasps are extremely dangerous jellyfish found in the tropical waters of the Pacific and Indian Oceans. Fortunately, few divers encounter them.

Portuguese Man-of-war: The Portuguese man-of-war (Figure 4-7) is often mistaken for a jellyfish, but it is actually a hydroid. Nevertheless, it inflicts a toxic sting in jellyfish fashion. The Portuguese man-of-war is powered by the wind. It inflates its bladder to seek a new feeding

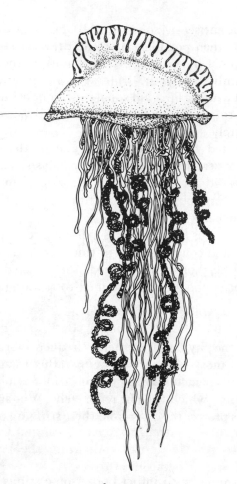

Figure 4-7. Portuguese man-of-war.

ground and deflates the bladder when content. Its menacing attribute is the long tentacles, ranging from 10 to 50 feet, which trail behind it.

The Portuguese man-of-war presents a particular problem to divers. Although the bladder is easily detected on the surface, the tentacles traveling well below the bladder may not be visible to the scuba diver. Each tentacle, containing thousands of nematocysts, is capable of total body coverage. Thus, when a diver swims through a mass of tentacles, a large quantity of toxin is injected into the victim.

Interestingly, the Portuguese man-of-war, while resembling a single jellyfish, is actually a host of individual organisms living together. Also, sea turtles enjoy eating the man-of-war, which is just one reason why divers should refrain from riding turtles.

Fire Coral: Although referred to as a coral by divers, fire coral is actually a hydroid in the phylum Coelenterata. It contains nematocysts which inflict a painful, burning sting. Fire coral resembles a small, hard coral cluster, usually tan or reddish brown in color with white fringes. It is found in most tropical waters throughout the world, but especially in Florida and the Bahamas. Fire coral should be avoided and protective clothing should be worn in case of accidental contact.

Prevention and Treatment of Stings

Additional stinging organisms may also be found underwater, either living individually or coexisting with other organisms (for example, sea anemones living in sponges). To avoid stinging nematocysts, the diver should wear protective clothing on all exposed body parts, especially the hands. If the diver finds that wearing a wet suit is uncomfortable in tropical waters, a long-sleeved shirt, jeans, and cotton gloves will provide adequate protection. It is also advisable to look up while surfacing to avoid jellyfish and Portuguese man-of-war stings. Divers should also refrain from touching the face with gloves after the dive. "Look with your eyes, not with your hands" is a rule intended to protect both the diver and the organism of interest.

Although all of the coelenterate stings are painful, only the man-of-war and the sea wasp are considered dangerous. All such stings may be treated in the same fashion. Basic solutions, such as alcohol, ammonia, and baking soda, neutralize the acidic sting of most coelenterates. Additionally, meat tenderizer containing the papaya enzyme papain works well in destroying the toxin.

4.2.3 ORGANISMS THAT BITE

While the larger marine-life organisms have notorious reputations and can potentially attack divers, actual instances are extremely rare. Because the media and many nondivers publicize the dangers of the larger fish, novice divers often learn to fear them, thus impairing underwater performance. Hopefully, this section will dispel the negative and morbid rumors associated with barracuda, moray eels, octopus, sharks, and other "sea monsters." Divers should learn to appreciate and respect these animals, not to fear them.

Barracuda

While there are many species of barracuda, apparently they all have the same demeanor; they are strong, sleek, and swift, with sharp teeth

Figure 4-8. Barracuda. (Courtesy National Oceanic and Atmospheric Administration)

and powerful jaws (Figure 4-8). The Great Barracuda may attain lengths up to 6 feet and have three distinct rows of sharp teeth. Because the barracuda is so well equipped, divers have mistakenly labeled them as ferocious. Also the barracuda's curiosity has not helped in bolstering its negative reputation.

Barracuda are found in almost all tropical waters, either schooling or swimming alone. These territorial fish will often follow and may even circle divers, but never will they attack. While not considered dangerous, the barracuda should not be chased, provoked, or fed by divers.

Moray Eel

Moray eels (Figure 4-9) also induce unnecessary anxiety among divers. In truth, moray eels are generally quiet, shy, and docile. Moray eels are nocturnal, meaning they are active at night and relatively passive during the day. Like the barracuda, morays have powerful jaws and intricate patterns of sharp teeth. Interestingly, moray eels ventilate their gills by constantly opening and closing their mouths. Many

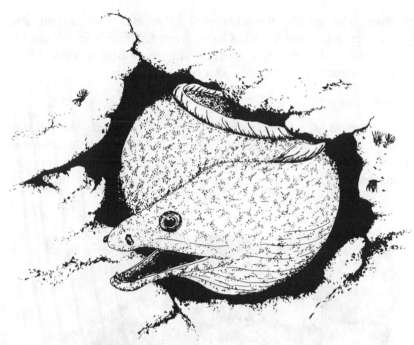

Figure 4-9. Moray eel.

novice divers misinterpret this action as an attack posture, thus promoting the moray's dangerous reputation.

Moray eels may attack when provoked. Divers can accidentally agitate the moray by reaching a hand into a coral crevice or hole without first alerting the occupant. Although the potential danger of moray eels has been exaggerated by the media, nevertheless, petting and feeding moray eels is not recommended for sport divers.

The old tale stating that once it bites, the moray eel will not let go is apparently false. If bitten, the diver should remain calm and refrain from fighting with the eel, which will release quickly.

Octopus

The octopus is also overrated as a diving hazard. Intelligent and shy, the octopus prefers hiding in holes rather than socializing with divers. These creatures may vary in size from a few inches to several feet. The octopus is equipped with a parrotlike beak, and some can inject poison. However, bites are extremely rare, and even when provoked, many octopuses will flee. Nevertheless, playing with or provoking this animal is not recommended. Although the octopus is found in nearly all salt waters throughout the world, it usually prefers deeper waters. Some octopuses may weigh in excess of 100 pounds. The Giant Pacific Octopus resides in the Pacific Ocean from California to Alaska but is not considered dangerous. However, the small Blue-Ringed Octopus found in Australian waters can inject potent toxin.

Sea Snakes

Sea snakes may be found either floating on the surface or swimming around rocks and corals on the bottom. They resemble land snakes with one major exception—they possess a paddle-shaped tail. Many sea snakes display contrasting bands of color running the length of their bodies (Figure 4-10).

Figure 4-10. Sea snake.

Although some sea snakes are poisonous, they are not considered a real threat to divers. Because sea snakes have small mouths and teeth, wet suits offer good protection. The best protection against sea snake bites, however, is caution and respect. Sea snakes are most frequently found in the warmer waters of the Pacific and Indian Oceans. They are not found around the continental United States.

Sharks

Surprisingly, most sharks are not dangerous to humans. Moreover, shark bites are among the least likely of all injuries divers may experience. Of the more than 300 different species of sharks in existence, less than 20 may be considered dangerous to divers. Internationally, fewer than 50 attacks occur annually (only a small percentage of victims

are divers), with less than half being fatal. Most sharks prefer deeper
water and, of the humans it might attack, divers are the least likely
candidates. Scuba divers do not usually attract sharks because they
blend in well with the aquatic environment. The movements of a
swimmer on the surface, however, closely resemble the thrashing of
a wounded fish.

THE FAR SIDE   By GARY LARSON

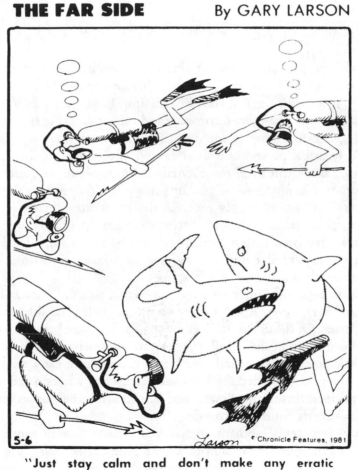

"Just stay calm and don't make any erratic
movements."

Although sharks have been considered to be unpredictable, the
following generalities hold true:

1. Most sharks like warmer water, especially 70°F and above.

2. Sharks have a lateral line running the length of the body which detects vibrations. Thrashing and erratic movements in the water can alert sharks from great distances.

3. Sharks possess a fine sense of smell, which assists them in finding wounded prey.

4. Sharks, having poor eyesight, are more attracted to objects with bright, contrasting colors, especially in the evening or in murky water.

5. Many sharks are more active at night and feed at that time.

Sharks, in general, are not attracted to divers because they are fairly inconspicuous underwater. Quite possibly, many sharks may fear the large, 7-foot (with fins) "manfish," exhaling large, noisy bubbles into the water. Some sharks are territorial, and a diver entering their domain might generate a shark's interest. This interest, however, is often limited to a few passes, or a short period of circling the diver. Upon sighting a shark, the diver must remain calm, move slowly, and stay on the bottom. Fleeing frantically to the surface may only attract the shark.

Divers may unknowingly provoke sharks by attempting to take a close-up photograph or obtain a better look. Lately, underwater photographers have been bitten while creating shark "feeding frenzies" for research and film documentaries. Towing speared fish on a line is another accidental means of attracting sharks.

A shark especially interested in or attracted to a diver may circle or even bump the diver. Apparently, "bumping" helps the shark measure up the diver. Of the divers bumped by sharks, few have been bitten.

A violently upset shark will demonstrate aggressiveness by assuming an attack posture. The shark's response resembles a cat's reaction to seeing a dog. A provoked shark is characterized by a hunched or arched back, pectoral fins turned down, nose turned up, and vigorous undulating movements from side to side.

Shark defense equipment includes the *bang stick* (a pole with a power-head), *shark billy* (simply a stiff pole), *shark dart* (a gas gun which inflates the shark), *air bags* (inflatable bags to climb into), and *shark cages*. However, these items may be considered unnecessary for sport divers and are mostly used by the diving professionals working with sharks.

Undeniably, sharks are more feared than they should be. The truth is that most divers will never even sight a shark. Divers should treat sharks just like any other large fish that might be encountered in the ocean, the same way outdoor sports enthusiasts would respect large wild land animals, such as the bear.

THE FAR SIDE   By GARY LARSON

Selected References

Boehler, T. *The Pro Manual*. Colton, Calif.: National Association of Underwater Instructors, 1977, II.93–II.137.

Miller, J.W. (Ed.). *NOAA Diving Manual*. Washington, D.C.: U.S. Government Printing Office, 1979, 15.1–15.15.

Mount, T., and Ikehara, A.J. *The New Practical Diving*. Coral Gables, Fla.: University of Miami Press, 1979, pp. 5–48.

Chapter 4 Review

The instructor should correct the student's answers, record the results, and return them to the student. Both teacher and student should sign after the last question.

REVIEW QUESTIONS	ANSWERS
1. The sport diving limit is _____ feet.	1. _____
2. Define flood tide and ebb tide.	2. _____
3. List three safety strategies for diving in a current from a boat.	3. _____ _____ _____
4. Explain the following currents: (a) longshore (b) rip, and (c) undertow.	4. (a) _____ (b) _____ (c) _____
5. What is a thermocline?	5. _____
6. What problem might barnacles present?	6. _____
7. How many sea urchins harm divers?	7. _____
8. List three species of poisonous fish.	8. _____ _____ _____
9. What is the treatment for nematocyst stings?	9. _____
10. Do barracuda pose a real threat to divers?	10. _____

REVIEW QUESTIONS	ANSWERS
11. How might a sting ray injure a diver?	11. _____
12. Approximately how many species of sharks are there?	12. _____
13. List three characteristics common to sharks.	13. _____ _____ _____
14. Are sea snakes common around the continental United States?	14. _____
15. Describe the personality of a Moray eel.	15. _____ _____
16. How many major ocean currents (gyres) are there?	16. _____ _____
17. How deep is the deepest point in the ocean?	17. _____
18. What percentage of the earth's surface is covered by water?	18. _____
19. Are octopuses aggressive?	19. _____
20. The average depth of the ocean is _____ feet.	20. _____

REVIEW QUESTIONS	ANSWERS
I have graded, recorded, and returned this student's responses.	Instructor's Signature: Date:
I have seen my corrected review questions and now know the appropriate answers. Note: The answer sheet may either be taken out or retained with this book.	Student's Signature: Date:

PART II

Enjoyment Through Safety

Introduction

~~~~~~

This part of the book deals with attitudes and safety practices. The objective is to motivate you to develop a good diving attitude, one which promotes safety and increases your diving pleasure. Scuba diving is not a high-risk sport, and just about anyone can learn to dive—deaf, blind, and even other handicapped people become safe divers. It's not your athletic ability that makes you a good diver, but rather your attitude. The chapter on stress and scuba should give you an understanding of why a few divers become nervous while diving, how to deal with them, and how to prevent stress in yourself. The chapter on defensive diving and scuba rescue provides you with information which will make you a stronger, safer diver, capable of helping others in need.

Chapter 5

~~~~~~

Stress and Scuba

Although some students of scuba diving fear dangerous marine life or possible equipment failure while underwater, mishaps in these areas seldom occur; rather, some divers become their own worst enemies underwater. In the sport of scuba diving, loss of control can be described as panic—the major contributing factor to most accidents. Novice and experienced divers alike must constantly train themselves to prevent this loss of control or panic in order to avoid accidents. The psychological aspects of diving are probably the most important facets of diver training.

5.1 Definitions

Stress and anxiety are two very ambiguous and difficult terms to differentiate. Although they have extremely similar meanings, there are subtle but important differences between them.

Stress is a state that evokes effort on the part of the individual to maintain or restore equilibrium. The agents producing such a state are called *stressors* and may be physical or psychological. The response to stress may include many physiological and psychological reactions which attempt to restore the organism to a balanced state. This response is often referred to as the "fight or flight" reaction because the individual responds by either attacking or retreating from the stressor.

Anxiety refers to fear or apprehension which a person experiences in the face of real or imagined dangers. Some sports psychologists make a further distinction by describing that state of fear or apprehen-

137

sion experienced by an individual just prior to engaging in a risky or threatening activity as *state anxiety*.

Most scuba diving literature uses the term *stress* when discussing the psychological aspects of the sport. The term *anxiety* is often associated only with personality traits,[1] and anxiety is thought by many to be a phobic response; thus the term usually carries a negative connotation.

It is important to note that stress reactivity is perfectly normal and healthy. However, if the stress becomes extreme and continues unchecked, it may lead to *panic*, which can be dangerous. Panic is an emotional and volatile human reaction which occurs in the presence of a real or imagined danger; it is characterized by a total loss of logic and mental control.

5.2 Stress and Underwater Performance

Different individuals respond to identical stressors in different ways. Some enter rapidly into a stress state, others show increased alertness and apparently improved performance, and still others appear to be "immune" to the stress-producing qualities of the environmental conditions.[2]

Human performance underwater is influenced by varying levels of psychological stress. Stress prior to a dive can make the diver more aware of the problems and procedures of the dive, while overwhelming stress during a dive can disable the diver.[3] A diver in the panic state becomes all action and movement but is not capable of thinking clearly. Panicked divers are almost impossible to assist and incapable of helping themselves.

In general, moderate amounts of stress may actually enhance performance. As shown in Figure 5-1, which illustrates the Yerke-Dodson Law, optimum performance for complex tasks usually occurs when stress is neither extremely high nor extremely low. In some situations, high states of arousal enhance performance, but in others the same levels of stress can be detrimental.

Relaxation techniques (see Section 5.6.3) can be effective in significantly reducing stress levels and thus improving performance. It is

1. R. Martens, *Sport Competition Anxiety Test* (Champaign, Ill.: Human Kinetics Publishers, 1977), p. 8.

2. M.D. Appley and R. Trumbull, *Psychological Stress* (New York: Appleton-Century-Crofts, 1967), p. 11.

3. A.J. Bachrach, *Diving Behavior: Human Performance and Scuba Diving* (Chicago: The Athletic Institute, 1970), pp. 119–137.

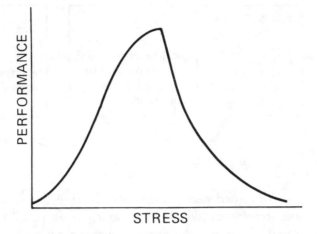

Figure 5-1. Relationship between stress and performance.

important to note that stress must be controlled, but not necessarily completely eliminated, in order to promote safe diving.

5.3 Causes of Stress

5.3.1 PHYSICAL STRESSORS

The physical stressors present in the diving environment include cold water, limited visibility, strong currents, and rough waves. The physical state of the diver may also present stressors, including fatigue, cramps, rapid respiration, overloading (performing too many tasks at one time), and time pressure (racing against the clock). Lack of physical fitness and poor swimming ability are major contributors to these forms of stress. Additionally, the equipment used in scuba diving is generally cumbersome and therefore causes the following stressors: confinement or restriction of movement, overweight, fatigue, and discomfort.

Any one of these physical stressors may increase the stress level of the diver. When several physical stressors occur simultaneously, the diver may feel threatened, resulting in dangerously high levels of psychological stress.

5.3.2 PSYCHOLOGICAL STRESSORS

Peer pressure, the pressure placed by peers on fellow divers, keeps stress levels relatively high. Humans are very social beings, and peer approval is extremely important to most individuals. Winning the admiration and respect of others is a goal most people attempt to

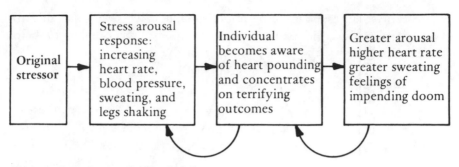

Figure 5-2. Stress feedback loop.

achieve. This self-imposed peer pressure can be significant, and when colleagues make statements like "If I can do it, so can you," additional pressure is created. Failure in the face of peers is a definite ego threat. Any possibility of failure is also an ego threat. A damaging blow to one's pride may be inflicted if a diver fails at a task or refuses to attempt or complete a task. The combination of peer pressure and ego threat increases stress levels among scuba divers. Research findings at the University of Maryland have consistently shown that peer pressure, ego threat, concern about receiving a good grade, and concern about receiving the certification card are the most significant stressors for college students in dive courses.

The possibility of underwater dangers is also a cause of stress, although it takes a back seat to peer pressure. Humans know they are not fish, but they do adapt very well to the underwater world with the aid of sophisticated equipment. Subconsciously, some divers fear drowning because they are entirely immersed in the water for an extended period of time. They realize that if equipment problems do arise they do not possess the ability to breathe in the water without a mechanical device.

Psychological stress produces a stress reaction in the body which in itself is often the cause of additional stress. The stress reaction is part of a feedback loop perpetuating and augmenting the stress response (Figure 5-2).[4]

5.4 Symptoms of Stress

Excessive stress, which can lead to loss of control underwater, usually begins well before the diver enters the water. By being able to detect

4. D.A. Girdano and G.S. Everly, *Controlling Stress and Tension: A Holistic Approach* (Englewood Cliffs, N.J.: Prentice-Hall, 1979), p. 116.

these telltale signs of extreme apprehension, divers may be able to help themselves avoid panic and other divers may be able to help them, either before the dive begins or in the water.

5.4.1 PHYSIOLOGICAL RESPONSES

Psychological stress is accompanied by several physiological responses, including increased heart rate, respiration, muscle tension, and perspiration. These increased energy expenditures lead to additional stress problems of hypoxia, hyperventilation, fatigue, and exhaustion, which in turn pave the road to panic. Changes of voice and shaking hands also indicate heightened stress levels.

Since a stressed diver breathes more often and exhales more forcefully while underwater, the frequency and intensity of the exhaled air bubbles can alert other divers to a problem. Another symptom of high stress levels that is easy to detect underwater is the "wide-eyed look." When divers are overly stressed underwater, they will often open their eyes extremely wide and stare at a person or object. Because underwater communication requires good eye contact, this sign of stress is easily recognizable.

The physiological symptoms of panic are similar to those of excessive stress. These symptoms include involuntary hyperventilation, the wide-eyed look, dilated pupils, excessive muscle tension, and increased heart rate and respiration. These responses lead to breathing difficulties, fatigue, exhaustion, and muscle cramps, which add to the existing panic state and can easily cause drowning. Scuba experts refer to this progression as the panic syndrome, and it is the most significant threat to the diver in the water.

5.4.2 BEHAVIORAL RESPONSES

Many dive masters and instructors rely on certain behavioral cues to detect nervous divers. Divers should learn to spot these signs of stress in themselves and their partners.

Before the Dive

Most of the behavioral patterns seen before the dive are forms of procrastination, which are defense mechanisms used by the diver to delay entering an uncertain or threatening situation. Subconsciously, these nervous divers are seeking help. Examples of these behavioral patterns follow.

Introversion: The diver who withdraws from the rest of the group and remains continually quiet throughout the day might be dwelling on the possible negative aspects of the dive.

Tardiness: Some divers will be continually late for several meetings convened the day of the dive. A diver who misses the car pool for a ride to the dive site or the dive orientation meeting, who is late picking up equipment, or who is the last one to suit up might be procrastinating because of fear.

Mental Errors: Divers who are excessively nervous will often make simple mistakes prior to entering the water. Placing the regulator on the tank backward, putting the fins on upside down, and getting hair under the mask are just a few of the many mistakes that can occur. Some of these mistakes are made innocently enough, but some divers may subconsciously make these mistakes to delay the dive.

Forgetfulness: There is much to be remembered for a scuba dive, and it is, therefore, easy to overlook something. But when divers forget several items (bathing suit, mask, wet suit, money), this may indicate another type of defense mechanism used by the nervous diver.

Extreme Cockiness: Many very competent divers are ashamed and embarrassed when they experience excessive apprehension prior to the dive. To mask the fear, they will often brag about how easy the dive will be or make a big joke about the entire experience. These people probably possess more anxiety than they would like to admit.

Irritability: Some scuba students display a loss of patience and a quick temper on the day of the open-water dive. Any slight change in plans or a delay propels these divers into a mild tantrum. This sudden irritability is quite possibly a manifestation of the stress built up in them, which they cannot mentally accommodate and must, therefore, impose on others.

During the Dive

Once in the water, a stressed diver may display other behavioral patterns.

Inefficient Swimming: Rather than moving through the water smoothly and slowly to conserve air and energy, a highly stressed diver will swim erratically in the water. Usually the arms and legs will move wildly underwater as the diver becomes overly dependent on the muscles and fins to make progress. Inefficient swimming manifests itself in many ways. While on the surface the highly stressed diver may tread water extremely high out of the water. If an anchor line or trail line is being used, the diver becoming panicky can often be found "clinging and clambering" on it.[5] A diver in this state is simply too nervous to swim smoothly through the water. Swimming inefficiently leads to excessive fatigue which often leads to panic.

Equipment Rejection: Divers who are highly stressed tend to lose faith in the scuba equipment. While on the surface, the diver may quickly and abruptly remove the mask and/or regulator. Underwater, the diver may continually readjust one piece of equipment, like the weight belt, or frequently fuss with just about every item of equipment being used.

Fixation: Some highly stressed divers will not be attentive to or aware of what is going on around them but, instead, may concentrate or stare at one person or object. Also, a diver who appears listless or apathetic underwater may be a victim of excessive stress. Some experts refer to this concept as *narrowing*, which may be either mental or perceptual.

Human Errors: When making procedural mistakes and errors in judgment while underwater, the diver may become overly stressed and unable to function properly. A key contributing factor to panic is a mistake, either mental or physical, made by the diver while attempting to correct a small problem. Typically, after divers become overly stressed, they make mistakes which ultimately lead to a total loss of control. For example, the mistake a diver might make in dealing with the problem of too much lead is either not removing lead from the weight belt or not using the B.C.D. Failure to compensate for the excessive lead might eventually lead to fatigue, cramps, and ultimately panic.

Perhaps the most critical factor in the panic progression (Figure 5-3) after stress increases is whether or not a problem arises. If a problem does occur, it is usually accompanied by another increase in stress levels. Problems include being overweighted, losing one's buddy, or running out of air, among others. Fortunately, quite often no problems occur even though the diver is highly stressed. If a problem

5. R.N. Smith and H.C. Allen, *Scuba Lifesaving and Accident Management* (Key West, Fla.: National YMCA Underwater Activities Program, 1978), p. 9.

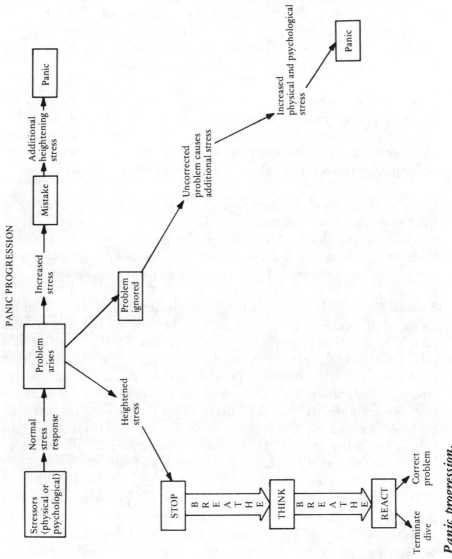

Figure 5-3. Panic progression.

does not arise, no threat is posed to the diver. If a problem does develop, it must be confronted by the diver regardless of how insignificant it appears to be.

5.5 Treatment of Stress

Excessive stress displayed by divers is a problem largely because the stress reaction distracts them from concentrating on the specifics of the dive. If a diver displays the physiological and/or behavioral symptoms described in Section 5.4 before the dive begins, the dive should be delayed or canceled. The stressed diver should be counseled with the aim of decreasing stress and increasing concentration on the task at hand. Several methods may be used to help a highly stressed diver.

Talk: Taking the time to explain all the dive procedures in detail is perhaps the easiest and most efficient way to help the diver. While doing this, however, the instructor should not draw attention to the diver's nervousness. The dialogue between the instructor and the diver should be friendly, informative, and full of encouragement.

Accentuate the Positive: Highly stressed divers find themselves in a poor mental state for the dive because they often dwell on the negative aspects of the dive. In order to combat this, the instructor might want to focus verbally on all the positive facets of the dive (for example, the good weather, the unusually good visibility, and the warm water temperature) while deemphasizing the negative aspects.

Fight Distraction with Distractions: Excessive stress distracts the diver from functioning properly underwater. One way to eliminate this distraction is to give the divers something to do while diving which will keep them occupied and distracted from their nervousness. Some examples are helping to collect samples, identifying certain forms of marine life, and keeping track of depth and time. The diver *must not*, however, be overburdened with too many tasks.

Buddy-up Weak with Strong: Every attempt should be made to pair up the stressful diver with a strong, confident diver, preferably a talkative and responsible person who will go out of the way to be helpful. However, as diver training continues, the weaker diver must be given progressively more responsibility to prevent him or her from becoming a dependent diver, and therefore a liability.

Use a Buddy-Line: Even in clear water, a buddy-line can help to reduce stress by increasing contact and communication with the dive partner. Actually holding the hand of the nervous diver might also be beneficial.

Offer Praise and Encouragement: The instructor might help the extremely stressed diver by continually offering praise and encouragement, even when the diver makes mistakes.

Practice the Calming Response: A deep-breathing exercise has been developed recently which promotes relaxation and enhances respiratory efficiency in a matter of minutes.[6] It is easy to learn and practice and may be used on land prior to the dive or underwater. The technique, called the Calming Response, is an adaptation of the "Quieting Response" developed by Dr. Charles Strobel. The Calming Response combines yogic breathing (diaphragmatic or stomach breathing) with autogenic phrases. As the diver inhales deeply, the stomach (not the chest) is pushed out and then drawn in during exhalation. During the slow, deep inhalation, the diver mentally says, "I feel calm." During the slow, full exhalation, the diver mentally says, "I feel warm."

It should be remembered that the instructor or dive partner should have a friendly and encouraging manner while attempting to help an extremely nervous diver. Above all, instructors who are unable to help a diver cope with excessive stress prior to the first dive must have enough courage to tell the diver not to dive.

Perhaps the most efficient way to combat excessive stress while the diver is in the water is to remove the victim slowly and carefully from the situation. Another method of treating a stressful diver underwater is to have the diver stop, breathe deeply, and then think about the situation (the diver can do this even if he/she is alone). Gaining control during a stressful situation is extremely important. In order to stop the chain of events which may lead to panic, the following progression is recommended:

STOP → BREATHE → THINK → BREATHE → REACT

6. G.S. Everly, "A Psychophysiological Technique for the Rapid Onset of a Trophotropic State," *IRCS Medical Science* 7 (1979): 423.

Conscious breath control should permeate each of the three stages.

Once on the surface, the victim should be made positively buoyant as discretely as possible, in order to avoid additional stress, by dropping the weight belt and/or inflating the B.C.D. At this time, the victim may be treated for stress in the same fashion as during the predive state. Verbal reassurance, encouragement, and accentuating the positive while minimizing the negative aspects of the dive will all aid in reducing stress.

5.6 Prevention and Control

5.6.1 THE DIVER'S AREAS OF RESPONSIBILITY

Preventing excessive stress, which may lead to panic, should be of paramount importance to all divers. If three general areas of responsibility are attended to by each diver, stress levels can be kept under control. These three areas are the water, the equipment, and the divers themselves.

Water

One way of preventing excessive stress is to attempt only those dives which are conducive to safety and enjoyment. Each diver should know the conditions of the water prior to entering it. The unknown or unexpected easily breeds apprehension. Therefore, each diver should consider the following conditions before attempting a scuba dive: wave action, weather conditions, visibility, dangerous marine life, entry conditions, bottom conditions, and dive conditions specific to the environment (e.g., cave, lake, ocean). Above all, a diver should not engage in a scuba dive for which he or she has had no specific training.

Equipment

Not only must all gear being used by the diver be in good working order, but the diver must also be *familiar* with the specific gear to be used. New or unfamiliar gear should be used in the safe environs of the swimming pool, not the open water. All scuba equipment should be overhauled or serviced by a certified scuba specialist at least once a year. Additionally, divers should understand the basic mechanical principles of the scuba equipment. Being familiar with one's gear and knowing how the equipment works and that it is in good condition will all help to reduce stress because confidence in the equipment will be established.

Diver

Perhaps the most important area of responsibility is the physical and psychological well-being of the diver about to enter the water. The following physical factors should be kept in mind to avoid excessive stress:

1. Maintain physical fitness.
2. Overlearn skills through practice and repetition.
3. Know your physical limitations.
4. Practice buddymanship.

Some of the psychological aspects that should be considered prior to diving are confidence, emotional state (do not dive when depressed or upset), relaxation skills and techniques* (including deep-breathing exercises), mental practice or rehearsal of diving skills,* and anticipation of possible problems and solutions.

5.6.2 RESPONDING TO A PROBLEM

When faced with a problem underwater, a diver may have three possible reactions:

1. The diver can react quickly to the problem and attempt to correct it immediately; however, quick action is not always the best action while underwater. Quick action often leads to mistakes or errors in the corrective procedures. The cliché "haste makes waste" applies directly to scuba divers underwater.

2. The diver can totally ignore the problem or rationalize and judge the crisis as insignificant. Eventually, this uncorrected problem will add additional stress to the diver.

3. The diver can stop immediately and do *nothing* to interrupt the chain of events. Doing nothing at all is preferred to acting rashly underwater. After stopping all swimming activity in the face of an underwater crisis, the diver should immediately practice slow, controlled, deep breathing. After breath control is achieved, the

---

*While many courses may not have sufficient time to include these aspects, there are some very good cassette tape programs available; for example, an audio cassette tape series, "Controlling Stress and Panic," by R.J. Allen and T.J. Griffiths (Scuba Safety Services, P.O. Box 1385 State College, PA 16804).

diver should think rationally about the problem. While thinking of the correct course of action to remedy the situation, rhythmic breathing should be continued. Corrective action should not be taken until an itemized plan is formulated and slow breathing restored.

Thus, the preferred reaction to a problem is the same as for controlling a stressful situation:

STOP ⟩ BREATHE ⟩ THINK ⟩ BREATHE ⟩ REACT

Even though a well-trained diver knows the proper action to implement in the face of danger, he/she should stop, think, and restore controlled breathing prior to reacting to the situation. This course of action will most likely ensure that the corrective measures will be completed in a slow and deliberate fashion. STOP THINK REACT with an emphasis on deep breathing is a progression that is directly opposite to the panic reaction which incapacitates the diver. If divers would learn to STOP THINK REACT when a problem occurs, the panic progression would be thwarted and ultimately the possibility of drowning would lessen. After divers *STOP* and *THINK* clearly, then they may *REACT* by either correcting the problem carefully underwater, preferably with the assistance of the diving partner, or terminating the dive, at least temporarily.

5.6.3 STRESS REDUCTION METHODS

Because stress is caused by environmental, social, mental, and physical factors and occurs in many different and varying situations, no single technique is recommended to prevent, reduce, and control excessive stress. Divers faced with high levels of stress must develop a program of various techniques to learn to relax, control stress, and ultimately improve diving performance. Once again, scuba divers should not attempt to eliminate all stress, but must try to learn to keep it under control. Increased diver stress can actually enhance the dive by making it more exciting, challenging, and even safer. This is true because a moderately stressed diver tends to focus more on particular aspects of a dive than the totally relaxed diver. Conversely, excessive stress will impair performance, thus making the dive more dangerous.

Psychological Evaluation

It is essential that every scuba candidate evaluate certain key personality traits before getting involved in the sport. Some of the more important traits are the following:

Positive Self-esteem: This is a prerequisite of successful scuba diving. The ability to see oneself in a positive light and to feel good about oneself is a must for scuba diving candidates. Individuals who downgrade themselves or who are experiencing emotional problems should refrain from scuba diving. While it is true that scuba diving can and does build confidence in divers, students with emotional problems tend to focus on the negative aspects of their lives, and the physical and psychological demands of the sport only add to their problems.

Confidence: This is closely associated with positive self-esteem and means believing in oneself to get the job done. Unconfident students repeatedly underrate themselves during scuba training, which erodes their ability to perform scuba skill correctly. These students often program themselves for failure. Poor self-expectation repeatedly leads to poor performance. All scuba certification courses require a simple prerequisite swim test. Scuba candidates should realize that anyone passing the initial swim test possesses enough skill to pass the course.

Anxious Reactive Personality: A few divers may be described as having anxious reactive personalities. Anxious reactive individuals exaggerate the existing stress and actually perpetuate it after the stress is gone. People prone to this reaction can become mentally and physically incapacitated in the face of the mildest stressor. Needless to say, anxious reactive personalities probably should not engage in scuba diving. The anxiety feedback loop, which anxious reactive personalities often experience, was illustrated in Figure 5-2.[7]

Relaxation Techniques

There are many effective methods of preventing and reducing excessive stress. These techniques are only briefly outlined in this section; for additional information, the references at the end of the chapter should be examined.

7. *Controlling Stress and Tension*, p. 116.

Meditation: Meditation is a state of mind or consciousness. Most meditation techniques used today are based on specific concentration and contemplation practices of ancient Yoga and Zen Buddhism. To meditate effectively does not require the use of burning incense, a Yogi, or a fancy, secretive mantra. Regardless of the stereotypes associated with meditators, meditation does promote relaxation and reduce stress. Many athletes use meditation to enhance their concentration and thus improve physical performance.

Biofeedback: Biofeedback is an educational tool giving information which can aid in self-control. With biofeedback as a relaxation technique, electrical equipment monitors physiological activity to the subject and provides feedback through visual and/or audio signals to inform the subject of the activity. Although biofeedback is very efficient in promoting relaxation and reducing stress, it is not as financially feasible as meditation. The systems which have become most popular include the muscular, brain wave, and cardiovascular systems. The muscular system is often monitored to detect muscle tension and to promote relaxation. This is achieved through the electromyograph (EMG), which is an instrument that measures electrical energy emitted by the muscle.

Deep-breathing Exercises: Proper breathing is the key to achieving relaxation just as it is the key to safe scuba diving. Practicing breathing techniques strengthens and conditions the pulmonary system, enhances circulation of the blood and promotes oxygenation, calms the nerves, and ultimately promotes relaxation. The practice of breathing techniques not only facilitates neuromuscular relaxation, but also helps to prevent respiratory ailments.[8]

Neuromuscular Exercises: Neuromuscular relaxation reduces tension in the muscles, and because the muscles make up such a large portion of the body's mass, significant reduction in body tension results. The following ingredients are required to practice muscle relaxation exercises correctly: proper breathing pattern, a quiet room, and a reclined or semireclined body position.

Mental Rehearsal: One method of reducing stress in diving is by rehearsing the key diving skills mentally before entering the water. Experts

8. *Ibid.*, pp. 203–207.

believe that mental practice is *just* as important as physical practice and that basic diving skills and emergency techniques should be mentally practiced on a regular basis. The mental scenes created by the diver should be as vivid as possible, and the diver should perform the skill perfectly in the mind. Thus, the physical skills become ingrained in the mind and stress is reduced because the diver has mentally rehearsed the proper procedure to follow in a given situation.

One popular form of mental rehearsal is called psycho-cybernetics.[9] Maxwell Maltz popularized this mental practice program in the 1960s, and many people, especially athletes, have since used this technique to reduce stress and enhance performance. Psycho-cybernetics incorporates several psychological strategies in order to improve performance. A positive self-concept, mental practice through imagery, and relaxation are all essential to the Maltz technique. When divers practice this program they must first work diligently on improving the self-concept and learn to approach everything, including diving, with confidence. Second, all skills to be performed in real life should be rehearsed mentally beforehand. The key to this mental practice is the performing of each skill perfectly in the mind, without errors or mistakes. Last, improving the self-concept and mentally rehearsing skills must be done while in a relaxed state; they cannot be forced or pressured into being. The works of Maxwell Maltz are inspiring and are recommended to all divers who lack confidence or suffer from excessive stress.

Selected References

Allen, R., and Griffiths, T. *Controlling Diver Stress and Panic*. Audio Cassette Tape Program. Piscataway, N.J.: New Century Publishers, 1983.

Appley, M.D., and Trumbull, R. *Psychological Stress*. New York: Appleton-Century-Crofts, 1967.

Bachrach, A.J. *Diving Behavior: Human Performance and Scuba Diving*. Chicago: The Athletic Institute, 1970, pp. 119–137.

Bachrach, A.J., and Curley, M.D. "Diver Stress—Control and Prevention." In *Proceedings of Man and the Sea Conference, 1980*. Philadelphia: Center for Marine Studies, Temple University, 1980, pp. 16–21.

Bachrach, A.J., and Egstrom, G.H. "Diver Panic." *Skin Diver* 20 (1971):36–37, 54–55, 57.

9. M. Maltz, *Psycho-cybernetics* (New York: Bantam Books, 1960).

Brady, J.I. *Manual Performance Underwater*. Doctoral dissertation, Texas Tech. University, 1976.

Brown, B. *New Mind, New Body*. New York: Harper and Row, 1974.

Deppe, A.H. "Overload and Sensory Deprivation: Time Estimation in Novice Divers." *Perceptual and Motor Skills* 29 (1969):481–482.

Fenz, D., and Epstein, S. "Stress: In the Air." *Psychology Today* 3 (1969):28.

Girdano, D.A., and Everly, G.S. *Controlling Stress and Tension: A Holistic Approach*. Englewood Cliffs, N.J.: Prentice-Hall, 1979.

Gorrie, D.D. "A Curriculum Guide for SCUBA Diving Instruction." Doctoral dissertation, Oklahoma State University, 1976.

Griffiths, T. "Stress and Scuba," *Ascent Lines* 7 (1978):14.

———. "Anxiety, Stress, and Scuba Diving Performance." *Ascent Lines* 8 (1979):6.

———. "The Signs of Stress." *Ascent Lines* 8 (1979):7.

———. "Sport Scuba Diving: It's a Man's World." *Ascent Lines* 8 (1979):5–6.

Griffiths, T., Steel, D., and Vaccaro, P. "Anxiety Levels of Beginning Scuba Divers." *Perceptual and Motor Skills* 47 (1978):312–314.

———. "Relationship between Anxiety and Performance in Scuba Diving." *Perceptual and Motor Skills* 48 (1979):1009–1010.

———. "Anxiety of Scuba Divers: A Multidimensional Approach." *Perceptual and Motor Skills* 55 (1982):611–614.

Griffiths, T., Steel, D., Vaccaro, P., and Karpman, M. "The Effects of Relaxation Training on Anxiety and Underwater Performance." *International Journal of Sport Psychology* 12 (1981):176–182.

Hardy, J. "Diver Stress." *NAUI News*, July 1976, pp. 2–3.

———. "Part Two: Diving Accidents—Why?" *NAUI News*, July 1976, pp. 2–3.

Kraft, I.A. "Panic, Training and Personality." *NAUI News*, February 1979, pp. 2–5.

Martens, R. *Social Psychology and Physical Activity*. New York: Harper and Row, 1975.

———. *Sport Competition Anxiety Test*. Champaign, Ill.: Human Kinetics Publishers, 1977.

Mount, T., and Ikehara, I. *The New Practical Diving*. Coral Gables, Fla.: University of Miami Press, 1979.

Oxendine, J.B. *Psychology of Motor Learning*. New York: Appleton-Century-Crofts, 1968.

Pelletier, K.R. *Mind as Healer, Mind as Slayer*. New York: Dell Publishing, 1977.

Radloff, R., and Helmreich, R. "Stress: Under the Sea." *Psychology Today* 3 (1969):28.

Schenck, H., and McAniff, J. *U.S. Underwater Diving Fatality Statistics, 1976*. Report No. URI-SSR-78-12 and Report NOAA Grant No. 4-3-158-31. Rockville, Md.: U.S. Department of Transportation and U.S. Department of Commerce, 1978.

Schenck, H., McAniff, J., and Capapezz, E. *Skin and SCUBA Diving Fatalities Involving U.S. Citizens*. SCUBA Safety Report Series, Report No. 2. Kingston: University of Rhode Island, 1972.

Smith, R., and Allen, R. *Scuba Lifesaving and Accident Management*. Key West, Fla.: National YMCA Underwater Activities Program, 1978.

Spielberger, C.D., Gorsuch, R.L., and Lushene, R.E. *Manual for State-Trait Anxiety Inventory*. Palo Alto Calif.: Consulting Psychologists Press, 1968.

Chapter 5 Review

The instructor should correct the student's answers, record the results, and return them to the student. Both teacher and student should sign after the last question.

REVIEW QUESTIONS	ANSWERS
1. Define state anxiety.	1. _____
2. Moderate amounts of stress during diving may actually improve underwater performance. True or false?	2. _____
3. List three physical causes of stress.	3. _____ _____ _____
4. List three psychological causes of stress.	4. _____ _____ _____
5. List three physiological symptoms of diver stress that can be seen before the diver enters the water.	5. _____ _____ _____
6. List three predive behavioral symptoms of diver stress.	6. _____ _____ _____
7. List three behavioral symptoms of diver stress in the water.	7. _____ _____ _____

REVIEW QUESTIONS	ANSWERS
8. List three ways to treat diver stress prior to entering the water.	8. _____ _____ _____
9. What is the most significant threat to the diver in the water?	9. _____
10. Mention a form of treatment for in-water diver stress.	10. _____

I have graded, recorded, and returned this student's responses.	Instructor's Signature: _____ Date: _____
I have seen my corrected review questions and now know the appropriate answers. Note: The answer sheet may either be taken out or retained with this book.	Student's Signature: _____ Date: _____

Chapter 6

~~~~~~

Defensive Diving and Scuba Rescue

In this chapter you will learn about a safety concept borrowed from driver education. Defensive diving basically means developing an anticipatory attitude which allows you to adapt to unpredictable actions of your partner, your equipment, or the environment. As a defensive diver you will learn to avoid mishaps before they happen by imagining possible hazards and then mentally rehearsing the appropriate defense. Three phases of defensive diving will be discussed in this chapter: before the dive, during the dive, and after the dive.

Please do not interpret this as a pessimistic approach to diving. *Driver* education programs have been using this technique for years with great success.

The scuba rescue section introduces some basic lifesaving techniques which could be used to assist a dive partner in need. Although you will probably never have to use these skills, *knowing* what to do in a crisis will certainly promote confidence in yourself.

6.1 Defensive Diving

6.1.1 BUDDYMANSHIP

Perhaps the best way to prepare a safe dive is to plan it with the person you'll be diving with—your buddy. Divers dive in buddy pairs in order to render assistance if and when a problem should arise. Proper planning with your dive buddy usually circumvents any problems that might possibly occur. Good buddymanship requires thoughtful planning, coordination, cooperation, and communication, before, during, and after the dive. It is the first step in defensive diving and certainly makes the dive more enjoyable.

Although buddymanship should be characterized by good teamwork, this is not always the case. A dependent person, who is often inexperienced and/or timid, will usually be a dependent diver, which is not a good situation. On the other hand, the independent person may be a self-centered dive partner, never helping his/her buddy and often leaving him/her behind, on land and in the water.

6.1.2 BEFORE THE DIVE

Rehearsing defensive diving prior to the dive should be an integral part of dive planning, although it is often overlooked. The underlying theme for defensive diving during the predive stage is the hypothetical "what-if" attitude. When dives are planned with possible problems in mind, defensive tactics can be rehearsed both mentally and physically beforehand, thereby promoting safety. Perhaps the best way is to imagine everything that could go wrong while diving and visualize the appropriate corrective measures.

One technique used to practice defensive diving as a part of dive planning is to list all potential hazards which could possibly be encountered within the three domains of diving and then list the appropriate defenses for them. For example, the diver could plan defenses for rip current, jellyfish, and poor visibility within the domain of *environment*. Hazards in the domain of *diver* could include leg cramps, hyperventilation, and anxiety, and hazards in the domain of *equipment* could include running out of air, mask flooding, and regulator freeflow.

It is important to note that this technique should not be used to dwell on all the negative aspects of diving, thus promoting undue stress; rather, it should be used as a problem-solving technique which requires emotional fitness and common sense. After listing all the potential problems, the diver should sit down in a quiet, comfortable setting and mentally rehearse the appropriate responses to such emergencies. An emphasis must be placed on breath control and relaxation because they are directly opposed to the panic response. Before rehearsing each skill, several minutes should be spent relaxing with eyes closed while concentrating on a slow, deep, rhythmic breathing pattern.

After deep breathing and relaxation are accomplished, the diver then chooses an uncomfortable situation which could possibly be encountered on a forthcoming dive. Whatever skill or situation is chosen, the diver must visualize it perfectly, making the mental images as clear and as vivid as possible. Procedural mistakes and negative thoughts should be discouraged from entering the mind during mental rehearsal. Divers should see themselves performing perfectly and with confidence. Throughout the mental practice session, breath control and relaxation must be maintained, and the skills should be practiced at a slow, relaxed pace. The skill to be practiced in the following example of mental rehearsal used as a defensive diving technique is clearing the mask after a sudden flooding during an open water dive:

Close your eyes and relax. Work on your breathing . . . Inhale . . . Exhale . . . Relax. Inhale . . . Exhale . . . Relax. Breathe slowly and deeply. O.K. You're swimming along in a fresh water quarry with about fifteen feet visibility. The water is rather cold but not unbearable. The water depth is about thirty feet and you can see the sunlight penetrating the surface and filtering down to you. You're watching your buddy carefully as you follow him, but you are also being entertained by a small school of fish, mostly bluegills and perch. All of a sudden, without warning, your partner accidentally kicks your mask off your face. The cold water shocks you as it hits your face, and of course you have lost just about all your vision.

Stop . . . Breathe deep . . . Think. You cannot see well at all. You are taking in a little water through your nose but *relax.* You have plenty of air. *Think* . . . your mask is off your face and you cannot see, but you can breathe which is far more important. Breathe deep . . . you can feel your mask on your forehead (seldom does it ever come off your head completely). Don't move. Just breathe and relax. Reach up to your forehead with both hands. Feel your mask. You've got it, now pull it down gently back onto your face. Do this slowly, don't rush. You have plenty of time. Press the mask firmly on your face. Now before you attempt to clear it take several deep breaths. Think about the sequence you must follow to clear the mask. O.K. Now go ahead and clear it. That's right, look up towards the surface, press the top, now exhale slowly. Feel the cold water slowly descend down your face until it all empties from the bottom of your mask. *You did it! You can see!* Your buddy is standing two feet in front of you with a big grin on his face. Now he's writing something on his slate. It's just one word. "Sorry" the note says. He now shakes your hand for a job well done.[1]

This is just one example of mentally rehearsing underwater scenes to master the art of defensive diving. In addition to practicing these skills mentally, practice should also be conducted in pools and in open

1. R. Allen and T. Griffiths, *Controlling Diver Stress and Panic* (Scuba Safety Services, P.O. Box 1385 State College, PA 16804). [audio cassette program]

water training areas. All potential hazards should be mentally and, whenever possible, physically rehearsed until the appropriate responses become automatic, and then these responses should be reviewed periodically in the water. Again, mental rehearsal as a defensive diving tool should be practiced for all possible encounters with the three domains: the environment, the diver, and the equipment.

The result of this type of defensive diver training is that for any given hypothetical situation, the diver can state the correct response with confidence and assertiveness. In this fashion, the diver approaches each dive mentally prepared to handle any incidents.

6.1.3 DURING THE DIVE

Diving defensively while on a dive trip requires a trained and analytic eye. Defensive diving during this stage serves as a type of troubleshooting. While suiting up, defensive divers must visually and mentally probe the environment for strong currents and waves; check the equipment, making certain all is in good working order (including the buddy's); and examine the actions of themselves and their partners for signs of stress or overexertion.

Just prior to entering the water, divers should recheck all aspects of the scuba system, including buckles, straps, gauges, and weight belts. Self-rescue techniques may be rehearsed on the dock or beach by closing the eyes and actually feeling for the B.C.D. inflator, weight belt buckle, CO_2 cartridge inflators, regulator, and so forth. This is best accomplished by having the dive buddy call out each safety item or procedure to the rehearsing diver. One diver calls out specific skills, such as "drop your weight belt," "recover your regulator," and "inflate your B.C.D.," while the rehearsing diver actually performs each skill with eyes closed. After all procedures are reviewed by one diver, the buddy performs the skills. All hand signals should be reviewed together, following the review of equipment and procedures by both buddies. This defensive diving technique should be performed in a quiet place with a minimum of distractions to allow for maximum concentration.

The process of defensive diving continues in the water as the divers survey all three domains (environment, diver, equipment) and communicate with each other continuously. Each diver attempts to see potential problems as far ahead of encountering the incidents as possible. Defensive divers underwater are looking out for each other and carefully monitoring the water and the equipment. Anticipating problems before they arise is the key to defensive diving, together with understanding the specific defenses for handling specific problem situations. When a diver detects a potential problem area, the proper defense must be selected carefully and then applied authoritatively.

6.1.4 AFTER THE DIVE

Defensive diving techniques should continue immediately following each dive. The dive partners should sit down together and evaluate their performance. All aspects of the dive should be reviewed, and notations should be recorded in the log book (Figure 6-1). Keeping an accurate log book and reviewing the data in it is an excellent contribution to defensive diving. If all went well and if even slight problems were not encountered, proper notation of this fact should also be recorded. Dive log data will usually include date, time, place, weather, and type of dive; water temperature, visibility, maximum depth, and bottom time; buddy's name and underwater observations (including marine life); and amount of lead worn and air used.

Talking to other divers about their underwater excursions will often provide valuable information which should be stored for future use. Evaluating problems other divers have encountered will help defensive divers solve those problems, should they arise.

6.2 Scuba Rescue

Scuba rescue is an important aspect of defensive diving which promotes safety through preventive lifesaving techniques and rescue maneuvers. The discussion in this section is a brief introduction to scuba lifesaving skills and is not intended to be comprehensive. Although these techniques are quite basic, they are nevertheless extremely effective. However, reading about them is insufficient; the skills must be practiced regularly both in the pool and in the open water.

By now the reader has learned that scuba diving is an equipment-oriented, and, perhaps, equipment-dominated, sport. While many divers scorn the quantity and bulkiness of the equipment required for diving, defensive divers with an appreciation for scuba lifesaving welcome the gear. Lifesaving in the water can be made incredibly simple if the rescuing diver *stops* and *thinks* before *reacting* in an emergency situation, utilizes the equipment every diver wears, and recruits help from others to make the rescue. Of course, the best scuba lifesaving techniques are the preventive techniques covered in this chapter and the first half of Chapter 9, which allow divers to correct problems before they necessitate rescues.

DIVING LOG

Dive No. _____

Date _____

Total Underwater Hours to Date _____

Total Time This Dive _____

Total Hours _____

PRE-DIVE INFORMATION

POST-DIVE INFORMATION

Location _____

Water Temperature _____ Visibility _____

Description of the Bottom _____

Purpose of Dive _____

Maximum Depth of Dive _____

Average Depth _____

Diving Buddy _____

Bottom Time _____

Decompression _____

Time out of the Water _____

Accessibility from beach _____

Total Dive Time _____

Air Temperature _____

Air Consumption: Use NASDS Scuba Time Calculator or

Surface Conditions _____

Weather Conditions _____

$$\frac{PSI\ Consumed}{TTD} = \frac{33 + Depth}{33} = \frac{Surface\ Air\ Consumption}{PSI/Min.}$$

Time in the Water _____

Nav. Compass Reading to Locate Dive Spot _____

Wave Height _____

Remarks _____

_____

_____

Witness _____

Certification _____

©

Figure 6-1. Diving log. (© *National Association of Scuba Diving Schools*)

6.2.1 FIVE STEPS TO EASY RESCUE

1. Whenever possible, dive with some type of stable float on the surface in the immediate vicinity. Inner tubes and surf-mats are ideal for this purpose. A tired diver may grab the inflatable device or it can be pushed by a rescuer to a panicky diver to assist the victim and protect the rescuer.

2. Whenever possible, never attempt a rescue alone. Always call for assistance before approaching the victim.

3. Whenever possible, keep a safety team out of the water to make rescues when needed, offer assistance to a rescuer, and summon additional help. Regardless of the type of diving group, safe diving practices dictate that at least two divers should remain out of the water to serve as lifeguards.

4. Whenever possible, alert divers and nondivers alike that a rescue is about to be made. The rescuer should then instruct the aides in what must be done while the rescue is attempted. For instance, nondivers should constantly point to the victim to help the rescuer get there more quickly and to mark the spot in case the troubled diver suddenly submerges. Other aides should summon additional help and toss or carry some type of float or line to the rescuer.

5. Always use equipment designed to produce positive buoyancy. Dropping the weight belt and/or inflating the B.C.D. must be of primary importance when the actual handling of a troubled diver is required.

NOTE: Most divers must be cautious about attempting a rescue because they are not properly trained in lifesaving, lack assistance, or lack proper rescue equipment. This is true especially in the case of a panicky diver.

6.2.2 ELEMENTARY FORMS OF SELF-RESCUE AND BUDDY ASSISTANCE FOR FATIGUED DIVERS

Elementary forms of rescue and assists in the water call for the use of the diver's equipment to provide positive buoyancy, which enables the diver to rest on the surface and summon additional help if necessary. These forms of rescue require a combination of using some equipment for assistance while discarding other items which cannot be used to aid, and may even endanger, the diver.

Two very important items should be used without hesitation to provide self-rescue or buddy assistance in the water. In order of preference, they are the *B.C.D.* and the *weight belt*. Whenever a diver experiences fatigue, psychological stress, or cramps, the B.C.D. should be inflated slightly to provide immediate positive buoyancy. While being supported on the surface with the B.C.D., divers can either tend to the problem themselves or summon the assistance of the dive partner. In most cases, problems are best treated on the surface where unrestricted breathing and communication can take place.

If inflating the B.C.D. is not possible for any reason, the weight belt should then be dropped. Doing this underwater, however, may be a risky proposition because it can in some cases lead to a rapid, uncontrolled ascent. The weight belt should be dropped only if the B.C.D. cannot be inflated, but certainly should be dropped when the situation merits it. Too many divers fail to drop the weight belt when necessary for fear of losing it. When the weight belt does have to be dropped, it should be stripped completely away from the diver before being dropped to avoid entanglement with other items, like the diver's knife or fins. It is very helpful for divers to wear brightly colored weight belts so that assisting divers can easily spot the belt.

A *whistle* attached to the diver's vest provides a valuable means of seeking additional help. Yelling for help is often too fatiguing and is not as efficient as a whistle.

When a problem arises either underwater or on the surface, all equipment not required for safety should be dropped. Cameras, goodie bags, and spearguns can always be recovered after the problem is solved, and rescue and assistance will certainly be made more cumbersome if these items are not discarded.

Once positively buoyant on the surface, the diver should rest, relax, and maintain deep breathing. Survival skills, such as survival floating and treading, should be used, but swimming back to shore or boat should be discouraged until the diver is completely recovered and has assistance.

When assisting another diver in need of help, several suggestions should be remembered:

1. Talk to the diver in need of help before actually coming in contact with him or her.

2. Persuade the diver to relax and use the equipment to promote positive buoyancy.

3. Physically assist the diver only when you are certain that the diver is not panicky and you will not be endangering yourself.

4. Use a surface float (inner tube with diver's flag) for additional buoyancy whenever possible, placing the float between the tired diver and rescuer.

5. Assist the tired diver back to the shore, dock, or boat by using one of a variety of tows (discussed in Section 6.2.4). Towing a diver is recommended only after the most vital problems have been corrected. Ideally, a third party on shore should be delegated to pull the victim in, using a float with a line attached.

6.2.3 CONTROL AND RESCUE OF THE PANICKY DIVER

Panicky divers in the water are not only hazards to themselves but also endanger the rescuer's safety. Panicky victims are extremely difficult to assist because they cannot help themselves, due to the irrational behavior which accompanies panic, and because they are unable and unwilling to listen to the rescuer. For these reasons, panicky victims must be approached with caution.

When approaching a panicky diver, the rescuer should stop approximately 8–10 feet from the victim to assess the situation and to avoid being grabbed by the panicky diver. The primary objective of the rescuer is to make the victim positively buoyant by ditching the weight belt, inflating the B.C.D., or both. Although there are several ways to produce positive buoyancy for panicky victims, only two are discussed here: the rear surface approach and the front underwater approach.

The Rear Surface Approach

The preferred method (many experts believe that this is the only way to rescue a scuba diver) of approaching a panicky diver is from the rear. This type of approach should be considered first because it allows the rescuer to control the victim before the victim has a chance to grab the rescuer. One disadvantage of this approach is that it makes it more difficult for the rescuer to inflate the B.C.D. and/or drop the weight belt.

When approaching a panicky diver from the rear, the rescuer should first attempt to summon additional aid by calling for help or using the whistle. While swimming to the victim, the rescuer must not overdo it. Although the approach should be made quickly, if the rescuer swims too fast to get to the victim undue fatigue may hinder the rescue and transport of the panicky diver. The eyes of the rescuer should be focused constantly on the victim, while other divers not in the water should point to the victim to help the rescuer locate him/her. Just prior to contacting the victim (8–10 feet away), the rescuer should stop and tread water to assess the seriousness of the situation, decide how to handle the victim, and determine what defensive tactics will be used if the victim lunges at the rescuer.

When contact is finally made, the rescuer can place a hand under the victim's tank valve to hold the victim up on the surface and simultaneously use the free hand to inflate the B.C.D. The rescuer must be prepared to back off quickly if the victim attempts to grab the rescuer. Once the victim is made buoyant and is calmed by the rescuer, a tow can be initiated.

The Front Underwater Approach

The advantage of the front approach is that the rescuer may be able to instruct and reassure the victim verbally, during the approach, making the rescue simpler and safer. One disadvantage is that a diver who is overanxious to be rescued may grab and endanger the rescuer. This rescue is difficult to perform without practice. Again, before making contact with the victim, the rescuer should stop 8–10 feet from the victim to decide on the best action.

Submerging to approach the victim underwater is highly recommended whenever the water is sufficiently clear. This allows the rescuer to make the victim buoyant without risking a front headhold. The victim will not submerge to grab the rescuer. When performing the front underwater approach, the rescuer surface dives 8–10 feet from the victim and then makes contact by holding the victim's legs between the ankles and knees, at the same time pushing the victim slightly up toward the surface to offer support. The rescuer should then maintain contact while working the hands to the victim's waist in order to drop the weight belt. When releasing the weight belt, the rescuer is advised to open the buckle first and then strip the belt completely away from the panicky diver. If, after providing positive buoyancy, the victim is still struggling, the rescuer may want to turn the victim around before surfacing to tow the victim. This action is recommended when there is any chance that the victim may still grab the rescuer.

In the event that the victim still attempts to grab the rescuer, which is quite unlikely because of the bulky equipment, the rescuer must defend himself by tucking the chin to protect the mask and face, automatically inflating the victim's B.C.D., and, if necessary, pressing the victim away by placing the heels of the hands on the victim's hips and pressing up and away. The front underwater approach is not a simple maneuver and is recommended only for those divers trained in lifesaving. For this reason, all scuba divers are strongly urged to enroll in a complete lifesaving course offered by the Red Cross or YMCA. Although most scuba divers will never need to attempt a rescue, knowing how to save someone instills confidence.

6.2.4 TOWS

Transporting a troubled diver to safety is one of the last considerations when attempting a scuba diving rescue. If the victim can be made buoyant and stabilized on the surface, there is often no need to rush him/her out of the water if help is on its way. Eventually, during the process of a rescue, towing the victim may be necessary. If so, remember that

- both rescuer and victim must be buoyant,
- the victim's face must be kept out of water,
- both the victim and rescuer must be as horizontal (flat) in the water as possible,
- the rescuer must be able to kick freely without being hindered by dangling equipment or limbs, and
- firm contact with and control of the victim must be maintained.

Towing a victim to shore with the assistance of a towline (a line with a float attached) can make this lifesaving skill much easier. A ring buoy with an extended line attached to it is an ideal type of rescue device. The advantages of using a towline include more support of the victim, more protection for the rescuer if the victim panics, and less work for the rescuer, since another person on land or boat pulls both the victim and rescuer to safety.

When a rescuer uses a towline to carry a troubled diver to safety, one end of the line is held by another person out of the water while the rescuer swims the opposite end of the line, with the float attached, to the victim. Upon reaching the victim, the rescuer can either extend the float to the victim, or hold the float with one arm and the victim with the other arm. The former action is recommended for active, panicky victims, while the latter is suggested for passive or unconscious

Figure 6-2. Fin push. (Photo by Michael Oakes)

divers. Once contact with the victim is made, the rescuer signals the line tender to pull them in.

NOTE: Whenever possible, towlines with tenders assigned to them, in addition to some type of surface float to aid in scuba rescue, should be available when diving.

Although there are many different types of scuba rescue tows and carries, only four are discussed here because they are easy to learn, easy to use, and allow the rescuer to release the victim quickly if the victim endangers the rescuer. They are the fin push, armpit tow, tank-valve tow, and B.C.D. tow.

Fin Push

The fin push (Figure 6-2) is an excellent tow for passive victims. This tow allows the rescuer to swim naturally on the stomach without the victim's equipment or limbs impairing the rescuer's progress. In addition, with the rescuer swimming on the front and the victim resting on the back, the rescuer can visually monitor the victim and offer verbal reassurance.

To perform the fin push, the rescuer instructs the victim to float on the back with legs spread slightly apart. The victim's fins are placed on the rescuer's shoulders.[2] The rescuer then simply places the palms under the victim's calves and gently pushes the victim to safety using a relaxed flutter kick.

Figure 6-3. Tank-valve tow.

Tank-Valve Tow

The tank-valve tow (Figure 6-3) is recommended because it allows the rescuer to maintain secure contact without actually touching the victim. Additionally, the rescuer is offered more freedom of movement because holding the tank valve allows the rescuer to remain further

2. R.W. Smith and H.C. Allen, *Scuba Lifesaving and Accident Management* (Key West, Fla.: National YMCA Underwater Activities Program, 1978), p. 50.

behind the victim. Performing the tank-valve tow is accomplished by placing the hand under the tank valve with palm up and fingers spread apart. The victim is approached from the rear and is towed on the back while the rescuer swims on the side. A flat horizontal swimming position is recommended, with the towing arm held straight.

B.C.D. Tow

The B.C.D. tow (Figure 6-4) is similar to the tank-valve tow and may be used for skin divers or in rare cases when the scuba diver's tank must be jettisoned. (The tank would only be jettisoned when its weight is making the rescue impossible.) Rather than placing the palm under the tank valve, it is placed under the B.C.D. behind the victim's neck. All other towing techniques used in the B.C.D. tow are identical to the tank-valve tow.

Figure 6-4. B.C.D. tow.

Armpit Tow

The armpit tow (Figure 6-5) requires that the diver approach from the rear and make contact by placing the hand under the victim's shoulder. This tow offers more control and support of the victim, but the rescuer's legs may be hindered because they kick directly under the victim. When using the armpit tow, the victim lies on the back while the rescuer lies sideways in the water and uses a side-flutter kick for transport. Either the right hand of the rescuer is placed in the victim's right armpit or the left hand is placed in the victim's left armpit. The rescuer's arm used to hold the victim must be fully extended with elbow straight.

NOTE: The tank-valve tow, B.C.D. tow, and armpit tow all require the same swimming stroke; only hand placement differs between tows.

Figure 6-5. Armpit tow. (Photo by Michael Oakes)

6.2.5 RESCUE OF A SUBMERGED, UNCONSCIOUS DIVER

The thought of rescuing a submerged, unconscious diver is certainly not a pleasant one. However, a diver may be required to perform this type of rescue. This dire situation calls for special considerations and lifesaving techniques. Of course, the priority of the rescuer must be to get the victim to the surface as quickly as possible.

When a submerged, unconscious diver is first sighted, the rescuer should quickly strip the victim of the weight belt if progress to the surface is impeded. Then the rescuer should take a position behind the victim, maintaining good contact by holding the victim's armpit or tank valve with one hand while securing the second stage of the regulator in the victim's mouth with the other hand. Holding the victim securely with both hands, the rescuer should kick quickly to the surface. During the ascent, the victim's head should be held in a straight or neutral position, but not hyperextended.[3] At no time should resuscitation efforts begin for a nonbreathing diver underwater. All rescue attempts should be focused on returning the victim to the surface as fast as possible, where resuscitation can then be effectively performed. Once the surface has been reached, a call for help must follow immediately, and, at the same time, the B.C.D. should be inflated and resuscitation efforts should commence.

6.2.6 RESUSCITATION

Of paramount importance in the rescue of a nonbreathing diver is immediate and effective resuscitation. Therefore, all scuba divers, whether novice or expert, should be trained in mouth-to-mouth resuscitation and cardiopulmonary resuscitation. These courses are conducted frequently by the American Heart Association and the American Red Cross. For those readers who are unfamiliar with these resuscitation techniques, a brief synopsis of the skills involved are found in Appendix B. The following discussion of in-water resuscitation assumes that the reader has mastered these procedures.

To perform artificial respiration on the surface, both victim and rescuer must be made buoyant. As mentioned earlier, this is usually accomplished by first dropping the victim's weight belt and then inflating the B.C.D. if necessary. Although the rescuer's B.C.D. might require inflating, dropping the weight belt of the rescuer is not usually a necessity. Having both B.C.D.s fully inflated may also prove too

3. *Ibid.*, p. 47.

cumbersome to perform effective ventilation. Mouth-to-mouth or mouth-to-snorkel resuscitation is then begun.

Mouth-to-Mouth Technique

The mouth-to-mouth technique is obviously not as easy in the water as it is on land, After positive buoyancy is achieved on the surface, the masks of both victim and rescuer are usually removed, although some instructors recommend keeping them on. Then the rescuer takes a position alongside the victim's head, next to the victim's left shoulder. The left side is recommended because most life-support apparatus is located on the left side (auto-inflators, weight belt buckles, and shoulder buckles).[4] The rescuer's left arm then slides under the victim's left arm to position the rescuer's left hand behind the victim's neck. This is referred to as the "do-si-do" position (Figure 6-6) because it closely resembles the square dance pattern. With the rescuer's left hand behind the victim's head, the victim's hair or hood is pulled downward to hyperextend the victim's neck, opening the airway. Then the palm of the rescuer's right hand is placed on the victim's forehead while the thumb and index finger of that hand pinches the victim's nostrils shut.

Mouth-to-mouth resuscitation is begun by administering four quick, successive breaths to fully inflate the victim's lungs. The victim's head

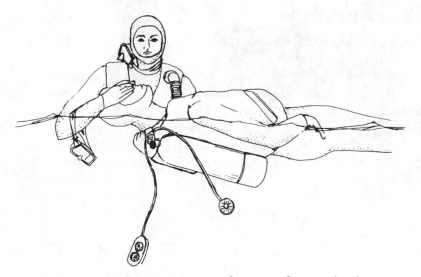

Figure 6-6. Do-si-do position for mouth-to-mouth resuscitation.

4. *Ibid.*, p. 51.

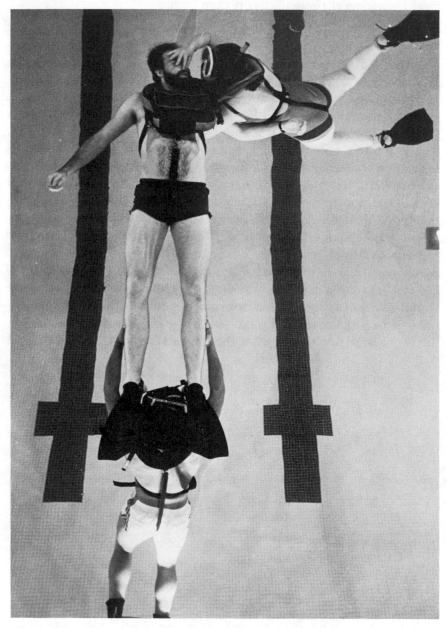

Figure 6-7. Fin push with mouth-to-mouth resuscitation.
    (Photo by Michael Oakes)

must be rotated toward the rescuer during in-water resuscitation because it is virtually impossible for the rescuer to climb up out of the water and position the mouth directly on top of the victim's. After four quick inflations are made, one breath every 5 seconds should be administered to the victim. Calls for help should be continued between breaths if assistance has not yet arrived. Resuscitation efforts must not, however, be stopped for more than 90 seconds once mouth-to-mouth has commenced.

Resuscitation efforts are of primary importance; victim transport should be considered secondary when effective ventilation is being made. Once a second rescuer arrives, the new helper should be positioned at the feet of the victim to provide victim transport by means of the fin push. Of the various tows available, the fin push provides maximum propulsion without interfering with the resuscitation efforts of the primary rescuer. During the transport, mouth-to-mouth must continue without interruption (Figure 6-7).

When the rescuer providing artificial respiration does not have additional help for victim transport (a situation which should never occur), kicking the fins toward the victim's feet will provide adequate propulsion. However, mouth-to-mouth resuscitation should not be interrupted while towing the victim to safety.

Mouth-to-Snorkel Technique

When mouth-to-mouth resuscitation becomes impractical due to rough water or inadequate buoyancy, the snorkel may be used for in-water artificial respiration. Mouth-to-snorkel breathing is the preferred method of resuscitation for many scuba divers but does require practice in a variety of conditions.

To begin mouth-to-snorkel breathing, the rescuer should be positioned directly behind the victim's head. The victim's head should be held at the chin and pressed against the rescuer's chest. Using the free hand, the rescuer may shake water from the snorkel and then place it in the hand providing the chin pull. While exchanging the snorkel between hands, care must be taken to bend the snorkel end up to avoid reflooding the tube with water. The masks may be kept on.

The snorkel mouthpiece must be manipulated between the middle and ring fingers of the chin-pulling hand without losing contact with the victim. After the mouthpiece is properly placed in the hand controlling the victim's head, the rescuer must press the snorkel flange over the victim's mouth and apply constant pressure with the fingers to ensure an airtight seal. The victim's nose may then be sealed with

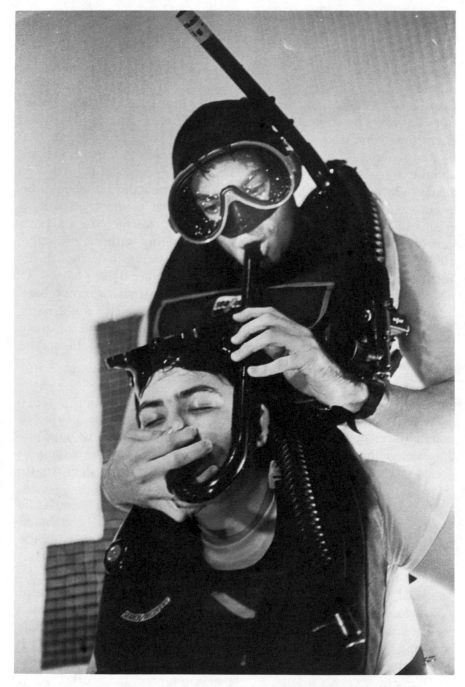

Figure 6-8. Mouth-to-snorkel resuscitation. (Photo by Michael Oakes)

the thumb and index finger of that same hand.[5] If the mask is left on this may help to seal the nose.

When the snorkel mouthpiece is properly placed and sealed in the victim's mouth, rescue breathing commences by placing the end of the snorkel tube in the rescuer's mouth and exhaling forcefully into the tube (Figure 6-8). After each exhalation, the rescuer's mouth should be removed from the tube to allow the victim's air to escape.

The following suggestions will promote effective mouth-to-snorkel breathing:

1. Exhale harder when using the snorkel for rescue breathing to overcome the dead-air space found in the tube.

2. Try to place the snorkel flange between the victim's teeth and lips for an improved seal.

3. Practice mouth-to-snorkel breathing with a variety of tubes to find the snorkel which can be easily manipulated for best results.

Regulator Technique

Recently, a new technique for in-water rescue breathing has been developed for scuba divers. Apparently, certain scuba diving regulators can be used in the water for resuscitation and may even be more effective than mouth-to-mouth or mouth-to-snorkel breathing. A scuba regulator can only be used for this purpose if it can deliver acceptable air pressure (15–35 cm H_2O). The scuba regulator can deliver more oxygen to the victim (20 percent) than the mouth-to-mouth or mouth-to-snorkel technique. With the victim's neck hyperextended to open the airway and the mask in place to make a nose seal, the regulator is placed in the victim's mouth and the purge button is gradually depressed for 2 seconds, then released for 3 seconds. This, of course, should only be attempted on the surface.[6]

It appears that scuba divers are better equipped to make rescues than other water sports enthusiasts. Divers can quickly make victims positively buoyant and can choose from a variety of resuscitation techniques, such as mouth-to-mouth, mouth-to-snorkel, and even

5. *Ibid.*, p. 56.
6. N. Eastman, J. Ghapery, and G. Landrum, "The Scuba Regulator as a Resuscitator for In-Water Rescue Breathing," *The Physician and Sportsmedicine* 10 (March 1982):116–123.

regulator-to-mouth. Additionally, in all three cases, the victim's mask may remain in place to ensure a nose seal.

6.3 Diving Accidents

There are many causes of scuba diving accidents, but the major contributing factor to underwater fatalities is drowning due to panic. Surprisingly, many scuba diving fatalities occur before the dive even begins. This scenario often reveals a diver getting into trouble by either entering rough or dangerous water or entering a diving environment (cave, ice, deep wreck) for which he/she is totally untrained. A problem arises, the diver panics, and drowning follows, often even before the diver gets underwater.

Understanding the causes and conditions that lead to underwater accidents should help divers to avoid hazardous situations. The possibility of accidental death is *not* a major area of concern for certified divers because accidents occur to untrained divers. For certified divers who exercise good judgment, scuba diving is indeed a safe sport.

6.3.1 STATISTICS

Since 1970 the University of Rhode Island, in conjunction with the National Oceanographic and Atmospheric Administration (NOAA) and U.S. D.O.T., has been carefully analyzing scuba diving accidents in the United States and compiling annual statistics.[7] These statistics are summarized in the following sections.

The number of fatal scuba diving accidents has ranged from 66 to 147 per year since 1970. More than half of these deaths are drownings due to panic. The Associated Press reported a study by the American Medical Association which showed that scuba diving is much safer than some other "risk-taking" sports. The number of deaths per 100,000 participants in various sports is as follows: riding race horses, 12.8; sky diving, 12.3; hang gliding, 5.6; mountain climbing, 5.1; scuba diving, 1.1; motorcycle racing, 0.7; and college football, 0.3.[8]

7. H.V. Schenck and J.J. McAniff, *U.S. Underwater Diving Fatality Statistics, 1976*, Report No. URI-SSR-78-12 and Report NOAA Grant No. 4-3-158-31 (Rockville, Md.: U.S. Department of Transportation and U.S. Department of Commerce, 1978), pp. 3–19.
   8. *Washington Post*, November 18, 1982, p. E10.

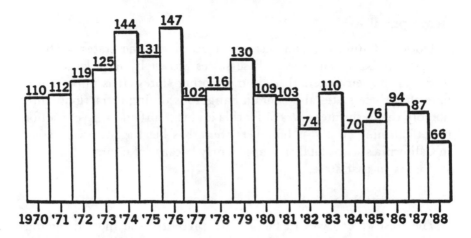

Figure 6-9. *United States nonoccupational underwater diving fatalities, 1970–1988. (Courtesy National Underwater Accident Data Center, URI)*

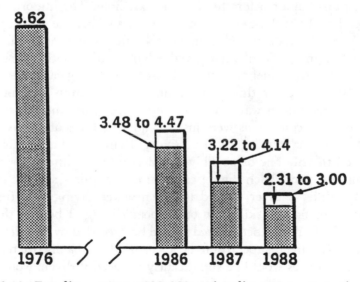

Figure 6-10. *Fatality rate per 100,000 active divers, nonoccupational underwater diving, 1976 vs. 1986, 1987, and 1988. (Courtesy National Underwater Accident Data Center, URI)*

Geographical Area

Florida, California, and recently Hawaii are the states with the largest number of fatalities. These states attract by far a larger share of divers to their waters than do most other states. It is important to note that these states also contain dangerous diving attractions, most notably the freshwater caves of Florida and the surf and kelp of California. Beginning in 1974, however, there has been a downward trend in California's scuba fatalities, apparently because of upgraded training standards in that state.

Environment

The freshwater caves in Florida are presently the most dangerous diving environment. A second leading category implicated in scuba diving deaths is rough surface conditions, such as high waves and strong currents. Entanglement in kelp, weeds, lines, and ropes have all contributed to accidents underwater. Ice diving is yet another contributing environmental factor leading to fatalities.

Untrained divers engaged in ice diving and cave diving become lost and run out of air before finding the exit hole. The important fact to remember about these environmental causes is that the victim probably should *not* have been diving in the specific environment without advanced training. Too often divers plan to dive without regard for changing environmental factors. Most cave diving fatalities occur to those untrained for this very unique and dangerous type of diving. Those perishing in waves and currents were either inferior swimmers or the water conditions were just too adverse for scuba activity.

During the training process, scuba diving candidates are usually exposed to only one or possibly two diving environments outside the swimming pool. Each diving environment requires specific training. For example, a diver trained for open-water diving in a freshwater quarry will not be skilled in ocean boat diving. I believe that every new type of diving encountered should be preceded by specific training under the direct supervision of a certified scuba instructor. Scuba diving fatalities would be significantly reduced if divers would refrain from diving in situations for which they have not been specifically trained. Additionally, divers must learn to abort dives when the weather and water conditions are not suitable for diving.

Depth

Contrary to what many novice divers believe, most scuba fatalities occur in *shallow*, rather than deep, water. In fact, approximately 50 percent of all scuba diving accidents occur between a depth of 40 feet and the surface. For example, during 1976, 50 percent of all fatalities occurred in 30 feet of water or less, with many of these accidents happening on the surface. Many experts would agree that regardless of the actual depth where the fatalities occur, most scuba accidents *begin* on the surface.

Medical Causes

The largest number of medical causes of fatalities was found in the "exhaustion, embolism, and panic" categories. Heart attack, nitrogen narcosis, and head injuries were other causes found contributing to scuba fatalities, but all these other causes combined do not begin to approach the number found in the category of "exhaustion, embolism, and panic."

Equipment

Equipment malfunction was implicated only in a minority of scuba fatalities. The largest number of equipment-related accidents was caused by running out of air. Although lack of air supply falls into the equipment area, this usually occurs due to human error rather than equipment failure. Other equipment-related causes were improper use of the weight belt, poor maintenance of regulators, and entanglement in improperly secured belts and buckles. When equipment malfunction was found as a direct cause of an accident, usually the equipment in question was grossly neglected by its user.

Dangerous Marine Life

Shark attack has been identified as a cause of death only *once* in recent years. Marine life with notorious reputations, such as the barracuda, the octopus, and moray eels, seldom, if ever, attack divers.

6.3.2 PREVENTION

To avoid diving accidents, remember the following safety suggestions:

1. Do *not* dive in a new environment without special training.
2. Avoid diving in rough or dangerous water.
3. Know when *not* to dive.
4. Practice buddymanship.
5. Practice and review diving skills whenever possible in a pool.

6. Try to relax prior to and during the dive in order to avoid excessive stress.

7. Anticipate problems.

8. If excessive stress develops and/or a problem arises,

STOP   BREATHE   THINK   BREATHE   REACT

9. If a problem cannot be corrected while underwater, slowly and carefully ascend to the surface. Reaching the surface should be attempted by swimming normally. If ascending becomes difficult and a normal swimming ascent is not possible, the following emergency ascents are recommended in the order presented below:

   a. shared ascent using an auxiliary or pony bottle (octopus) regulator (victim breathing from an additional emergency second stage on the rescuer's regulator)

   b. emergency free swimming ascent (diver *must exhale continuously*)

   c. buoyant ascent (drop weight belt first, then, if necessary, inflate B.C.D.; *exhale continuously*)

   d. emergency buddy-breathing.[9]

Selected References

Allen, R., and Griffiths, T. *Controlling Diver Stress and Panic.* Piscataway, N.J.: New Century Publishers, 1983.

Dueker, C.W. *SCUBA Diving Safety.* Mountain View, Calif.: World Publications, 1978.

Eldridge, L. "Women in Diving: Psychological Considerations." Proceedings of the Sixth International Conference of Underwater Education. Colton, Calif.: National Association of Underwater Instructors, 1975.

Sleeper, J.B., and Bangasser, S. *Women Underwater.* Crestline, Calif.: Deep Star Publishing, 1979.

Smith, R.W., and Allen, H.C. *SCUBA Lifesaving and Accident Management.* Key West, Fla.: National YMCA Underwater Activities Program, 1978.

9. J. Hardy, "Part Two: Diving Accidents—Why?" *NAUI News*, July 1976, p. 6.

Chapter 6 Review

The instructor should correct the student's answers, record the results, and return them to the student. Both teacher and student should sign after the last question.

REVIEW QUESTIONS	ANSWERS
1. Define defensive diving.	1. _____
2. Potential problems while diving can arise from three general areas. What are they?	2. _____ _____ _____
3. Identify the defenses for the following potential hazards: environment—jellyfish, shark, poor visibility, rip current, strong ocean currents; equipment—mask flooding, regulator freeflow, insufficient lead, out of air, loss of regulator; diver—hyperventilation, predive anxiety, head cold, excessive fatigue, leg cramps.	3. Use a separate piece of paper.
4. List five ways of using equipment to rescue a diver without attempting a swimming rescue.	4. _____ _____ _____ _____ _____
5. Name three different types of in-water resuscitation.	5. _____ _____ _____
6. Should mental rehearsal be practiced before, during, or after the dive?	6. _____

REVIEW QUESTIONS	ANSWERS

7. What type of information should go in the log book?

7. _____

_____

_____

8. When is the front underwater approach recommended?

8. _____

9. List three principles of a good lifesaving tow.

9. _____

_____

_____

10. Which lifesaving approach is recommended for a panicky diver?

10. _____

11. What piece of diving equipment is valuable in assisting the fatigued diver?

11. _____

12. The fin push is recommended for what type of victim?

12. _____

_____

I have graded, recorded, and returned this student's responses.

Instructor's Signature:

_____

Date:

_____

I have seen my corrected review questions and now know the appropriate answers.
Note: The answer sheet may either be taken out or retained with this book.

Student's Signature:

_____

Date:

_____

Answer to Review Question 3

ENVIRONMENT

Potential Hazard	*Defense*
1. *Jellyfish*—May sting the diver if touched.	1. Wear protective clothing in the water, especially on hands, arms, and legs. Do not touch jellyfish.
2. *Shark*—Could bite, but probably won't. More likely to cause diver fear and panic.	2. STOP – BREATHE – THINK – BREATHE – REACT! Work on breathing and try to relax. Move close to your buddy and back into a reef, wreck, or other large object. *DO NOT* swim quickly to the surface. When the shark swims away, slowly get out of the water.
3. *Poor Visibility*—May cause anxiety and loss of buddy.	3. Use buddy-line or light when appropriate. Swim slowly. Terminate dive if visibility is too low.
4. *Rip Current*—A strong, narrow, short-lived current which could pull a diver away from shore and cause fatigue.	4. Look for rips by surveying the water's surface before entering. If caught in a rip, RELAX, inflate B.C.D., swim *PARALLEL* to shore. Signal for assistance.
5. *Strong Ocean Currents*—Could cause diver fatigue.	5. Make sure boat has sufficient equipment, such as surface trail lines, extra down lines, two anchor lines, for coping with currents. Begin dive into or against current so that return may go with the current at the end of the dive. Save at least half the total air supply for a safe return to the boat. If unable to make it back to the boat because of strong currents, inflate B.C.D. and whistle for assistance.

EQUIPMENT

Potential Hazard

Defense

6. *Mask Flooding*—Could possibly surprise diver, leading to breathing difficulties.

6. STOP – BREATHE – THINK – BREATHE – REACT! Work on slow rhythmic breathing. Mentally review how the mask should be cleared. Take a deep breath. Clear the mask by exhaling through the nose slowly while looking up and gently pressing the top of the mask with your hand against your forehead.

7. *Regulator Freeflow*—May be difficult to breathe from and may deplete air supply rapidly.

7. STOP – BREATHE – THINK – BREATHE – REACT! Remember that a freeflowing regulator is usually breathable. If so, signal your buddy to the surface and swim to boat or shore. Get another regulator. If freeflow is so severe that breathing is not possible, signal buddy for assistance. Perform either octopus assisted ascent, swimming free ascent, buoyant ascent, or buddy-breathing ascent. Come up under control; stay calm.

8. *Insufficient Lead*—The result will be a buoyant diver who must work excessively to stay underwater.

8. Do not fight positive buoyancy! Return to the shore or boat to add additional weights.

9. *Out-of-Air*—A situation which should never occur, but if it does, may cause an uncontrolled ascent.

9. STOP – BREATHE (if possible) – THINK – BREATHE (if possible) – REACT! Signal buddy for assistance. Swim to the surface slowly using either emergency swimming ascent, octopus assisted ascent, buoyant ascent, or buddy-breathing ascent.

10. *Loss of Regulator*—Should never occur, but may worry a diver if it does.

10. Simply reach the right hand over and behind the right shoulder to the tank valve where the regulator originates on the first stage or stand vertically in the water with the head down and the feet up and the regulator mouthpiece should drop in front of the face.

DIVER

Potential Hazard

Defense

11. *Hyperventilation*—Due to anxiety or overexertion; may lead to panic.

11. Exit from the water as soon as possible. Concentrate on a slow, deep, rhythmic breathing pattern. Try diaphragmatic breathing.

12. *Predive Anxiety*—May lead to hyperventilation and diving errors.

12. *DO NOT ENTER THE WATER* until comfortable. Work on breathing, talk with buddy and dive master. Use meditation and mental rehearsal. Cancel the dive if you cannot relax.

13. *Head Cold*—May lead to sinus or middle-ear injury.

13. *DO NOT DIVE.*

14. *Excessive Fatigue*—May lead to panic.

14. STOP! Signal for assistance. Work on breathing. Swim slowly to surface. Make yourself positively buoyant and rest on surface. *DO NOT* swim to boat or shore alone.

15. *Leg Cramps*—Could cause panic.

15. STOP – BREATHE – THINK – BREATHE – REACT! Signal buddy for assistance. Make affected leg straight and pull fin toward the knee to stretch out the calf muscle. Make yourself positively buoyant and rest on surface.

Chapter 7

Air Sharing and Controlled Ascents

7.1 Controlled Emergency Ascents for Out-of-Air Situations

Out-of-air situations underwater are, of course, extremely threatening to the diver, but should simply never occur. Then again, automobile owners should never run out of gasoline, but they are known to do so. While the analogy between a scuba diver and a car driver may be fitting, divers must realize that when they run out of "fuel" underwater, survival requires more than just pulling over on the shoulder of the road, especially when diving at 100 feet. Just as drivers should have full gas tanks, properly functioning fuel gauges, good travel planning, and a watchful eye, scuba divers must be even more prudent, because running out of air underwater may be not just inconvenient, but catastrophic. Preventing out-of-air situations requires a tank with air, an accurate pressure gauge, proper dive planning and a watchful eye. There is no excuse for running out of air. All divers should make a habit of returning to the surface with 500 psi remaining in their scuba tanks.

If a diver does run out of air, an emergency ascent may be executed in a controlled or uncontrolled manner. The uncontrolled ascent is usually a product of diver panic and greatly amplifies the emergency of which the diver is already a part. Therefore, the controlled emergency ascent, regardless of the situation, is perhaps the primary goal of all scuba training programs.

Once an out-of-air situation is confirmed, divers must make every attempt to stay calm and to carefully consider options rather than rushing to the surface irrationally or grabbing the dive buddy.

Controlled emergency ascents may be either *dependent* or *independent* ascents. A *dependent* ascent means that air is shared and contact is maintained by two dive buddies enroute to the surface. An alternate air source (A.A.S.) is highly recommended for a dependent ascent. An *independent* ascent means that the out-of-air diver swims to the surface alone with or without supplemental air. The independent ascent is usually preferred because it is generally faster, easier, and safer than the dependent ascent.

7.2 Dependent Emergency Ascents

By far the most desirable dependent emergency ascent involves the use of an A.A.S. that allows both divers to breathe simultaneously by using their own second stages during the ascent. This may be accomplished in several ways.

Octopus Breathing

This method is often called auxiliary regulator breathing, or octopus breathing, and requires an extra second stage of a regulator attached to the first stage of a diver's primary regulator. With this safety attachment, two divers may share one diver's air with little coordination or effort. Although octopus breathing makes the troubled diver dependent on the doner's air supply, it has an advantage in that both divers have their own regulator mouthpiece, thus eliminating the need to share one. However, octopus breathing, while making dependent emergency ascents easier than buddy breathing, does require special training.

The auxiliary second stage should be readily available for use and should be located somewhere on the diver's chest. The mouthpiece should be brightly colored to enable a troubled diver to find it quickly. The spare second stage should have a longer hose to allow for more freedom between the divers when a shared ascent is necessary. Most divers prefer to have the auxiliary pass over their right shoulder so they can place it easily in their mouth in the event that their primary second stage malfunctions.

Some scuba instructors teach their students to pass the primary second stage to the out-of-air victim while the donor uses the spare auxiliary second stage to breathe. Although there are numerous reasons for this method of air-sharing, recent research findings at Penn State University suggest that this technique is awkward and slow for novice divers. Regardless of the reasoning for passing the primary second stage to the out-of-air victim, passing the octopus regulator now comes highly recommended.

Pony Bottle Breathing

Another type of dependent emergency ascent uses an additional small scuba system usually attached to the primary scuba tank. This system not only requires an additional tank but an additional regulator with a longer hose as well. The pony bottle has an advantage over the octopus regulator during emergency ascents because both divers have more air by way of two separate air supplies. Another advantage is that the pony bottle owners may use it for self-rescue if their primary air source runs out or their regulator malfunctions. This would then be considered an independent emergency ascent. The pony bottle is especially popular in ice, cave, and wreck diving, all of which require additional air supplies and advanced training.

Figure 7-1. Pony bottle. (Photo by Bill Hughes)

Emergency Buddy-Breathing

Once regarded as *the* emergency ascent technique, buddy-breathing is now considered almost obsolete as a controlled emergency ascent. Perhaps the key word in attempting to identify the problems associated with buddy-breathing is *control*, or better yet, the lack of control experienced while performing this skill. Buddy-breathing requires two divers to breathe from the same regulator while swimming to the surface (Figure 6-11). Not only is it difficult to coordinate breathing efforts, but it is also difficult to maintain buddy contact and the same rate of ascent. Keep in mind that while all this is occurring, two divers must pass a regulator back and forth between them.

When one diver is panicky, the seriousness and difficulty of the situation is amplified. When both divers are highly trained in buddy-breathing and both partners can remain calm during the exercise, regardless of the circumstances, then and only then should buddy-breathing be attempted; this is assuming other emergency ascent options are not available. The major problem with buddy-breathing as an emergency ascent is that both the air donor and the troubled diver are placed in vulnerable and awkward positions, because an alternate air source is not used. When divers are required to be so close together, freedom of movement is restricted thus making swimming to the surface difficult. Buddy breathing should still be taught and practiced, however, because it requires little gear, develops emergency skills, and better prepares divers for all situations.

7.2.1 GUIDELINES FOR A.A.S. USAGE

Regardless of what type of A.A.S. is used for the dependent emergency ascent, the following guidelines should be followed:

1. The A.A.S. should be located in the chest area and be freed for use by one hand with a simple action.
2. The A.A.S. should be brightly colored and clearly visible.
3. Dive buddies must familiarize each other with their particular A.A.S. and review emergency air-sharing procedures during the pre-dive check prior to getting into the water.

Once a true out-of-air emergency has been confirmed, the following steps should be taken slowly and carefully:

1. Signal out-of-air.

2. Signal for air-sharing.

3. Establish contact with the donor.

4. The A.A.S. should be guided into the victim's mouth without being forcefully taken from the donor.

5. When comfortable rhythmic breathing has been established, the donor then initiates the ascent.

7.3 Independent Emergency Ascents

Many diving experts now recommend independent emergency ascents over dependent ascents. Controlling buoyancy, maintaining breath control, and ascending at a controlled rate is difficult enough for one diver to master under stress. When two divers must do this simultaneously while tethered to each other by an air hose, it becomes extremely difficult. When the buddy system fails, a dependent ascent is impossible. Many diving instructors encourage their students to go alone to the surface in an out-of-air emergency. In this case, only the out-of-air diver is jeopardized during the ascent, thus following the basic water safety principle "one victim is better than two."

Emergency Swimming Ascents

The emergency swimming ascent is an independent means of attaining the surface for safety. A confident and skilled diver may prefer swimming to the surface without relying on another diver. However, the major drawback of this type of ascent is that the diver in need will not receive any supplemental air on the way unless, of course, the out-of-air diver carried an additional air source. Although emergency swimming ascents have been accomplished successfully from great depths, most experts recommend this type of ascent from shallow or moderate depths only.

To perform the emergency swimming ascent in an out-of-air situation, the diver simply swims to the surface while exhaling constantly. While ascending, the regulator should be kept in the mouth and exhalation should be continuous. The diver should also extend the left arm upward and control buoyancy by inflating/deflating the B.C.D. with the left hand. The diver making an emergency swimming ascent must swim at a moderate pace and remain calm. A relaxed diver, swimming at a moderate pace and exhaling throughout the ascent, should not have any difficulties reaching the surface. While swimming to the surface, any residual air in the tank and regulator may expand allowing the diver to get a little more air on the way to the surface.

Figure 7-2. Spare Air™. (Courtesy Submersible Systems)

Spare Air™

An exciting new development in alternate air sources has recently been introduced by Submersible Systems. Spare Air™ is a miniature, self-contained scuba bottle/regulator unit approximately the size of a flashlight. Spare Air™ is very easy to handle and has no air hose. Research conducted at Penn State University found the Spare Air™ unit to be faster and easier to use than other techniques studied. These tests were conducted in clear, warm-water swimming pools and depth was not a factor. The Spare Air™ units, however, have only a limited supply of air.

To use the Spare Air™ unit the diver simply holds it in one hand, turns the air knob on with the other and slowly swims to the surface while breathing from it.

Buoyant Ascents

When a diver attempting an emergency ascent finds that progress to the surface is too slow, a buoyant ascent may be considered. The buoyant ascent usually assures the diver of getting to the surface but the trip there is more risky than the first two ascents discussed. The buoyant ascent involves dropping the weight belt and/or inflating the buoyancy compensator device. The potential hazard in performing the buoyant ascent is that the rate of ascent may become excessive as the diver approaches the surface. If the buoyant ascent is the only practical means of getting to the surface, divers must remember to exhale constantly and flare the body if ascent becomes rapid. While octopus breathing and emergency swimming ascents are preferred over buoyant ascents, which may become uncontrolled and increase the likelihood of a lung rupture, it is better to reach the surface with problems than to never get there at all.

Buoyant ascents are made easier and safer with a power B.C.D. inflator supplying air to the buoyancy compensator. Using the push button inflator allows the diver to achieve positive buoyancy without overfilling the B.C.D., thus promoting a safer, more controlled ascent. If for any reason the B.C.D. cannot be inflated, the weight belt should be jettisoned.

7.4 Emergency Ascent Training Problems

Paradoxically, emergency ascent training designed to produce safer, more competent divers actually risks the safety of the scuba diving trainee. Emergency ascents, even when practiced in the most ideal situations, are difficult and dangerous. The danger lies in the actual ascent to the surface; ascending too rapidly or not exhaling sufficiently could prove to be disastrous to the candidate due to lung overexpansion.

While many instructors circumvent the dangers of actual emergency ascents by having their students either buddy-breathe horizontally around the perimeter of the swimming pool or "blow and go" as they swim horizontally the length of the pool, these simulations do not realistically represent the mechanics involved in an actual ascent. Other instructors may go a step further in simulated swimming pool "ascent" training by introducing stressors like time and sensory deprivation while these techniques are being practiced. These drills do have merit, but, again, do not realistically re-create an actual ascent.

Open-water training in emergency ascents can be difficult to supervise. One advantage of stressing octopus breathing and Spare Air™ is that these techniques may be practiced safely in the open water from shallow depths with minimal risk to the diver trainees.

Actual ascent training in the open water does have merit for some types of scuba classes, but it must be remembered that one third to one-half of all air embolisms occur during this specialized training.

In light of this information, actual open-water ascent training should be reserved for only those classes in ideal conditions with expert supervision; novice divers probably should not be subjected to this specialized training. Instead, more time should be devoted to preventing out-of-air situations.

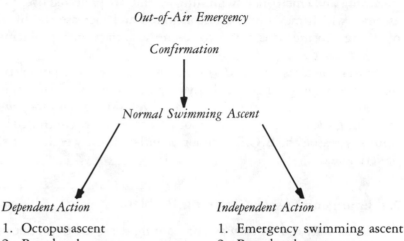

Figure 7-3. Summary of Emergency Out-of-Air Ascent Options.

Selected References

Fead, L. *Easy Diver*. Crestline, Calif.: Deepstar Publications, 1977.

Gravers, D., and Wohlers, R. *PADI Advanced Dive Manual*. Santa Ana, Calif.: Professional Association of Diving Instructors, 1980.

Griffiths, T. *A Guide to Your Open-Water Dive*. Key West, Fla.: National YMCA Underwater Activities Program, 1978.

Chapter 7 Review

The instructor should correct the student's answers, record the results, and return them to the student. Both teacher and student should sign after the last question.

REVIEW QUESTIONS	ANSWERS
1. Define an alternate air source (A.A.S.).	1. _____ _____ _____ _____ _____
2. List three different types of A.A.S.	2. _____ _____ _____
3. What is the difference between a *dependent* and *independent* controlled emergency ascent?	3. _____ _____ _____ _____ _____ _____
4. What is the easiest way of preventing an out-of-air situation?	4. _____ _____ _____
5. Where should the A.A.S. be located?	5. _____ _____ _____
6. What is an octopus regulator or octopus second stage?	6. _____ _____ _____

REVIEW QUESTIONS	ANSWERS

7. What is a pony bottle?

7. _____
_____
_____

8. What is Spare Air™?

8. _____
_____
_____

9. How does buddy breathing differ from using an A.A.S.?

9. _____
_____
_____

10. What is the best way for dive buddies to familiarize each other with their particular A.A.S.?

10. _____
_____
_____

11. Once a true out-of-air emergency has been confirmed, what steps should be taken to reach the surface safely?

11. _____
_____
_____
_____

12. How does an emergency swimming ascent differ from a buoyant ascent?

12. _____
_____
_____
_____

REVIEW QUESTIONS	ANSWERS
I have graded, recorded, and returned this student's responses.	Instructor's Signature:
	Date:
I have seen my corrected review questions and now know the appropriate answers. Note: The answer sheet may either be taken out or retained with this book.	Student's Signature:
	Date:

Chapter 8

~~~~~~

Accident Management

by Jim Corry

In addition to the usual cuts, broken bones, and abrasions that the general public suffers, sport divers occasionally suffer unique, compressed-gas injuries that few Emergency Medical Technicians understand or are prepared to handle. These injuries are decompression sickness and air embolism. Both of these maladies require immediate treatment with hyperbaric oxygen in a recompression chamber. Divers suffering from only pneumothorax, mediastinal emphysema, or subcutaneous emphysema will probably not be treated in a chamber if they are not also suffering from air embolism or decompression sickness. Nitrogen narcosis or "rapture of the deep" is caused by the narcotic effect of the nitrogen in the diver's breathing medium and disappears when the diver moves into shallower water or surfaces.

8.1 Decompression Sickness

Decompression sickness is generally brought about by the diver absorbing too much gas, nitrogen in particular, from the compressed air breathed while diving. If the diver stays too long at any given depth and returns to the surface without making allowances for elimination of the inert gas dissolved in solution, the nitrogen in the body will begin to bubble similar to the carbon dioxide in a soft drink that is opened too quickly. This can occur even if the diver adheres to standard, proven decompression schedules ("tables"). Occasionally, it can result in pain so great that the diver is bent over in agony or has difficulty walking. This is why decompression sickness is often referred to as the "bends." A large proportion of divers may have bubbles in the venous side of the circulation (venous gas embolism) which are easily filtered by the lungs without symptoms. Large quantities of such bubbles may result in respiratory impairment called the "chokes." Bubbles forming in the tissues and venous return of the brain, spinal cord, or inner ear may cause serious neurological symptoms. Decompression sickness has also been called the "staggers" as a result of this inner ear impairment. Decompression sickness is a very complicated problem as a function of where the bubbles go and how an individual's body reacts to those bubbles on a given day. It must be emphasized that the observed signs and symptoms of decompression sickness are not necessarily serious and spectacular; they can be very subtle.

REMEMBER: Decompression sickness has its origin in bubble formation. It may result in vascular obstruction by gas, tissue, or fat; a reduction in available circulating blood; asphyxia due to pulmonary impairment; pain; central nervous system injury; permanent disability; or even death.

8.2 Air Embolism

Air embolism or arterial gas embolism (AGE) is usually associated with lung over-pressure accidents. As the diver ascends from a dive, the pressure exerted on the body by the water decreases. This results in expansion of the air in his/her lungs. The diver must breathe normally on ascent or risk over-pressurization (over-inflation) of the lungs. If the lung is over-pressurized from a depth as shallow as even four feet of sea water (4 fsw), air may rupture the alveoli and enter the pulmonary circulation. This will return to the heart where the air passes into the arterial circulation. This air (bubble) typically is transported to the brain where blockage of blood flow will occur depriving the brain of oxygen. Individuals who have a history of smoking or lung problems such as asthma or bronchitis may be at greater risk of pulmonary over-pressure accidents.

Recent research has revealed that an air embolism can also occur if venous bubbles are shunted from the right ventricle to the left ventricle of the heart through a hole called a foramen ovale. This patent (open) foramen ovale may exist in 20%–30% of the normal adult population.

REMEMBER: Air embolism generally has its origin in a pulmonary over-pressure event but may also be the result of arterialization of venous gas emboli. These circulating, arterial bubbles can cause spectacular results by interrupting blood flow to the brain, heart, or other tissues.

8.2.1 SIGNS AND SYMPTOMS

Decompression Sickness

1. Joint Pain
2. Chest Pain
3. Headache/Dizziness
4. Back and/or Abdominal Pain
5. Confusion
6. Shortness of Breath
7. Numbness and/or Paralysis
8. Tingling in Extremities
9. Partial Blindness
10. Loss of Bowel and/or Bladder Control

Air Embolism

1. Vision Disturbance
2. Dizziness/Nausea
3. Weakness
4. Confusion
5. Headache
6. Paralysis
7. Chest Pain
8. Unconsciousness
9. Bloody Froth*
10. Other Neurological Disturbances

*The typical scenario involves the diver suffering a pulmonary over-pressure accident during ascent, signaling for assistance on the surface upon realization of a problem, and becoming unconscious, face-down in the water. Although not regularly seen, bloody froth at the mouth is most likely the result of aspiration of fluids into the lungs or lung damage induced by bubbles. Absence of this sign should not dismiss suspicions of arterial gas embolism.

8.3 The Emergency Plan—Managing the Diving Accident

In order to implement an emergency plan at the scene of a diving accident, the diving leader must have given some thought to such an event and have a written plan prepared.

Consideration should be given to ensuring that the right equipment is always available, such as demand-style oxygen equipment with an adequate oxygen supply, first aid kit, backboard and straps, appropriate rescue devices such as rope throw bags and flotation devices, note-taking equipment such as paper and pencil, and reliable/dependable communications equipment such as a marine radio, CB radio, or regular/cellular telephone.

It should be well documented what first aid measures will be taken dependent upon the type and severity of injury.

Communication with appropriate Emergency Medical Services (EMS) personnel capable of dealing with the unique medical problems of a diver should be established. You should be prepared to briefly explain the pertinent facts concerning both the victim and the injury to those you initially contact. You will also need to be prepared to provide EMS, hospital, or chamber personnel with a comprehensive briefing of history, symptoms, and first aid rendered. Good planning would include knowing what resources are available and who to call depending upon the type of injury.

Planning should include the means of transporting the victim, be it by ambulance, aircraft, boat, or private vehicle.

Personnel who respond to the victim should be adequately trained to use appropriate rescue equipment, evaluate the victim, render appropriate first aid, communicate for help, and transport the victim as appropriate. All supervisory personnel should understand the emergency plan in its entirety. All divers should be briefed on the emergency plan and know where it and the emergency equipment is stored.

The important thing is to give some thought to and develop an emergency plan. Prior planning really will prevent a poor performance in the event of an emergency.

8.4 Assessment of the Victim

It is very difficult for even diving medical experts to differentiate between decompression sickness and air embolism without a patient history. Many air embolism victims are also suffering from decompression sickness. During your secondary survey, ask questions of the victim or the diving buddy that will assist the physician:

1. Have you been scuba diving or breathing any sort of compressed gas recently?

2. What was your dive profile on this dive and all others during the past 24 hours?

3. Which dive table or computer did you use and how close to the no-decompression limits did you dive?

4. Were there any equipment problems during the diving?

5. Was there any sort of forced, rapid ascent during any dive?

6. Did you or your buddy run out of air at any time?

7. Did you or your buddy drop your weight belts at any time?

Above all, keep a record of how the victim's symptoms have changed or are changing in your presence. Attempt to reconstruct the victim's diving profile during the preceding 24–72 hours.

Perform a good, head-to-toe neurological examination looking for any deficits in sensory, motor, or reflexive function. A good clue is whether the overall muscular strength is the same on both sides of the body (bilateral). The quality of the victim's walking ability also provides good information. The victim's buddy is an excellent source of information for the diving physician. Attempt to take the diving buddy with the patient in order to provide information to the physician or chamber medical team. Do not allow the victim to perform in-water recompression. This will only "feed" nitrogen to the offending bubbles. Both in-water recompression and decompression with oxygen should not be attempted due to the risk of convulsions from high pressure oxygen toxicity.

8.5 Treatment

Since it can be difficult to differentiate between decompression sickness and air embolism, this treatment protocol is regarded by diving physicians and Emergency Medical Technician educators to be the best for field treatment of both while maintaining consistency with other treatment protocols being taught in most Emergency Medical Technician programs.

1. Ensure Airway, Breathing, and Circulation (ABC), and provide CPR as required.

2. Calm and reassure the victim.

3. Perform a patient assessment with full diving history.

4. Administer fluids. The diver will undoubtedly be dehydrated from breathing very dry compressed air as well as from the diuretic effects of immersion. The ideal fluids are intravenously administered Ringer's solution or normal saline. Dextrose in water should not be administered. Intravenous fluids should be started immediately. In the absence of IV capability, balanced, oral fluids such as one-half strength Gatorade may be used. This fluid administration should be the same as for shock victims: IF MORE THAN ONE HOUR FROM MEDICAL HELP, ALLOW THE VICTIM ORAL FLUIDS AT THE RATE OF 4 FLUID OUNCES EVERY 15 MINUTES AS TOLERATED. Oral fluids should be withheld if transport time is less than one (1) hour. Urine output should be monitored and recorded.

5. Administer 100% oxygen. Oxygen is a diatomic, colorless, odorless, tasteless gas responsible for 21% of the air we breathe. During the management of a diving accident, it is critical to administer as high a concentration of oxygen as possible to the victim. The oxygen serves to reduce the partial pressure of the offending nitrogen, deals with resulting tissue edema and hypoxia, and generally assists the breathing of the victim. The ultimate goal is to deliver 100% oxygen to this victim from the time the accident is recognized until medical authorities order it discontinued or the oxygen supply is exhausted. Due to equipment limitations, we find that only a demand valve with a tight sealing oronasal mask will actually deliver 100% oxygen to the victim. Constant flow devices (inhalators) realistically will only deliver low, inefficient concentrations (25%–70%) depending upon the metered flow rate and/or device (nasal cannula, simple elongated face mask, partial rebreather mask, etc.) used to deliver the oxygen to the victim. If only a limited supply of oxygen is available, it should be administered in heavy concentration by demand valve from the time the accident is recognized until the supply of oxygen is exhausted. A non-breathing victim may be supported using a positive pressure demand valve or a pocket mask with an oxygen inlet connected to 10 + liters per minute of constant flow oxygen. If only constant flow oxygen is available, it should be administered through a non-rebreather mask at an ideal flow rate of 10 + liters per minute. If a large quantity of oxygen is available in this situation, higher flow rates may be utilized.

Even though the oxygen may cause symptoms to disappear, the victim should still be transported for professional medical evaluation and hyperbaric oxygen treatment.

A variety of aluminum and steel high pressure cylinders are available for field administration of oxygen as illustrated below:

TABLE 8-1 Medical Oxygen Cylinder Specifications

ALUMINUM (Luxfer USA, Ltd.)

Type	Service Pressure (psi)	Liters	Cubic feet	E.W. w/o Valve (lbs.)
Medical 9	2015	249	8.8	3.9
D	2015	413.2	14.6	5.5
Jumbo D	2216	636.8	22.5	9.0
E	2015	682.0	24.1	8.1
M 60*	2216	1748.9	61.8	23.1
Medical M*	2216	3495.0	123.5	40.6

Medical 9 = "C"

STEEL (Pressed Steel Tank Company)

Type	Service Pressure (psi)†	Liters†	Cubic feet†	E.W. w/o Valve (lbs.)
D	2015/2216	410.4/450.0	14.5/15.9	7.5
E	2015/2216	682.0/744.3	24.1/26.3	10.5
(Norris Cylinder Company)				
M*	2015/2216	3178.1/3497.9	112.3/123.6	61.0
G*	2015/2216	6378.9/7021.2	225.4/248.1	115.0
H*	2015/2216	7148.6/7861.7	252.6/277.8	116.0
J*	2015/2216	8549.4/9387.1	302.1/331.7	140.0

*Do not accept regulators with pin-indexed yoke (CGA-870 fitting); require CGA-540 fitting.
†Secondary figures apply if cylinder is " + " rated for 10% overfill. The service pressure on both aluminum and steel cylinders is roll stamped into the shoulder of the cylinder.

6. *Place victim in appropriate accident management position.* The following are general guidelines for the positioning of a diving accident victim. The immediate evacuation of the victim should not be compromised in order to adhere to these general guidelines. The rescuer(s) should be creative in adapting these guidelines to their unique evacuation situation.

a. Place all victims supine (flat on back).

b. If you suspect cerebral air embolism based on symptoms and diving history, elevating the victim's legs may help. If the victim's condition worsens, return victim to a supine position.

c. If the victim is nauseated, place the victim on his/her left side for airway management.

All victims suffering dysbaric injuries should be placed in a supine (flat on back) position. A head low (Trendelenburg) position has been indicated in the past for the victim obviously suffering from cerebral air embolism (AGE) only. The idea is to vasodilate the cerebral (arterial) circulation to either drive the offending bubbles deeper into the cerebral circulation or actually pass some of the offending bubbles over into the venous return. Unfortunately, this position induces cerebral edema and respiratory discomfort. It may also cause additional cerebral injury. It is probably good only during the first hour after the accident has occurred. The head low position will be dictated by the comfort level of the victim who likely will not be able to tolerate it any longer than thirty (30 minutes). As such, a full body tilt (modified Trendelenburg) should be avoided. Raising only the legs may prevent respiratory discomfort and still aid the cerebral circulation. If the victim is made worse by lifting the legs, the victim should be returned to a horizontal position. If the victim becomes nauseated, he should be placed on his/her left side. Some authorities advocate a 15 degree left tilt of the body to trap bubbles in the ventricle(s) of the heart. The effectiveness of this additional positioning has not been well documented. This left tilt is primarily indicated for airway management in the nauseated victim. The individual with air embolism should be encouraged to remain supine. Some anecdotal information indicates that this individual may be made worse if allowed to elevate the head after having been supine.

7. *Transport to nearest medical facility/recompression chamber as dictated by local protocol.* The sooner a victim is transported to and treated in a chamber, the better he/she will probably resolve. Even if the symptoms have diminished or disappeared, this victim should be professionally evaluated. If several days have passed since the original accident, it is not too late for chamber treatment. Some success has been seen in treating victims in a chamber up to twenty-eight (28) days after the accident. Many chambers in use today are primarily for

non-diving medical treatments. Some of these chambers are not necessarily ideal for the treatment of injured scuba divers. The ideal chamber
is capable of containing the patient and support personnel, can be
pressurized to 165 fsw (6 ATA), and will allow extended hyperbaric
oxygen therapy. Aside from being within reasonable transport distance,
a chamber should be selected in the following order:

  a. Multi-place chamber with built-in breathing system (BIBS) cap-
     able of pressurization to 6 ATA;

  b. Mono-place chamber with built-in breathing system (BIBS) and
     transfer under pressure (TUP) capability; or

  c. Mono-place chamber with built-in breathing system (BIBS).

If this diver is in full arrest or otherwise seriously deteriorating, immediate helicopter evacuation from the accident scene to the nearest
available chamber is indicated. The pilot should be instructed to fly
at an altitude of 500–1000 feet above sea level or as low as is safely
possible to prevent further reduction of pressure on the diver. Commercial aircraft cannot appreciably increase cabin pressure without physically decreasing altitude. One major airline has stated that they would
only consider such a reduction in altitude if the victim was in critical
condition. Aircraft such as a Lear jet or C-130 can be pressurized to
sea level (1 ATA) and the flight crews advised as such.

   Any further questions regarding availability of emergency chambers,
diving medicine, or training in accident management/oxygen administration may be directed to:

  Divers Alert Network (DAN)
  Box 3823, Duke University Medical Center
  Durham, North Carolina   27710
  (919) 684-8111   (24-hour: Emergency)
  (919) 684-2948   (Office)

A comprehensive training course titled "Emergency Oxygen Administration and Field Management of Scuba Diving Accidents" has been
jointly developed by the National Association for Search and Rescue
(NASAR) and the National Association of Underwater Instructors
(NAUI) with the cooperation of the Divers Alert Network (DAN).
Included in this program are such topics as the basics of oxygen
administration; equipment selection, use, and applications; basic

maintenance; causes, symptoms, prevention, and basic physiology of both air embolism and decompression sickness; hyperbaric chamber operations and treatment; drowning; and field evaluation, care, and transportation of the compressed-gas injured victim. Half of this 8–10 hour workshop is devoted to hands-on skill sessions. This program is approved by the Undersea and Hyperbaric Medical Society (UHMS), the Council for Continuing Education Units, and the National Registry of Emergency Medical Technicians for continuing education credits. Further information is available from:

National Association for Search and Rescue (NASAR)
P.O. Box 3709
Fairfax, Virginia   22038
(703) 352-1349

National Association of Underwater Instructors (NAUI)
P.O. Box 14650
Montclair, California   91763-1150
(714) 621-5801

Selected References

Anthony, C. and G. Thibodeau. *Textbook of Anatomy and Physiology*. St. Louis, MO: The C.V. Mosby Company, 1983.

Bennett, Peter and David Elliot. *The Physiology and Medicine of Diving*. 3rd ed. New York: Best Publishing Company, 1982.

Campbell, John. *BTLS Advanced Prehospital Care*. 2nd ed. New York: Brady Books, 1988.

———. *BTLS Basic Prehospital Trauma Care*. New York: Brady Books, 1988.

Camporesi, Enrico, M.D. Personal conversation. August 25, 1988.

Caroline, Nancy. *Emergency Care in the Streets*. New York: Little, Brown & Co., 1983.

Daugherty, C. Gordon, M.D. Personal correspondence. October 8, 1988.

Davis, J. and T. Hunt. *Hyperbaric Oxygen Therapy*. Chicago, IL: Undersea Medical Society, 1977.

Hill, R. Kelly, M.D. "Medical Answers," *NDA News*. September–October 1988.

———. Personal conversation. August 27, 1988.

McIntyre, Kevin and A. Lewis. *Textbook of Advanced Cardiac Life Support*. New York: American Heart Association, 1983.

Moon, Richard, M.D. Personal conversation. September 9, 1988; October 24, 1988.

————. Personal correspondence. August 31, 1988; October 19, 1988.

Pilmanis, Andrew, Ph.D. *Chamber Operator's Manual*. [Self-published] 1983, 1986.

————. Personal conversations. May 1983 to present.

Safar, Peter and Nicholas Bircher. *Cardiopulmonary Cerebral Resuscitation*. 3rd ed. Philadelphia, PA: W.B. Saunders Co., 1988.

Strauss, Richard, M.D., ed. *Diving Medicine*. London: Grune and Stratton, 1976.

Vann, Richard, Ph.D. Personal conversation. September 27, 1988.

West, John. *Respiratory Physiology—the Essentials*. Baltimore, MD: Williams & Wilkins, 1984.

Chapter 8 Review

The instructor should correct the student's answers, record the results, and return them to the student. Both teacher and student should sign after the last question.

REVIEW QUESTIONS	ANSWERS

1. List five pieces of equipment needed to implement an emergency plan.

1. _____

   _____

   _____

   _____

   _____

2. Whom should you call first when a diving accident occurs?

2. _____

   _____

3. What information are you expected to give the EMS (Emergency Medical Services) at the accident scene?

3. _____

   _____

   _____

4. When assessing a victim, list five questions you should ask.

4. _____

   _____

   _____

   _____

   _____

5. List in order of priority seven types of treatment for both decompression sickness and air embolism.

5. _____

   _____

   _____

   _____

   _____

   _____

   _____

REVIEW QUESTIONS	ANSWERS
6. The best source of availability of emergency recompression chambers in the United States is _____.	6. _____
7. Describe the appropriate accident management position.	7. _____ _____ _____
8. Are fluids recommended for a diving accident victim?	8. _____ _____
I have graded, recorded, and returned this student's responses.	Instructor's Signature: _____ Date: _____
I have seen my corrected review questions and now know the appropriate answers. Note: The answer sheet may either be taken out or retained with this book.	Student's Signature: _____ Date: _____

PART III

Beyond the Basics

Introduction

In this part of the book you will read about the art of scuba diving. It will teach you the little but important hints that make your diving more pleasant. You should appreciate the *lack* of scientific data in this chapter. Its homespun and cookbooklike approach to diving will maximize your diving pleasures while minimizing the hassles you may have with organizing your dives. Diving is fun, and this section sees to it that it will be enjoyable for you.

Chapter 9

~~~~~~

Dive Planning

As a well-trained diver, you will realize that you must plan each dive with conscientiousness and common sense. Good dive planning will not only increase your diving pleasure but also make your dives safer and more time and energy efficient. Although the process of dive planning is thoroughly detailed in the following pages, you must remember that this chapter is designed to *assist* the certified diver rather than to teach someone how to dive. For your easy, step-by-step dive plan, the chapter is divided into the following sections: The Week of the Dive, The Day Before the Dive, Predive Planning, The Immediate Dive Plan, and Postdive Planning.

9.1 The Week of the Dive

The week preceding the dive is perhaps the most important phase of dive planning. The days leading to the dive should be full of preparations to avoid a last-minute rush the night before the dive. All scuba equipment should be completely checked and adjusted at least 1 week in advance because if any gear requires maintenance, it may take longer than a couple of days to complete the work. Equipment checks made the night before the dive often lead to frantic searches for replacement scuba gear. Also, a written checklist of all required equipment should be prepared during the week to ensure that all will be packed the day before the dive.

The week preceding the dive should be considered a period of information gathering. Much of the time required for this long-range planning can be spent on the telephone contacting the diving partner, the dive master or group leader, the local authorities (dive shop, marina, hotel, Coast Guard, and boat captain), and the weatherman.

Speaking to diving personnel well in advance of the dive allows the diver to gather all pertinent diving information and assimilate it. The information sought from key diving personnel should include dive objective; meeting time and place; directions to the dive site; environmental conditions; water and weather conditions; idiosyncrasies of the dive site, boat, and dive objective; special diving and personal equipment required; and surface floats and rescue equipment needed. Long-range planning permits the diver to prepare psychologically for the dive and mentally rehearse appropriate diving skills and techniques. This is an important aspect of the defensive diving techniques discussed in Chapter 6.

The week preceding the dive should provide ample time for rest and maintenance of a good diet. As the day of the dive approaches, alcohol intake (if any) should be reduced and any fatigue-producing activities should be curtailed.

9.2 The Day Before the Dive

Because scuba diving involves so much equipment and so many unpredictable factors, like weather and water conditions, it is prudent to be completely prepared to dive 1 day in advance, in case it is necessary to make last-minute changes and alternative dive plan decisions.

After contacting key diving personnel and collecting all pertinent diving data during the preceding week, the diver should focus attention on checking, adjusting, and packing all necessary scuba gear the day before the dive. The gear inspected during the week should have been laid out to facilitate packing. Before placing any equipment in the gear bag, the diver must make certain that each item is indelibly marked with the owner's initials. Placing all scuba equipment, with the exception of the tank and weight belt, into one gear bag will prevent the diver from forgetting items. A *written* checklist (Figure 9-1) should be referred to while loading the gear bag; mental checklists have been proven to be unreliable in sport diving.

Loading the gear bag appears to be a simple task, but it is an involved process. Properly packing the equipment is an art which makes suiting up for a dive easier and more enjoyable. Systematically loading the gear bag will eliminate disorganization while unpacking prior to the dive; thus it is an important facet of dive planning.

A) The following items are *absolutely necessary* for your dive. Check each item off as you place it in your dive bag:

   1. ( ) Mask, fins, snorkel

   2. ( ) Tank and backpack (Tank filled to rated capacity)

   3. ( ) Wet Suit*: ( ) Jacket
               ( ) Pants
               ( ) Hood
               ( ) Boots
               ( ) Gloves

*These items are properly fitted when they "feel" snug to tight (they will loosen somewhat in the water)

   4. ( ) Regulator and submersible gauge

   5. ( ) Buoyancy compensator device ("B.C.D." with whistle attached)

   6. ( ) Weight belt with weights attached (between 12 to 15 lbs. depending on your size—with at least 22-lbs. weights to "fine tune" your final buoyancy)

   7. ( ) Dive knife

B) Additional dive equipment that could be required:

   1. ( ) Diver's watch

   2. ( ) Depth Gauge

   3. ( ) "No Decompression" tables

   4. ( ) Dive flag (may be provided by staff or boat captain)

   5. ( ) Underwater message slate

   6. ( ) Buddy-line

   7. ( ) Underwater Compass

C) Other items you may wish to bring to facilitate safety, comfort, or relaxation:

   1. ( ) Extra warm clothing and towels

   2. ( ) A hat (prevents heat loss in cold climates and sunburn in warm locations)

   3. ( ) A thermos full of something hot (or cold) to drink

   4. ( ) Something to eat

   5. ( ) Motion sickness tablets if required

   6. ( ) Sunburn lotions

   7. ( ) A plastic sheet or canvas ground cover upon which to place your gear

Figure 9-1. Sample dive checklist.

8. ( ) A friend to travel with (team up while traveling)

9. ( ) A thinking cap

10. ( ) Dive Log

NOTE: Get all your gear ready the night before a dive and put it in one bag or carrying case. Carry a "route of travel" map with you and plan to arrive at least 15 minutes prior to scheduled starting time.

*Equipment will vary with water temperatures.

Diver "Don'ts"

Several special conditions have been found to be major contributors to diving mishaps. If you or your buddy are influenced by any of the following, you should postpone your dive.

1. X Alcohol	5. X Sinus infection
2. X Drugs	6. X Extreme anxiety
3. X Head colds	7. X Fatigue
4. X Ear infections	8. X Depression

Figure 9-1. (continued)

Basically, when packing scuba equipment, gear that is to be donned first should be packed *last*. This procedure will save the diver from rummaging through the gear bag in search of "lost" equipment. Before placing the equipment in the bag, all gear should be spread out on the floor. As each item is placed into the bag, it should be inspected one last time to be certain it is functioning and adjusted properly. The mask, fins, and snorkel should be packed first because they are donned last. The other scuba gear should be packed according to preference of donning order. Many divers prefer to pack their regulators and gauges in a small, protective carrying case and load them into the larger gear bag last, on top of the other equipment. As the gear is stowed away, each item should be checked for readiness as described in the following paragraphs.

9.2.1 MASK

The mask strap should be checked for signs of deterioration. If the strap appears dried out and shows signs of cracking, it must be replaced. The day before the dive is perhaps the best time to clean the faceplate. Soap, toothpaste, or a defogging agent should be rubbed onto the inside of the glass and allowed to remain there until just prior to the dive.

9.2.2 FINS

The heel straps should be adjusted to fit the foot to save time and avoid aggravation the day of the dive. The condition of the straps should be checked along with the buckles.

9.2.3 SNORKEL

Before packing the snorkel, it should be checked for cracks. If joints are located between the barrel and the mouthpiece, they should be glued. The tooth-spacers or bits should also be checked for damage. The snorkel should be attached to the mask with a snorkel-keeper and adjusted to the diver's mouth.

9.2.4 WET SUIT

Before packing the wet suit (including hood, boots, gloves, jacket, and pants), the material should be checked for tears and holes. If any are found, they can be quickly and easily repaired with a fast-drying, contact neoprene cement available in dive shops. All zippers and tabs must be sprayed with silicone to protect them from breakage and to increase the ease of suiting up.

9.2.5 B.C.D.

Most importantly, the B.C.D. should be checked for leaks. This is best accomplished by fully inflating the B.C.D., then squeezing it gently while looking and listening for air leaks. The CO_2-firing mechanism should then be checked by removing the CO_2 cartridges and pulling the firing pin (Figure 9-2). This is also a good time to lubricate the firing mechanism with silicone spray. The cartridges must not have holes in the stems. Some divers prefer not to place the cartridges back into their detonators because of the chance of accidental firing during transportation. A whistle should be attached to the vest for emergency use.

9.2.6 REGULATOR

The regulator can be checked properly only by placing it on a tank and turning on the air. After pressurizing the regulator, the hoses and second stage can be checked for air leaks. At this time, the hoses should also be checked for deterioration, particularly bulges or bubbles in the rubber. Test the regulator by inhaling *and* exhaling fully, but *do not* depress the purge button because this may push contaminants into the internal workings of the second stage. The air pressure gauge

Figure 9-2. Checking the B.C.D. (© Geri Murphy, 1981)

should also be checked at this time by making certain it reads zero before pressurizing the regulator and reading it once again after the air is turned on.

9.2.7 GAUGES

All gauges and instruments should be inspected and then packed. Many divers prefer to dive with an instrument console attached to their regulator because if the regulator is packed for the dive, the gauges and instruments will automatically be included.

9.2.8 TANK AND VALVE

The air supply should be checked the day before the dive to avoid a last-minute trip to the dive shop for an air fill. The O-ring in the valve should also be checked to ensure that it is round, not flat, and not dried out. The tank backpack, belts, and buckles should all be adjusted and checked for operation.

9.2.9 WEIGHT BELT

The weight belt buckle should be inspected first, checking to see that it holds the belt securely but will release quickly in an emergency.

The weight should then be evenly distributed and secured in place around the belt to ensure comfort and balance in the water. A good suggestion is to take two extra pound weights to "fine-tune" one's buoyancy in case the diver is too light in the water. Weight belts should not be placed in the bag because they may damange other instruments and gauges.

9.2.10 ACCESSORIES

Accessories to be placed into the gear bag include a diver's knife (secured in a scabbard), the decompression tables, a diver's flag, an underwater slate, and a diver log.

9.2.11 SPARE EQUIPMENT

The following items should not be considered as optional, equipment, but rather as essential diving gear: extra O-rings, extra CO_2 cartridges, extra mask and fin straps, and certification card.

9.2.12 FACILITATING EQUIPMENT

The following items should also be packed and will certainly enhance the safety, comfort, and enjoyment of the dive:

- silicone spray,
- adjustable crescent wrench,
- screwdriver,
- neoprene cement,
- extra clothing and towels,
- a hat (prevents heat loss in cold climates and sunburn in warm climates),
- thermos (hot or cold as applicable),
- extra change for emergercy telephone calls,
- map to dive site,
- emergency phone numbers (see below),
- swimsuit,
- food, and
- ground cover (tarp) to keep gear on.

The following telephone numbers should be brought with you to the dive site:

DIVING ACCIDENT NETWORK (D.A.N.)   919-684-8111
POLICE _____
COAST GUARD _____
HOSPITAL _____
WEATHER AND MARINE FORECAST _____
BOAT CAPTAIN _____
DIVE SHOP _____
LAKE OR QUARRY OWNER _____
DIVE PARTNER _____
DIVE MASTER _____

Additionally, it is a good idea to let family and friends know of your dive plans and leave with them phone numbers where you can be contacted.

9.3 Predive Planning

Upon arrival at the dive site, predive planning commences imme-diately. Divers must be flexible during this stage so that they will not attempt to carry out plans made in advance which are not practical at the present time. In addition, it is important to avoid certain conditions that have been found to be major contributors to scuba diving accidents. If divers are influenced by any of the following, the dive must be postponed: alcohol, drugs, head cold, ear infection, sinus infection, extreme anxiety, fatigue, and/or depression.

If an informal or social group is diving, a dive master, bottom-time keeper, and safety team must be appointed. Divers must *never* enter the water and dive all at the same time. This is a dangerous practice. Many lives could have been saved in the past if at least one buddy team of divers delayed its dive to serve as a rescue team for the remainder of the group.

After appointing facilitating personnel, the environment should be carefully inspected. Wind, waves, surface currents, boat traffic, and all other pertinent information should be carefully monitored. Special attention should be focused on potential hazards. When comparing diver capabilities with environmental conditions, the limitations of the least experienced divers should be considered.

Opinions of other divers, bathers, boaters, and lifeguards should be sought as the dive conditions are evaluated. If the conditions are not suitable, the dive should be canceled or postponed.

9.3.1 EQUIPMENT CHECK

As the equipment is removed from the gear bag, it should be checked before being donned. The list which follows is one recommended progression:

1. Check the tank for air (at least 2,000 psi) and the valve for the O-ring.

2. Adjust the straps and buckles on the backpack.

3. Attach the regulator to the tank, turn on the air, and test the tank with the regulator close to the point of entry.

4. Check all gauges.

5. Check the B.C.D. for leaks and test all types of inflators.

6. Adjust the weight belt, test the buckle, and place the belt next to the tank.

7. Check and adjust the mask, fins, and snorkel.

8. Check and organize all wet suit items.

Many divers prefer to perform this equipment check prior to donning the wet suit because working with scuba gear becomes more difficult and fatiguing when a full wet suit is worn.

9.3.2 SUITING UP

For safety and a lighter work load, it is imperative to cooperate with the dive buddy while suiting up. When putting on the wet suit, most divers prefer to start from the bottom and work toward the top to allow the arms more freedom of movement. Wearing pantyhose under wet suit pants makes this cumbersome task much easier. The boots are put on after the pants, then the hood is put on, followed by the jacket. The gloves are often the last item donned before entering the water to allow the diver's fingers to function effectively.

Donning the wet suit usually promotes overheating by the diver. To prevent this, the diver should get wet often by taking a cold shower or jumping into the water.

After the wet suit is donned, the diving partners must assist each other in putting on the scuba gear. One suggested progression is as follows:

1. Don the B.C.D. and adjust all straps to fit snugly.

2. Don the tank with the assistance of the dive partner.

3. Test all air systems both on the tank and on the B.C.D.

4. Make certain the tank straps and buckles do not cover the B.C.D.

5. Be sure the CO_2 cartridge pull-cords are not entangled with the tank, B.C.D., or weight belt straps.

6. Don the weight belt, making sure it is properly positioned and buckled so that it can be easily jettisoned.

7. Take special care when donning the mask to place the mask skirt on the face under the hood to ensure a proper seal.

8. Display the diver's flag.

9.3.3 BUDDY CHECK

1. Familiarize yourself with your buddy's equipment. Pay special attention to the position and operation of the B.C.D. inflators, both manual and mechanical. Actually inflate your partner's B.C.D.

2. Check to see that your buddy's weight belt is positioned properly and make certain that *you* can jettison it.

3. Physically review emergency skills and techniques with your partner; actually perform a simulated shared ascent on land (buddy-breathing or octopus breathing).

9.4 The Immediate Dive Plan

9.4.1 PLAN YOUR DIVE

1. Review the dive objective with your buddy and the dive master.

2. Evaluate all water conditions, including visibility, waves, and currents.

3. Check the no-decompression tables and record your depth and time limits on an underwater slate.

4. Determine entry and exit points.

5. Establish air-turnaround points (plan to begin your return when one-third, one-half, or two-thirds of your total air supply is remaining, depending upon the rigors of the dive.)

6. Review all hand signals.

7. Determine who will lead and who will follow.

8. Check in with the bottom-time keeper or dive master.

9.4.2 DIVE YOUR PLAN

1. Use a safe entry. Check the surface area below before dropping into the water and hold onto the mask while making the entry.

2. As soon as the entry into the water is accomplished, take time to flood the mask and clear it, and to do the same with the snorkel. This enhances comfort in the water.

3. While on the surface and before submerging, scan the area to familiarize yourself with landmarks, the boat, and entry and exit points.

4. Swim slowly to conserve energy, save air, and avoid cramps.

5. Continually equalize the pressure in your ears. Don't force the ears or sinuses; don't ascend or descend too rapidly.

6. Stay within the no-decompression limits.

7. Stop to rest whenever necessary.

8. Maintain visual contact with your partner at all times; stay an arm's length away. If for some reason you should lose contact with your dive buddy, scan the area quickly and if you do not make contact, swim directly to the surface. When your buddy notices that you are "missing," he/she should follow the same procedure. A buddy-line is useful in low-visibility water.

9. Control your buoyancy. Strive for neutral buoyancy throughout your dive. As you dive deeper you will become "heavier," and as you approach the surface you will become "lighter." Adjust your buoyancy accordingly.

10. Remember, buoyancy control is achieved by using your buoyancy equipment, *not your fins!*

11. Your various gauges are designed to help you, so check your DEPTH, TIME, and AIR CONSUMPTION constantly. They are of no use unless you check them often.

12. Enhance your visibility and that of other divers by swimming several feet above the bottom.

13. Terminate your dive *before* using your reserve supply, at approximately 500 psi.

14. When you decide to surface, signal "thumbs-up" to your buddy, then swim up under control. Look up at the surface, raise one hand to protect your head, and rotate 360 degrees when nearing the surface. Do not ascend too rapidly—follow your bubbles up (approximately 60 feet per minute). Maintain visual contact with your buddy.

15. Upon surfacing, inflate your B.C.D., signal "Okay," and communicate with your partner. Your mask and snorkel are pieces of safety equipment. Never remove them until you are safely aboard the boat or ashore.

IN CASE OF AN EMERGENCY

1. Stop and think clearly before reacting to the problem area.

2. Calm yourself and strive to restore a slow, rhythmic breathing pattern.

3. Signal your buddy for assistance.

4. Tend to the problem slowly and carefully. If the problem cannot be corrected underwater, swim to the surface using a controlled ascent.

5. If difficulties are encountered while surfacing, drop the weight belt, if necessary, and then inflate the B.C.D., if necessary.

6. During an emergency out-of-air ascent, *exhale continuously*.

9.5 Postdive Planning

Immediately following the dive, a dialogue with the buddies and the dive master should commence. Talking to the dive buddy and dive master is beneficial in evaluating the dive. The dive master may keep a group dive log or manifest as shown in Figure 9-3. Conversing with other divers after their dives are completed can also provide good information.

A log book (see Section 6.1.5) should be used to record all data, including depth, bottom time, air consumption, visibility, water temperature, and amount of weight worn. The date and time of the dive, along with the dive objective, are also important.

After evaluating the dive and recording all pertinent information in the log book, divers should attend to the equipment.

PENN STATE UNIVERSITY DIVING LOG
Diving Supervisor: Dr. Tom Griffiths

Date ——————— Time ——————— Place ——————— Weather ——————— Air Temp. ———————

Dive Objective ——————— Water Temp. ——————— Visibility ———————

NAME	Lbs.	IN Air	IN Time	OUT Air	OUT Time	B.T.	Depth	Comments	Lbs.	IN Air	IN Time	OUT Air	OUT Time	B.T.	Depth	Comments
1.																
2.																
3.																
4.																
5.																
6.																
7.																
8.																
9.																
10.																
11.																
12.																
13.																
14.																
15.																
16.																
17.																
18.																
19.																
20.																

Figure 9-3. Group dive log.

All equipment should be washed in clean, fresh water. It should then be repacked in the gear bag in the same orderly fashion as it was packed. Using the equipment checklist will prevent leaving items behind. After all gear is cleaned and packed, the dive boat, dock, or picnic area should be cleaned up.

Selected References

Fead, L. *Easy Diver*. Crestline, Calif.: Deepstar Publications, 1977.

Gravers, D., and Wohlers, R. *PADI Advanced Dive Manual*. Santa Ana, Calif.: Professional Association of Diving Instructors, 1980.

Griffiths, T. *A Guide to Your Open-Water Dive*. Key West, Fla.: National YMCA Underwater Activities Program, 1978.

Chapter 9 Review

The instructor should correct the student's answers, record the results, and return them to the student. Both teacher and student should sign after the last question.

REVIEW QUESTIONS	ANSWERS
1. Name the five different categories of dive planning in chronological order.	1. _____
2. Name three people who should be contacted the week of the dive.	2. _____
3. When should your gear bag be packed?	3. _____
4. What two things should be done while checking the regulator prior to the dive?	4. _____
5. List three dive accessories needed for each dive.	5. _____
6. List three items of "spare equipment" that should be packed for the dive.	6. _____
7. List three important phone numbers for divers.	7. _____

REVIEW QUESTIONS	ANSWERS

8. List five items or conditions that must be avoided before the dive.

8. _____

_____

_____

_____

_____

9. In case of an emergency under water, what should be done first?

9. _____

10. Postdive planning primarily deals with filling out your _____.

10. _____

I have graded, recorded, and returned this student's responses.

Instructor's Signature:

_____

Date:

_____

I have seen my corrected review questions and now know the appropriate answers.
Note: The answer sheet may either be taken out or retained with this book.

Student's Signature:

_____

Date:

_____

Chapter 10

~~~~~~

Repetitive Diving

by Dennis Graver

10.1 Nitrogen Absorption and Elimination

We have mentioned several times the limitations of time and depth on diving. In this chapter, you will learn the basis for these limitations, become familiar with dive computers, and learn how to use both the National Association of Underwater Instructors (NAUI) Dive Tables and the NAUI Dive Time Calculator to plan dives with correct time and depth limits.

The various gases comprising the air you breathe dissolve into your body according to the concentration of each gas in the air. Air is essentially nitrogen and oxygen and oxygen is consumed by the body. Thus the gas with which we are primarily concerned is nitrogen. We have a certain amount of nitrogen dissolved in our blood and tissues at all times. When we breathe at sea level, nitrogen molecules are exchanged for nitrogen previously dissolved in the body. The exchange rate between new and old nitrogen is constant; the amount of nitrogen in solution remains constant.

Ingassing of Nitrogen

When you are subjected to changing pressures under water, the balance of nitrogen absorption and elimination is upset. Under increased pressure, the air you breathe is denser, which means the concentration of nitrogen is increased. There is more nitrogen in the air you breathe than there is within your body. The result is an "ingassing" of nitrogen into the body until a state of equilibrium is reached between the amount of nitrogen being breathed and that dissolved into the system. The ingassing occurs rapidly at first, then proceeds more and more slowly until equilibrium results many hours later, assuming the pressure remains constant. There are no negative effects experienced while the ingassing of nitrogen occurs at moderate depths.

The different tissues of your body—fat, muscle, bone, etc.—absorb gas at differing rates. Nitrogen is absorbed quickly by muscle tissue, but very slowly by bone tissue. There are different ingassing rates for each kind of tissue. The cumulative effect of these various rates involves complicated mathematics; fortunately the rates are all taken into consideration in dive computers, tables, and calculators, so you need not concern yourself with varying absorption rates.

Outgassing of Nitrogen

After spending time under pressure, you absorb a quantity of nitrogen greater than that found in your body at sea level. When you ascend and reduce the pressure, the balance between the nitrogen in your system and the amount being breathed is mismatched again. There is a greater concentration of nitrogen in your blood and tissues than there is in the air you are breathing. The result is an "outgassing" of nitrogen from your body until a state of equilibrium is reached. The excess nitrogen passes from the body tissues to the blood, from the blood into the lungs, and is then expired. This process occurs rapidly during the first few minutes, but takes many hours to complete.

As long as the reduction of pressure is not too rapid for the amount of nitrogen present, the outgassing of nitrogen can occur without physiological problems. If the change in pressure is sudden, however, the nitrogen may come out of solution in your system so rapidly that bubbles form in your body. These bubbles can damage tissues and cause a painful condition known as "decompression sickness," "DCS" or the "bends."

A can of soda can be used to illustrate the principle of decompression sickness. Carbon dioxide is dissolved in the soda under pressure and remains in solution until the pressure is dropped suddenly by opening the sealed container. The rapid drop in pressure causes the carbon dioxide to form bubbles within the liquid and produce effervesence within the drink. If the pressure in the container was relieved very

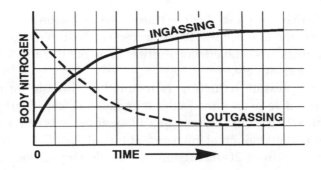

Figure 10-1. Nitrogen absorption. Above: Ingassing and outgassing (accumulation and elimination) of nitrogen in the body depicted graphically. Below: The bubbles form because of the sudden drop in pressure.

slowly, no bubbling would occur, and the soda would eventually be devoid of effervesence. To lessen the chance of bubbling within your body, it is important to control both the amount of nitrogen absorbed while diving and the rate at which it is eliminated from the body. This is the purpose of the information provided by dive time planners, which include dive computers, dive tables, and dive calculators.

Be aware that several factors can cause decompression sickness which would normally not occur. These factors include old age, obesity, fatigue, injuries, and the effects of drugs or alcohol. Be fit for diving, and dive conservatively.

A specific pressure reduction is required for bubble formation to occur. If you dive deeper than approximately 20 feet (6 m) and then ascend, the pressure change may be sufficient for bubble formation to take place if the amount of nitrogen absorbed is suffciently high. If you dive to depths of 20 feet (6 m) or less, decompression sickness is not likely to occur unless you reduce the pressure below that at sea level by going to altitude and thus further increasing "outgassing."

For depths of 21 feet (6.4 m) or greater, time limits called "dive time limits" have been established. The length of time spent at a given depth is not to exceed these limits or decompression sickness—a very serious condition—could be experienced during or after the ascent from the dive.

Time limits for various depths were established decades ago by the U.S. Navy based on field testing of military personnel. While the 1958 Navy time limits have been the standard of the diving community for many years and are still being used by many experienced divers today, physiological research and accident analysis of decompression have resulted in the recommendation by many highly qualified experts that lesser time limits than the U.S. Navy tables be used for recreational diving. Reduced time limits have been incorporated into the NAUI Dive Tables and Dive Time Calculator to reduce the risk of decompression sickness for recreational diving activities. Divers who choose to use time limits in excess of those currently recommended recognize and accept the increased risk associated with longer dive times.

TABLE 10-1

Depth	NAUI Limit	U.S.N. Limit
0–20′ (0–6 m)	No limit	No Limit
21–40′ (6.4–12 m)	130 mins.	200 mins.
41–50′ (12.5–15 m)	80 mins.	100 mins.
51–60′ (15.5–18 m)	55 mins.	60 mins.
61–70′ (18.6–21 m)	45 mins.	50 mins.
71–80′ (21.6–24 m)	35 mins.	40 mins.
81–90′ (24.6–27 m)	25 mins.	30 mins.
91–100′ (27.6–30 m)	22 mins.	25 mins.

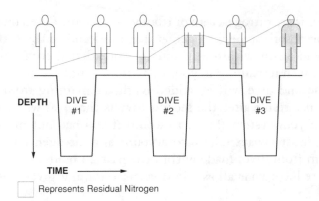

Figure 10-2. Residual nitrogen. The nitrogen remaining in the body from dives made within the past 24 hours. It accumulates from dive to dive.

NOTE: Diving to depths in excess of 60 feet (18 m) is discouraged for entry level (NAUI Openwater I) divers. Intermediate (NAUI Openwater II) divers are qualified to dive to a maximum depth of 80 feet (24 m); NAUI Advanced Scuba Divers are qualified to dive to a maximum depth of 100 feet (30 m); and NAUI Deep Diving Specialty divers are qualified to dive to 130 feet (39 m), which is the maximum depth limit for recreational diving.

You do not need to memorize the dive time limits. Most of them are included on your NAUI Dive Tables and on the NAUI Dive Time Calculator. The times are presented here merely to acquaint you with typical time limits for diving. Note, however, that the length of allowable time decreases as the depth increases.

The outgassing of nitrogen occurs at different rates for various body tissues, so the outgassing of different tissues becomes the controlling factor for the time limits of various depths. It helps to be familiar with the concept, which forms the basis for dive computers, tables and calculators, but a thorough understanding of the principle is not necessary at this point in your diving education. You will learn much more about ingassing and outgassing theory in your Advanced Scuba Diver course.

Residual Nitrogen

To understand the use of dive computers, tables, and calculators, you do need to become familiar with the concept of "residual nitrogen." You already know that many hours are required to either fully absorb or to fully eliminate nitrogen into or from your system. Based on this concept, if you absorb some nitrogen at depth, ascend to the surface, and then descend again within 24 hours of your first descent, there will still be nitrogen remaining in your body from your first dive. Nitrogen from the second dive will be added to that remaining from the first dive. The net result after the second dive is that you will have more nitrogen in your system than you would if you had not made a prior dive. You must always take into account any nitrogen remaining in your system from dives made within the past 24 hours. This "residual nitrogen" reduces your allowable dive time for any given depth.

10.1.1 DETERMINING TIME LIMITS

There are three ways in which you can determine how long you may dive and then ascend within the dive time limits. You may use information displayed by a dive computer or may plan your dive time using either the NAUI Dive Tables or the NAUI Dive Time Calculator. Each offers certain advantages and has certain limitations. You should become familiar with each method so you will be able to minimize the risk of decompression sickness by the proper use of any of your options.

As previously mentioned, different body tissues absorb and release nitrogen at different rates. Mathematical models have been developed to estimate ingassing and outgassing for various tissues, and dive computers with mathematical programs can continuously calculate the amount of nitrogen in several "compartments" (a component of the mathematical model used for the calculator) for any given depth. This information is used to determine time/depth limits which are displayed for the diver.

Dive tables are also based on mathematical models. The time limits provided by tables are in increments of ten feet (3 m) of depth and are based on the assumption that the entire time of the dive is spent at the deepest depth. This is one disadvantage of the use of the tables as compared to a dive computer. A dive computer calculates ingassing and outgassing in one foot (0.3 m) increments and only for the depth to which you are diving, even as that depth varies during your dive. With a computer you are not penalized by being required to count all of your dive time at the deepest depth. You absorb less nitrogen at shallower depths, so when you spend part of your dive in water shallower than the maximum depth of a dive, a dive computer takes this into consideration and computes only the amount of nitrogen a mathematical model predicts is absorbed or eliminated. The results

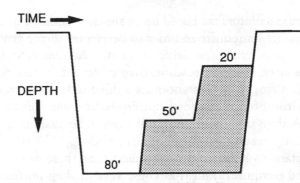

Figure 10-3. Multiple level dives. Involves diving at progressively shallower depths during a dive. The nitrogen absorption depicted by the shaded area is counted when dive tables are used, but not when a dive computer is employed.

of a dive with progressively shallower depths (called a multiple-level or "multi-level" dive) using a dive computer are longer dive time limits and less residual nitrogen penalty than when the fixed-calculation dive tables are used. Dive computers are expensive, however, compared to dive tables.

There are dive tables available which can compute multilevel dives. The manual planning and execution of multilevel dives are complex and are not recommended for recreational diving. If you wish to receive credit for reduced nitrogen absorption during multilevel dives, obtain and use a dive computer, but only after becoming proficient in dive table usage.

The following overview of dive tables will prepare you to learn to use the NAUI Dive Tables and Dive Time Calculator. A "letter group" designation is used in the tables as a simple means of expressing the amount of residual nitrogen within your body. The letters range in sequence from "A" to "L." A very small amount of nitrogen is represented by Group A, and the amount increases as the letter groups progress toward "L." You are designated with a group letter following a dive, and are assigned to lower groups as you outgas nitrogen while at the surface between dives. When you dive again to a given depth, your group letter at that time is used to determine an amount of time that would represent the residual nitrogen in your system. This time is then subtracted from the normal dive time limits, which results in a reduced time limit for your repetitive dive. The residual nitrogen time is also added to the amount of time you actually spend diving, and that total time is then used to determine a new letter group.

Manual dive calculators are based upon the dive tables, but eliminate the calculations tables require in order to determine letter group designations when more than one dive is made. A dive calculator also reduces errors often made in reading dive tables. It is easy to learn to use a dive calculator, but this should be done only after you become familiar with the procedures for planning dive time limits with the dive tables. A dive calculator may not always be available, but dive tables are usually readily available at dive sites.

It is important to know and understand that there are a variety of dive tables and computers and that these vary in the information they provide. Some are more conservative than others. Always use the type of table, calculator or computer with which you are familiar. If your dive buddy is using a different type, you should agree to abide by the most conservative dive planning information.

10.2 Dive Table Terms and Rules

To use the NAUI Dive Tables and Dive Time Calculator properly, you must become familiar with certain terms as well as rules which must be followed.

10.2.1 DIVE TABLE TERMS

Dive Schedule: The schedule of a dive is an abbreviated statement of the depth and duration of a dive and is expressed as depth/time, e.g., 70 feet (21 m)/40 = 70 feet (21 m) for 40 minutes.

Maximum Dive Time (MDT): The length of time that may be spent at a given depth without being required to stop during ascent to prevent the likelihood of decompression sickness.

Decompression Stop: The time a diver stops and waits at a specified depth during ascent to allow nitrogen elimination before surfacing.

Precautionary Decompression: Three minutes spent at a depth of 15 feet (5 m) as a safety precaution even though the Maximum Dive Time has not been exceeded. This procedure is recommended at the end of every dive. Time spent decompressing is considered "neutral" time and is not part of Dive Time.

Required Decompression: An amount of time specified by dive tables, a calculator or a computer to be spent at a specified depth (15 feet

[5 m]) for NAUI Tables and Calculator) whenever the Dive Time Limits are exceeded.

Actual Dive Time (ADT): The time from the moment you begin your descent until the time you return to the surface. (Time spent doing precautionary decompression may be excluded.)

Letter Group Designation: A letter symbol used to designate the amount of excess nitrogen in your system. The nearer the beginning of the alphabet, the less the amount of residual nitrogen in your system.

Surface Interval Time (SIT): Time spent on the surface between dives. During this time, excess nitrogen is eliminated from your body and your letter group designation changes, moving closer to the beginning of the alphabet.

Residual Nitrogen: The nitrogen remaining in your system from a dive or dives made within the past 24 hours.

Repetitive Dive: Any dive made within 24 hours of a previous dive.

Residual Nitrogen Time (RNT): On repetitive dives, the amount of time you must consider you have already spent at a given depth for a planned dive. This time is based on the amount of residual nitrogen remaining in your system from a previous dive. Residual Nitrogen Time is obtained from a table and is based on your letter group designation following your Surface Interval Time (SIT).

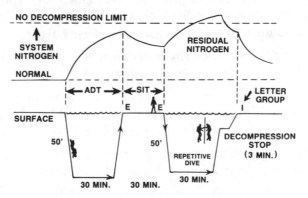

Figure 10-4. Dive table terms.

Adjusted Maximum Dive Time (AMDT): For repetitive dives, AMDT is the Maximum Dive Time for the depth of the dive minus the Residual Nitrogen Time (RNT) for the dive.

Total Nitrogen Time (TNT): This is the sum of your Residual Nitrogen Time (RNT) and your Actual Dive Time (ADT) following a repetitive dive. This total is used to obtain a new letter group designation after the repetitive dive. TNT is expressed as RNT + ADT = TNT.

10.2.2 DIVE TABLE RULES

1. On any dive, ascend no faster than 60 feet (18 m) per minute. This is only one foot (0.3 m) per second, and this slow pace is the *maximum rate* of ascent. The use of a timing device and depth gauge (or a dive computer) is required to measure your rate of ascent.

2. Use the exact or next greater number when referring to the dive tables. If a number in a table is exceeded, use the next greater number. For example, for depths from 40 to 130 feet (12–39 m), the dive tables increase in ten-foot increments, so a dive to 41 feet (12.3 m) is considered a 50-foot (15 m) dive and a dive to 61 feet (18.3 m) is counted as a 70 foot (21 m) dive.

3. When determining the dive schedule for a dive, use the deepest depth attained during the dive. If part of the dive was spent at 60 feet (18 m) while the majority of it was spent at 40 feet (12 m), the dive must still be considered as if the entire time were spent at 60 feet (18 m).

4. When making a series of dives, plan repetitive dives to the same or shallower depth as the previous dive. This allows you to outgas nitrogen on progressively shallower dives instead of carrying a large amount of residual nitrogen on deeper repetitive dives.

5. Consider all dives made shallower than 40 feet (12 m) as 40-foot (12 m) dives when planning repetitive dives.

6. A Surface Interval Time (SIT) of at least ten minutes is required before entering the Surface Interval Timetable. NAUI recommends a minimum of one hour between dives, however.

7. If a dive is particularly cold or strenuous, use the next greater bottom time. An example of this is included later in this section.

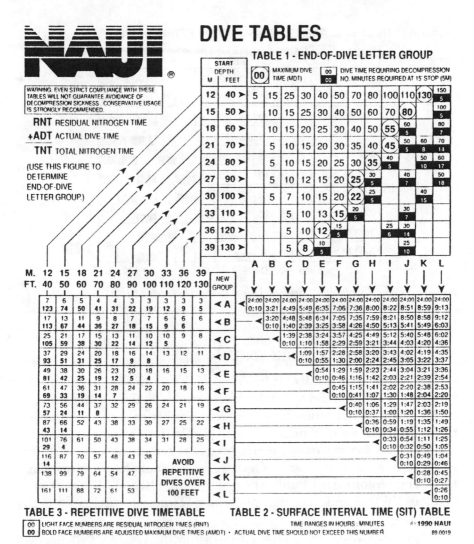

Figure 10-5. NAUI dive tables.

10.3 Finding Time Limits

Now that you know the concepts behind the tables, the terms used for them and the rules for their use, you are ready to learn how to refer to the NAUI Dive Tables. In this section, you will learn the general organization of the tables and how to use them to determine Dive Time Limits for both single and repetitive dives.

TABLE 1 - END-OF-DIVE LETTER GROUP

START DEPTH M	FEET	00	MAXIMUM DIVE TIME (MDT)								00 / 00	DIVE TIME REQUIRING DECOMPRESSION NO. MINUTES REQUIRED AT 15' STOP (5M)		
12	40 ➤	5	15	25	30	40	50	70	80	100	110	130 / 5	150 / 5	
15	50 ➤		10	15	25	30	40	50	60	70	80	100 / 5		
18	60 ➤		10	15	20	25	30	40	50	55	60 / 5	80 / 7		
21	70 ➤		5	10	15	20	30	35	40	45	50 / 5	60 / 8	70 / 14	
24	80 ➤		5	10	15	20	25	30	35	40 / 5		50 / 10	60 / 17	
27	90 ➤		5	10	12	15	20	25	30 / 5		40 / 7		50 / 18	
30	100 ➤		5	7	10	15	20	22	25 / 5		40 / 15			
33	110 ➤			5	10	13	15	20 / 5		30 / 7				
36	120 ➤			5	10	12	15 / 5		25 / 6	30 / 14				
39	130 ➤			5	8	10 / 5			25 / 10					

A   B   C   D   E   F   G   H   I   J   K   L

Figure 10-6. Table 1 - "End-of-Dive Letter Group" table.

10.3.1 GENERAL ORGANIZATION

The NAUI Dive Tables are based upon the U.S. Navy Decompression Tables and have been specially designed by NAUI for recreational diving. The NAUI tables are configured so that each of three tables flows into the next. You begin with Table 1, which is called the "End-of-Dive Letter Group" table. Not only does it give you a letter group designation at the end of a dive, it also contains the Maximum Dive Time information for depths from 40 to 130 feet (12 to 39 m). Look at Table 1 and note that Maximum Times are circled for each depth.

Table 1 is entered horizontally from the left. The numbers on the table represent bottom time in minutes. Find the row for the appropriate depth and move to the right along the line until you find a bottom time that meets or exceeds your dive time. Now follow that column downward, exit the table, and find the letter group designation that indicates the amount of nitrogen remaining in your system following a dive. For example, a person who dives to 50 feet (15 m) for 30 minutes would have an "E" letter group designation.

The longer you remain out of the water, the more excess nitrogen you eliminate. Crediting you with the loss of the nitrogen is the purpose of Table 2, the "Surface Interval Time (SIT) Table." It consists of blocks containing two numbers which represent the minimum and maximum times for assignment to a particular letter group. The times are expressed as hours and minutes (Hours:Minutes).

The SIT table is entered vertically coming down the column from Table 1 and followed downward until you find a range of times into which the length of your surface interval falls. Then follow that row horizontally to the left, exit the table, and receive a new letter group designation. For example, if you enter the table with an "E" letter group and have a surface interval of three hours, you will exit the table on the third horizontal line and end up with a new letter group of "C." Note that the maximum time in the table is 24 hours. All excess nitrogen is considered to be eliminated after 24 hours, so a dive after that amount of time is not a repetitive dive.

Table 3 is the "Repetitive Dive Timetable." It tells your Residual Nitrogen Time (RNT) based on your current letter group and your planned depth and provides Maximum Dive Times that are reduced by the amount of your RNT. Your Actual Dive Time (ADT) must not exceed the Adjusted Maximum Dive Time (AMDT). Your Residual Nitrogen Time (RNT) must be added to your ADT to obtain your Total Nitrogen Time (TNT). This formula is illustrated in the upper left corner of your NAUI Dive Tables.

To use Table 3, enter it horizontally from the right on the row representing your letter group designation after your SIT and move

NEW GROUP	A	B	C	D	E	F	G	H	I	J	K	L
◄ A	24:00	24:00	24:00	24:00	24:00	24:00	24:00	24:00	24:00	24:00	24:00	24:00
	0:10	3:21	4:49	5:49	6:35	7:06	7:36	8:00	8:22	8:51	8:59	9:13
◄ B		3:20	4:48	5:48	6:34	7:05	7:35	7:59	8:21	8:50	8:58	9:12
		0:10	1:40	2:39	3:25	3:58	4:26	4:50	5:13	5:41	5:49	6:03
◄ C			1:39	2:38	3:24	3:57	4:25	4:49	5:12	5:40	5:48	6:02
			0:10	1:10	1:58	2:29	2:59	3:21	3:44	4:03	4:20	4:36
◄ D				1:09	1:57	2:28	2:58	3:20	3:43	4:02	4:19	4:35
				0:10	0:55	1:30	2:00	2:24	2:45	3:05	3:22	3:37
◄ E					0:54	1:29	1:59	2:23	2:44	3:04	3:21	3:36
					0:10	0:46	1:16	1:42	2:03	2:21	2:39	2:54
◄ F						0:45	1:15	1:41	2:02	2:20	2:38	2:53
						0:10	0:41	1:07	1:30	1:48	2:04	2:20
◄ G							0:40	1:06	1:29	1:47	2:03	2:19
							0:10	0:37	1:00	1:20	1:36	1:50
◄ H								0:36	0:59	1:19	1:35	1:49
								0:10	0:34	0:55	1:12	1:26
◄ I									0:33	0:54	1:11	1:25
									0:10	0:32	0:50	1:05
◄ J										0:31	0:49	1:04
										0:10	0:29	0:46
◄ K											0:28	0:45
										0:10	0:27
◄ L												0:26
												0:10

Figure 10-7. Table 2 - "Surface Interval Time (SIT)" table.

M. 12 / FT. 40	15 / 50	18 / 60	21 / 70	24 / 80	27 / 90	30 / 100	33 / 110	36 / 120	39 / 130	NEW GROUP
7 / 123	6 / 74	5 / 50	4 / 41	4 / 31	3 / 22	3 / 19	3 / 12	3 / 9	3 / 5	◄ A
17 / 113	13 / 67	11 / 44	9 / 36	8 / 27	7 / 18	7 / 15	6 / 9	6 / 6	6	◄ B
25 / 105	21 / 59	17 / 38	15 / 30	13 / 22	11 / 14	10 / 12	10 / 5	9	8	◄ C
37 / 93	29 / 51	24 / 31	20 / 25	18 / 17	16 / 9	14 / 8	13	12	11	◄ D
49 / 81	38 / 42	30 / 25	26 / 19	23 / 12	20 / 5	18 / 4	16	15	13	◄ E
61 / 69	47 / 33	36 / 19	31 / 14	28 / 7	24	22	20	18	16	◄ F
73 / 57	56 / 24	44 / 11	37 / 8	32	29	26	24	21	19	◄ G
87 / 43	66 / 14	52	43	38	33	30	27	25	22	◄ H
101 / 29	76 / 4	61	50	43	38	34	31	28	25	◄ I
116 / 14	87	70	57	48	43	38	AVOID			◄ J
138	99	79	64	54	47		REPETITIVE DIVES OVER			◄ K
161	111	88	72	61	53		100 FEET			◄ L

Figure 10-8. Table 3 - "Repetitive Dive Timetable."

to the left until you intersect the column corresponding to the depth of your planned repetitive dive. Depths are listed across the top of the table. At the coordinates of the depth and the letter group you will find two numbers. The top number represents RNT for that depth; the bottom number represents the Adjusted Maximum Dive Time (AMDT) for the depth. If you compare the totals of the AMDT and the Residual Nitrogen Times for any depth, you will find they all total the Maximum Dive Time Limit for that depth in Table 1. The AMDT is found by simply subtracting RNT from Maximum Dive Time for a given depth. Table 3 has already done the work for you. Your Actual Dive Time must not exceed your AMDT during a repetitive dive.

An example of the use of Table 3 is a "C" letter group diver planning a dive to 50 feet (15 m). At the coordinates "C" and 50 feet (15 m), you find the number 21 over the number 59. This means the diver has 21 minutes of RNT and the duration of the ADT must not exceed 59 minutes. The diver proceeds with the dive, keeping the ADT within the 59 minute Adjusted Maximum Dive Time, then adds the ADT to the 21 minutes of RNT and uses the dive schedule of 50 feet (15 m)/TNT to re-enter Table 1 and obtain an End-of-Dive letter group. Note how the cycle has been completed with the three tables.

10.3.2 EXERCISES

Use the NAUI Dive Tables to find the Dive Time Limits for both single and repetitive dives.

1. What is the Maximum Dive Time for a dive to 60 feet (18 m) for your first dive of the day?

Answer: Because you have no residual nitrogen, you are allowed the Maximum Dive Time for the depth: 55 minutes.

2. What is your letter group designation following a dive to 55 feet (16.7 m) for 39 minutes?

Answer: Remember, when you exceed numbers in the tables, you use the next greater number. There is no 55-foot (16.7 m) depth in Table 1, so you use the 60-foot (18 m) schedule. The first time not exceeding 39 minutes in the 60-foot (18 m) row on Table 1 is 40. Thus the dive schedule for a 55-foot (16.7 m)/39 dive is actually 60 feet (16.7 m)/40 in the tables. Following the 40 minute column to the bottom of the table, you find that your letter group designation is "G" following this dive.

3. If your initial letter group is "G," what is your new letter group after a surface interval of one hour?

Answer: The correct answer is "F." To obtain it, enter Table 2 vertically at the Group G column and follow it down until you find the time range (0:41–1:15) corresponding to your surface interval. At that point on the table, follow the row to the left and obtain your new letter group.

4. With an "F" letter group, what is the Adjusted Maximum Dive Time for a dive to 50 feet (15 m)?

Answer: Table 3 is the Repetitive Dive Timetable providing the Adjusted Maximum Dive Time (AMDT) information. As an "F" diver going to 50 feet (15 m), the AMDT is 33 minutes. This is found as the lower number at the coordinates of F and 50 feet (15 m) in Table 3. Your Actual Dive Time must not exceed this number.

5. What is the Residual Nitrogen Time of a diver making the 50-foot (15 m) dive with an "F" letter group designation?

Answer: Table 3 also provides RNT times. At the 50-foot (15 m) and F coordinates, the top number (47) is the RNT.

6. With an ADT of 32 minutes on a dive to 50 feet (15 m) with a letter group of "F," what is the Total Nitrogen Time (TNT) of the dive?

Answer: TNT is the sum of ADT and the RNT, so TNT in this instance is the 32 minutes of ADT, plus 47 minutes of residual time, for a TNT of 79 minutes.

7. What is the End-of-Dive letter group for the dive in question six?

Answer: The dive schedule is 50 feet (15 m)/79. This information is taken to Table One to obtain an End-of-Dive letter group. For a depth of 50 feet (15 m), you find that the first time not exceeded by your TNT is 80 minutes. The letter group for a total time of 80 minutes is "J."

You have just used the NAUI Dive Tables to become acquainted with their arrangement. You should now be able to determine the Maximum Dive Time for single and repetitive dives and should also be able to determine your correct letter group designation following a dive. You will next learn how to use the tables so your combined dive plans do not exceed the Dive Time Limits.

10.3.3 DIVE TABLE PLANNING

When making repetitive dives, you will find that at times you are unable to dive to the depth you would like, for the duration you would like, due to the Adjusted Maximum Dive Times imposed upon you by residual nitrogen. In this part of Chapter 10, you will learn three ways to plan dives within the Dive Time Limits.

Limiting Your Actual Dive Time

The first means of keeping within the Maximum Dive Times is easy—limit your ADT. Your first dive of the day should not exceed the Maximum Dive Time for the depth of the dive, and your repetitive

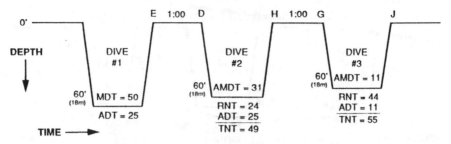

*Figure 10-9. Limited dive times. The dive time on the third dive is very
limited due to residual nitrogen from the previous dives.*

dives should not exceed the Adjusted Maximum Dive Time for your
planned depth. As you are about to see, this can be rather restrictive.

Suppose you wish to make three 25-minute dives to a depth of 60
feet (18 m). Assume a surface interval time of one hour between dives
and an ADT of 25 minutes for the first dive. Following the first dive
your letter group designation is "E." After a surface interval of one
hour, your letter group changes to "D." According to Table 3, your
AMDT for the second dive is 31 minutes. If you repeat the Actual
Dive Time of your first dive (25 minutes) your TNT for the second
dive is your ADT (25 minutes) plus your RNT of 24 minutes for a
total of 49 minutes. Your End-of-Dive letter group following the
second dive is "H." An hour after surfacing from the second dive,
your letter group is "G," and a "G" diver planning a dive to 60 feet
(18 m) is limited—according to Table 3—to a maximum ADT of 11
minutes. Now let's use this three-dive example to find other ways to
allow us to safely spend more time underwater.

Planning Your Surface Intervals

A good way to control your residual nitrogen, and your Adjusted
Maximum Dive Time for a repetitive dive, is with the surface interval.
The longer you remain at the surface between dives, the less nitrogen
remains in your system and the longer you can safely stay beneath the
surface on your next dive. What you want to be able to do is to
determine exactly how long a surface interval is required in order to
safely carry out a planned dive.

Let's use the third dive from our initial series of three dives as an
example. After the second dive, the letter group designation was "H."
To plan the dive, start with Table 3 and the bottom time you want
for the planned depth and work backwards. Here is how it is done:
For a desired ADT of 25 minutes at 60 feet (18 m), find the first

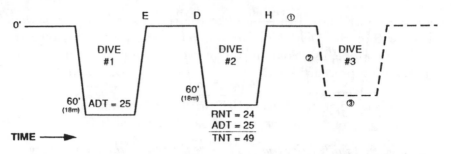

Figure 10-10. *Surface intervals. To avoid required decompression for the*
third dive, you can extend the Surface Interval Time ①,
limit the depth ②, *or limit Actual Dive Time* ③.

group in the 60 foot (18 m) column that has an AMDT equal to or
greater than 25 minutes. The group that does this is "E," which has
an AMDT of 25 minutes. You now have half of the problem solved.
All that remains is to determine how long it will take you to change
from letter group "H" to letter group "E," and Table 2 quickly provides
that information. Just look at the coordinates of letter group "E"
horizontally (the ending group) and "H" vertically (the starting group)
and find the minimum time required (1:42). By waiting just 42
minutes longer between your second and third dives, you can safely
make that third dive for 25 minutes. Planning your surface interval
is the second way to plan your dives.

Limiting Your Depth

Your third option is to increase your bottom time by limiting your
depth. If you were not able to extend your surface interval between
the second and third dives in our example series, and did not want
to make a dive of a very short duration, you could dive to a shallower
depth and safely spend more time diving. Let's see how that works
and how you would plan the dive.

Again, assuming a letter group designation of "G" following a one
hour surface interval after your second 25 minute dive to 60 feet (18
m), refer to Table 3 and look for the maximum depth which will
permit you to make a 25 minute dive with a letter group of "G."
Enter Table 3 on the "G" line and follow it to the left until you find
an AMDT equal to or greater than 25 minutes. In this instance, the
time is 57 minutes and the depth is 40 feet (12 m). You can see that
by diving 20 feet (6 m) shallower on your third dive you can make
your 25 minute dive. This is making good use of the dive tables.

You have just learned three ways to use the dive tables to plan your dives within the Dive Time limits. Now see if you can solve the following problems. Your instructor will provide more information on planning procedures.

1. After a dive to 65 feet (19.8 m) for 28 minutes and a surface interval of two hours, what is the maximum time you can dive on a second dive to a depth of 60 feet (18 m)?

2. After a dive to 70 feet (21 m) for 30 minutes, what is the minimum surface interval that will allow you to repeat the dive without exceeding the Adjusted Maximum Dive Time?

3. With a letter group designation of "E" following a series of dives, what is the maximum depth to which you can dive for at least 20 minutes?

10.4 Using the NAUI Dive Time Calculator

The NAUI Dive Tables are the basis for the calculator, which eliminates the calculations required with the tables. When you are familiar with the NAUI Dive Tables, it is very easy to learn to use the NAUI Dive Time Calculator.

Figure 10-11. *NAUI dive time calculator. The calculator is easier to use than dive tables.*

Tables 1 and 3 of the NAUI Dive Tables are combined on the base plate. Letter group designations appear around the circumference, and Actual Dive Times in minutes appear in the window. End-of-Dive letter group designations appear to the right of the ADT numbers in the disc window. Table 2—the Surface Interval Timetable—is printed on the disc and is identical to Table 2 on the NAUI Dive Tables.

10.4.1 DIVE PLANNING USING THE CALCULATOR

For your first dive of the day, find the "No Group" section on the base plate and align the depth arrow on the edge of the disc with the planned depth of your dive. The Maximum Dive Time for the dive appears as the largest number in the window. As an example, a "No Group" diver planning a dive to 60 feet (18 m) would have a Maximum Dive Time of 55 minutes.

Assuming you made your first dive of the day to 60 feet (18 m) and that your ADT for the dive was 23 minutes, your next step would be to determine your letter group designation following the dive. This is done by aligning the disc as described in the previous paragraph, reading bottom times from the center of the disc outward, and finding the first time you do not exceed. For our schedule of 60 feet (18 m)/23 minutes, the first time not exceeded is 25 minutes. Our End-of-Dive letter group appears to the right of the window next to 25: letter group "E."

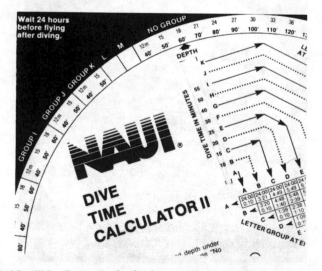

Figure 10-12. "No Group" of calculator. Use "No Group" portion of the calculator for the first dive.

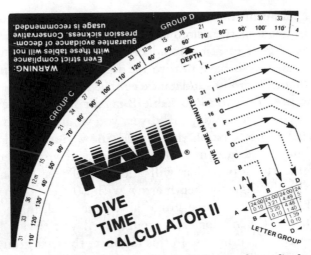

Figure 10-13. *"Group D" of calculator. It is simple to find repetitive dive time limits using the NAUI Dive Time Calculator.*

Letter group changes with surface intervals are determined the same as with the NAUI Dive Tables. An "E" diver after a surface interval of one hour would have a letter group designation of "D."

For planning of repetitive dives, find your new letter group on the circumference of the base plate and align the depth arrow on the disc with the planned depth of the repetitive dive. If, as a Group "D" diver, you wish to return to 60 feet (18 m), you will find in the window that your ADT is not to exceed 31 minutes. If you made a second dive of 23 minutes as a "D" diver, your End-of-Dive letter group (found adjacent to the first ADT number not exceeded in the window) would be 26 and your End-of-Dive group would be "H." Note that the design of the calculator eliminates Adjusted Maximum Dive Time and the need to add Residual Nitrogen Time to Actual Dive Time to obtain Total Nitrogen Time for the determination of your End-of-Dive letter group. All of this is rendered unnecessary by the design of the calculator, but the answers you obtain with the calculator are exactly the same as if you calculated the dive schedules using the NAUI Dive Tables.

The same three methods of dive planning used with the dive tables can be used with the Dive Time Calculator. You may limit your bottom time to the maximum number indicated for a given depth and group, extend your surface interval to obtain a lesser group letter, or dive to a shallower depth. As an example of dive planning using the calculator, assume you are a Group "F" diver and wish to dive for at least 25 minutes. Looking in the window below Group "F" on the calculator, you find, by moving the window back and forth, you may dive up to 19 minutes at 60 feet (18 m) and up to 33 minutes at 50 feet (15 m). Thus, you would have to dive no deeper than 50 feet (15 m) in order to remain 25 minutes and not exceed the Maximum Dive Time.

If you wanted to dive to 60 feet (18 m) for 25 minutes, but could not because you were a group "F" diver, you would need to determine the group letter designation that would allow you to make the dive and the minimum surface interval required to achieve that letter group. To determine the group that will allow a 60 feet (18 m)/25 dive schedule, simply align the depth arrow with 60 feet (18 m) in Group "F" and then work back one group at a time, realigning the depth arrow with 60' (18 m) for each group, until you find a MDT that equals or exceeds 25 minutes. In this instance, the first group allowing a Maximum Dive Time of 25 minutes is Group "E."

In some instances, the words "DO NOT DIVE" appear in the window of the calculator. This means you have too much residual nitrogen to permit a dive to the depth selected for a particular letter group. You will need to extend your surface interval to dive to the depth or select a shallower depth that indicates you may dive.

You can see already that using the Dive Time Calculator is easier than using the Dive Tables.

10.4.2 EXERCISES

Use the NAUI Dive Time Calculator to find the Dive Time Limits for both single and repetitive dives and for the planning of repetitive dives.

1. What is the Maximum Dive Time for a dive to 60 feet (18 m) for your first dive of the day?

Answer: You have no letter group designation for your first dive, so you align the depth arrow of the disc with 60' (18 m) under the "No Group" section of the base plate. Find that the Maximum Dive Time is 55 minutes.

2. What is your letter group designation following a first dive to 55 feet (16.7 m) for 39 minutes?

Answer: Just as with the dive tables, whenever a number is exceeded, you use the next larger number. There are no 55 foot (16.7 m) depths on the Calculator, so you must use the 60 foot (18 m) schedule. The first number under 60 feet (18 m) greater than 39 in the "No Group" section is 40 minutes. The dive schedule becomes 60 feet (18 m)/40 and the letter group is found to the right of the window beside 40—letter group "G."

3. An hour after your first dive, your letter group is "F." With this new group designation, what is the Maximum Dive Time for a dive to 50 feet (15 m)?

Answer: Align the depth arrow on the disc with 50' (15 m) in the Group "F" section of the base plate and read the Maximum Dive Time of 33 minutes in the window.

4. If a Group "F" diver makes a 32 minute dive to a depth of 50 feet (15 m), what is the End-of-Dive letter group designation?

Answer: Align the depth arrow on the disc with 50' (15 m) in the Group "F" section of the base plate and find the first time not exceeded by a 32 minute dive. In this case, that number is 33 minutes. Find the End-of-Dive group letter, which is "J," on the disc next to 33 in the window.

5. As a Group "H" diver, what is the minimum surface interval required to allow you to dive to a depth of 60 feet (18 m) for 25 minutes without exceeding the Dive Time Limits?

Answer: A Group "H" diver may not dive to 60 feet (18 m), as is stated in the window of the calculator. This is because a diver with this letter group designation has a large amount of residual nitrogen. Moving the depth arrow of the disc to 60 feet (18 m) to lower letter groups on the base plate shows that the time limits for Groups G, F and E are 11 minutes, 19 minutes, and 25 minutes, respectively. This means that you will need to attain letter group "E" before you can dive for at least 25 minutes without exceeding the Maximum Dive Time. Since you are in Group "H" and know you need to attain group "E," determining the surface interval is now merely a matter of referring to the Surface Interval Timetable and seeing how long it takes to move from group "H" to Group "E." At the coordinates "H" and "E" on the Surface Interval Timetable, we find the minimum time to be 1:42.

If you will check back to the dive table exercises you did previously, you will find you have just solved the same problems with the Dive Time Calculator you did using the Dive Tables and that the solutions are identical!

10.5 The Worksheet

A means to systematically keep track of depth, bottom time, surface intervals, letter group designations and other information is needed when working with the dive tables or the dive calculator. On the back of your NAUI Dive Tables is a Dive Planning and Recording Worksheet. This part of Chapter 10 explains how to use the Worksheet, which is recommended for the prevention of errors.

The NAUI Worksheet on your dive tables can be written on with a standard pencil and erased or scoured clean without damaging the tables. It is intended for use, so take a pencil when you go diving and write dive information directly onto your NAUI Tables Worksheet. Your NAUI Dive Tables are also waterproof, so you can record information on them in the water or refer to planning information previously entered.

The concept of the worksheet is quite simple. Time is plotted horizontally to the right, and depth vertically downward.

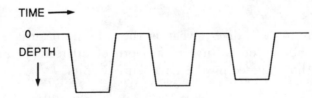

Figure 10-14. Basic dive worksheet. The concept of the worksheet is simple.

Four simple rules make the worksheet easy to use.

1. Enter the appropriate time (T) on each top corner of each dive profile. Include the appropriate letter group (LG) designation in the blanks above the times.

2. Enter the maximum planned depth (PD) for each dive profile (left side) prior to a dive and the actual depth (AD) after the dive (right side of the profile).

3. Enter either the Maximum Dive Time (MDT) or Adjusted Maximum Dive Time (AMDT) for each dive profile. The reason for MDT and AMDT being listed twice at the bottom of each profile is that the time limit for both the intended maximum depth plus the next greater depth should be included for contingency planning.

4. Enter the formula for Total Nitrogen Time (RNT + ADT = TNT) beneath each repetitive dive profile.

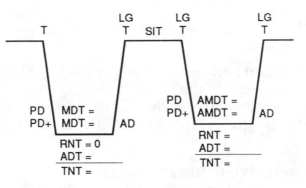

Figure 10-15. The basic rules for use of the worksheet. T = Time, PD = Planned Depth, AD = Actual Depth, LG = Letter Group, SIT = Surface Interval Time. The remaining terms have been previously defined.

Step one is to plan your first dive by entering the planned depth and MDT on the first dive profile. Enter the Maximum Dive Times (MDT) for the dive along the bottom line of the profile as shown in the example. Then record the time at the beginning of your descent on the upper left corner of the profile. When you return to the surface, the elapsed time is recorded in the upper right corner along with your End-of-Dive letter group. The deepest depth of the dive should be recorded on the right side of the dive profile.

When a repetitive dive is planned, the procedure is nearly the same except that you now use the Adjusted Maximum Dive Times at the bottom of the repetitive profile and (unless using the Dive Calculator), add your RNT to your ADT at the bottom of the profile to obtain Total Nitrogen Time (TNT).

When precautionary decompression is carried out, the time spent decompressing is shown next to a short horizontal line drawn through

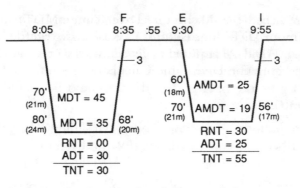

Figure 10-16. Example of a completed dive worksheet.

the ascent side of the dive profile. This appears as the number "3" in the above illustration.

Now let's record a series of dives on a worksheet as an example. You will then be given another series of dives to record for practice.

10.5.1 SAMPLE WORKSHEET PROBLEM

The first dive of the day is planned to a depth of 60 feet (18 m), begins at 9:30 a.m., and lasts for 23 minutes. The actual depth of the dive is 55 feet (16.8 m). You surface at 9:53 and remain out of the water until 10:37. Your next dive is to a depth of 50 feet (15 m) for a duration of 23 minutes. You surface at 11:00 and have a surface interval of 1:50. At 12:50 p.m., you begin your third dive to a planned depth of 40 feet (12 m), but you end up reaching a depth of 45 feet (13.7 m) with an ADT of 30 minutes. You surface from the third dive at 1:35 p.m.

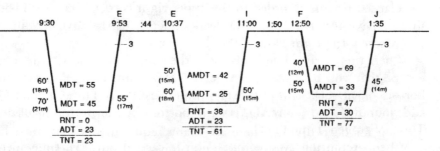

Figure 10-17. Sample worksheet problem.

NOTE: When the Worksheet is used in conjunction with the calculator, "RNT + ADT" for a sum of "TNT" is disregarded. Only the Depth and the ADT are required to determine the "End-of-Dive" letter group when using the Dive Time Calculator.

10.5.2 EXERCISE

Record the following dives on the worksheet and take them to class for review with your instructor. Work the exercise once using the NAUI Dive Tables and once using the NAUI Dive Time Calculator. Compare your results, should be the same.

Your first dive of the day begins at 8:00 a.m. and is to 60 feet (18 m) for 31 minutes. Time up is 8:31 and the surface interval time is 1:31. The second dive begins at 10:02 to a depth of 55 feet (16.8 m) and lasts for 24 minutes. Time of surfacing from the second dive is 10:26 and you remain out of the water for two hours. The third dive, started at 12:26, is to a depth of 50 feet (15 m) for 31 minutes. What are the time of surfacing and the End-of-Dive letter group?

Do not rely on your memory to keep track of dive times, maximum depths, or surface intervals. This information must be recorded. The NAUI Worksheet provides an easy and convenient way to accomplish this. Get into the habit of recording your dives on the Worksheet, and it will become easy to keep track of your diving. This also makes it easier to complete your log book at the end of the day.

10.6 Special Rules and Sample Problems

To be prepared to handle situations related to the dive tables, there are a few special rules and procedures you need to learn. How long do you decompress if the Maximum Dive Time is exceeded? What is the procedure for decompression? How can you keep from getting decompression sickness if you are to fly after diving? What if you want to go diving at some altitude above sea level or fly in a plane after diving? How do you handle a cold or strenuous dive? The answers to these questions follow.

10.6.1 DECOMPRESSION

Intentionally exceeding the Maximum Dive Time is unwise, unsafe, and discouraged. As you will learn in your Advanced or Specialty training for deep diving, there are many requirements that must be met to carry out decompression dives properly. Even if these requirements are met, dives requiring decompression are still discouraged.

Figure 10-18. Decompression at stop depth. If decompression is required, maintain the stop depth at chest level and limit activity to light exercise.

The long term effects of decompression diving are still not clearly understood, so this type of diving is deemed inappropriate for recreational purposes.

If you accidently exceed a Maximum Dive Time, you will need to decompress. This involves stopping at a depth of approximately 15 feet (5 m) during your ascent and remaining there for a specified number of minutes to allow excess nitrogen to be expelled. During a decompression stop, your activity should be kept to a minimum. You should have some means of support to help you maintain a constant depth during decompression stops. An ascent line, a decompression "bar" suspended from a boat, or the contour of the bottom in shallow water are examples of support. It is difficult to remain at one depth in shallow water without something to grasp. Swimming and hovering decompression are possible, but not easy. If you think you may need to decompress, have a means available to help you remain at a depth of approximately 15 feet (5 m).

Refer to Table 1 of the NAUI Dive Tables. You are already familiar with the Maximum Dive Time for each depth. To the right of the MDT are split squares containing two sets of numbers. The top number represents dive time, and the lower number represents the amount of decompression time required for that dive time. This decompression information tells you how long to remain at a depth of approximately 15 feet (5 m) to avoid decompression sickness if you should mistakenly exceed the Maximum Dive Times. For example, if your Total Nitrogen Time on an 80-foot (24 m) dive was 45 minutes, a ten minute decompression stop would be required.

Refer to your NAUI Dive Time Calculator. Required decompression information is handled differently on the calculator than it is on the dive tables. A separate Decompression Timetable is provided. To use the table, simply find in the first column the depth of your dive, find in the second column the first time that equals or exceeds your dive time in excess of the Dive Time limit for the depth, then decompress at 15 feet (5 m) for the time indicated in column three.

In addition to required decompression stops, you will want to stop at 15 feet (5 m) for three minutes as a safety precaution at the end of every dive. These "precautionary stops," while not required, are a good idea. Taking this action is recommended both to prevent decompression sickness and to maintain control of ascents near the surface. You may wonder how to document the time spent decompressing. Time spent doing decompression is simply "neutral" time. As an example, if you had an elapsed dive time of 45 minutes on a dive to 70 feet (21 m), you should stop at 15 feet (5 m) for three minutes. Determine your End-of-Dive letter group by using the schedule 70 feet (21 m)/45. Including stop time as part of your Actual Dive Time may also be done as an added precaution.

To document your decompression stops—either precautionary or required—enter the decompression time on your worksheet next to a short horizontal line drawn through the ascent line of the dive profile, as shown in Figure 10-16.

If decompression is required, refrain from further diving activities, or flying after diving for at least 24 hours.

10.6.2 OMITTED DECOMPRESSION

If you surface from a dive and discover required decompression was omitted, discontinue diving, rest, breathe oxygen if it is available, drink plenty of fluids, and watch for symptoms of decompression sickness. If you suspect you may have symptoms of the bends, proceed to the nearest recompression facility. No matter how well you feel, refrain from diving for at least 24 hours. Do not re-enter the water in an attempt to make up for the omitted decompression.

10.6.3 COLD/STRENUOUS DIVES

If you become cold during a dive or work hard, use the next greater time for your dive schedule. For instance, a first dive to 60 feet (18 m) for 40 minutes would be considered a 50-minute dive. If you become cold and work more than usual, use both the next greater time and depth.

10.6.4 FLYING AFTER DIVING

You are aware that decreasing the pressure below that at sea level following diving can lead to decompression sickness. What you need to know is how long to delay flying after diving to avoid problems related to decompression. Here are guidelines for going to altitudes of up to 8,000 feet (2,438 m) after diving. Note: Commercial airliners pressurize the cabins of the craft to maintain an altitude equivalent to 8,000 feet (2,438 m) or less. For recreational diving, NAUI recommends you wait at least 24 hours before flying. If you make dives requiring decompression (which you are advised not to do) or if required decompression is omitted, wait more than 24 hours before flying.

10.6.5 DIVING AT ALTITUDE

Atmospheric pressure decreases with altitude. This means the rate of change of pressure is greater when descending into water at altitude than it is at sea level. To take this difference into account, special altitude dive tables used and special procedures must be followed. The maximum rate of ascent changes with altitude, as do the decompression stop depths. Before diving at altitudes above 1,000 feet (300 m), you need to be trained in the use of the special tables and procedures. If altitude diving is common in your area, your instructor may provide additional information as part of your training, or recommend that you participate in a high altitude specialty training program subsequent to your being certified as an Openwater I or II Diver. High altitude training is beyond the scope or purpose of this textbook. For now, what you need to know is: Do not attempt high altitude diving without first completing a high altitude training program.

10.6.6 SAMPLE PROBLEMS

You have learned a great deal about the NAUI Dive Tables and the NAUI Dive Calculator and their uses. Now it is time to pull together all you know and apply it to typical diving situations. The following problems contain all of the aspects of dive table and dive calculator usage you will need to know for recreational diving. Explanations are included. When you understand how to work problems such as these correctly, you will be able to plan your dives to avoid decompression sickness.

1. Use the worksheet provided. Include a three minute precautionary stop at 15 feet (3 m) for all dives. Do not include the decompression time as part of dive time.

The first dive is to 60 feet (18 m) for 30 minutes and is followed by a 30-minute surface interval. The second dive is to 50 feet (15 m) for 30 minutes. Question: What is the End-of-Dive letter group after the second dive?

Answer: 60 feet (18 m)/30 results in Group "F." After a 30-minute SIT, the letter group remains "F." An "F" diver using the dive tables and going to 50 feet (15 m) has an RNT of 47 minutes which is added to the ADT of 30 minutes for a Total Nitrogen Time of 77 minutes. A schedule of 50 feet (15 m)/77 minutes results in an End-of-Dive letter group of "J." Note: The addition of the RNT to the ADT is not required when using the NAUI Dive Time Calculator. Simply look up the ADT of 30 minutes under 50 feet (15 m) in the Group "F" section and note that the End-of-Dive letter group is "J."

2. The first dive is to 55 feet (16.8 m) for 31 minutes followed by a SIT of an hour. The second dive is to 51 feet (15.3 m). What is the Maximum Dive Time for the second dive, and what is the End-of-Dive letter group if the Adjusted Maximum Dive Time is reached?

Answer: 55 feet (16.8 m) for 31 minutes is actually a 60 feet (18 m)/40 schedule resulting in a letter Group "G" designation. A one hour SIT leads to Group "F," and an "F" diver going to 51 feet (15.3 m) (60 feet [18 m] on the tables) has an RNT of 36 minutes. The Adjusted Maximum Dive Time (AMDT) for an "F" diver at 60 feet (18 m) is 19 minutes. Remember that your Adjusted Maximum Dive Time must include your ascent time (approximately one minute for this dive) so you will need to begin your ascent at or before 18 minutes of bottom time. Your TNT, if your ADT is 19 minutes, is 36 RNT plus 19 ADT for a total of 55 minutes. The dive of 51 feet (16.8 m)/55 is a 60 feet (18 m)/55 schedule producing an End-of-Dive letter group of "I."

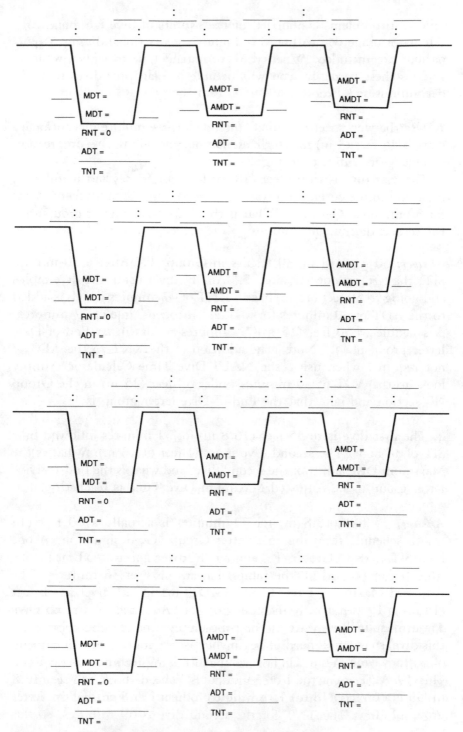

Figure 10-19. Blank dive worksheet for reader use.

3. After the second dive in the previous problem, a SIT of how long is required in order to make a 25 minute dive to 50 feet (15 m) without exceeding the Adjusted Maximum Dive Time? Also, what is your End-of-Dive letter group following the third dive if your ADT is 25 minutes? (Use the worksheet from the previous problem.)

Answer: To plan the minimum SIT with the dive tables, refer to Table 3 and determine the letter group required to allow the dive to be made. In this instance, to make a 25-minute dive to 50 feet (15 m), you need to achieve a Group "F" designation, which has an AMDT of 33 minutes. When you know the letter group required to make the dive, you go to the Surface Interval Timetable and work it in reverse to determine the minimum time needed to achieve the necessary letter group. Since you want the new group to be "F" and since your starting group is "I," the minimum time required is one hour and 30 minutes. Now let's determine the End-of-Dive letter group. Your ADT (including ascent time) is 25 minutes and your RNT for an "F" diver to 50 feet (15 m) is 47 minutes, producing a TNT of 72 minutes for a schedule of 50 feet (15 m)/80 and a letter group of "J." Note that when planning dives, you may at times need to use the tables in reverse order.

To solve this problem using the Dive Time Calculator, start at the Group "I" section on the base plate and move the depth arrow from one 50 feet (15 m) depth to the same depth for the next lesser letter group until the desired time of 25 minutes is permitted. In this instance, the first group allowing a 25-minute dive to 50 feet is "F." The Surface Interval Timetable on the calculator is used exactly the same way as that described for use of the table with the NAUI Dive Tables. A dive schedule of 50 feet (15 m)/25 minutes as a "F" diver produces an End-of-Dive letter group of "J."

4. Complete the Worksheet for three dives to 52 feet (15.8 m) for 25 minutes each with a SIT of one hour between dives.

Answer: This problem is tricky because it is not asking you to plan the dive to avoid required decompression and because decompression is required. It illustrates what can happen if you do not document your dive schedules and do not use the tables to plan your dives. Your first dive places you in letter group "E." A one-hour SIT leads to Group "D." A "D" diver returning to 52 feet (15.8 m) has an RNT of 24 minutes. The TNT for the second dive is 49 minutes, so the dive schedule is 60 feet (18 m)/50 and results in an End-of-Dive letter Group "H." An hour later, the new group designation is "G," and a "G" diver going to 52 feet (15.8 m) has an Adjusted Maximum Dive Time of 11 minutes (which is exceeded) and an RNT of 44 minutes. Although you should not exceed the AMDT, it is exceeded during this dive of 25 minutes. The TNT is 44 RNT plus 25 ADT for a total of 69 minutes. So you are required to decompress for seven minutes, as indicated by the tables, when the TNT is greater than 60 minutes and equal to or less than 80 minutes.

To use the Dive Time Calculator to determine the decompression requirement, find in the timetable at the bottom of the disc the exact or next greater time in excess of the time limit for the dive, then determine the decompression schedule. For this example, the ADT was exceeded by 14 minutes. Seven minutes of decompression is indicated for dive times at 60 feet (18 m) which exceed the limits by more than five minutes and up to 25 minutes.

By working with the tables and the calculator, you will soon feel very comfortable with their use. Your instructor will be glad to help you with any difficulties you have. Remember the importance of recording and planning your dives to prevent decompression sickness.

10.7 Using Dive Computers

When you are able to afford a dive computer, you will find this instrument allows you more dive time due to its capability to continuously calculate multi-level dives, only charging you for the nitrogen actually absorbed. You will also find dive planning is easier because you do not have to make calculations. You must not become totally dependent on a computer, however, because electro-mechanical devices are subject to failure.

Dive computers differ greatly. Different computers offer various features, and different mathematical models are used by different manufacturers. This results in dive schedules ranging from the conservatism of the NAUI Dive Tables to more liberal profiles. Since dive computer designs and features are subject to change, NAUI does not recommend particular types. We suggest you discuss the types and features of various computers with your instructor and your retailer and choose a model they recommend.

10.7.1 COMPUTER TERMS

There is some additional terminology with which you will need to be familiar in order to use a dive computer. These terms include:

Ceiling: Most dive computers do not use the standard depths for decompression stops, but instead calculate the shallowest depth to which you may ascend without risk of forming bubbles in your system. This minimum depth is called your "ceiling" and must not be passed. Whenever a computer displays a ceiling, you have entered a decompression situation, so you should dive with a computer in such a way as to prevent a ceiling from being established.

Scrolling: Before a dive, a computer will continuously flash the Maximum Dive Times for various depths in sequence. This feature is an aid for dive planning and is called "scrolling."

10.7.2 COMPUTER USAGE

A dive computer has the potential to become the "ultimate instrument" for diving activities. Some computers combine information that would usually require several instruments and present the information on a single digital display. A computer may be able to display several or all of the following items of information:

- Current depth
- Maximum depth attained
- Elapsed bottom time
- Surface interval time
- Temperature
- Minutes remaining within Dive Time Limits
- Minutes remaining based on air supply and consumption
- End-of-Dive letter group designation
- Rate of ascent
- Dive number
- Profile of the dive
- When flying is safe
- Scrolling of Dive Time Limits
- Ceiling

The following rules are to be followed when using a dive computer:

1. Each diver relying on a dive computer must have a separate unit. One computer may not be shared by a buddy team. A dive

computer used by one diver may not be used by another diver for a subsequent dive until the time period required for complete outgassing has been completed.

2. The dive computer instruction manual should be studied carefully and the computer used in accordance with the manufacturer's instructions. Completion of a dive computer specialty course is highly recommended.

3. If a dive computer fails at any time while diving, the dive must be terminated and appropriate surfacing procedures (precautionary decompression) should be initiated immediately.

4. You should not dive for twenty-four hours before using a dive computer.

5. Once a dive computer is in use, it must not be switched off until it indicates complete outgassing has occurred, or 24 hours have elapsed, whichever comes first.

6. When using a computer, non-emergency ascents are to be at the rate specified for the make and model of the dive computer being used. Several computers specify ascent rates that are slower than the rate used for the dive tables.

7. A five-minute decompression stop is recommended for all dive computer repetitive dives to 60 feet (18 m) or greater even if the computer does not indicate a ceiling.

8. Repetitive and multi-level divers should start the dive or the series of dives at the maximum planned depth, followed by subsequent dives or depths of shallower exposure.

9. Repetitive dives in excess of 100 feet (30 m) should not be made.

Some people suggest planning dives with the dive tables or a dive calculator as a contingency plan for computer diving. Due to the multilevel calculating capability of the computer, this practice is not usually feasible, although it is possible with some computers. You usually cannot revert to the dive tables in the event of a computer failure or the accidental switching off of your computer. Your only options in this event are to discontinue diving for 24 hours or to limit any subsequent dives during the day to depths of 20 feet (6 m) or less.

Computer diving is easier than diving with manual calculations, but you should always be able to use the dive table and dive calculator calculations in the event a computer is not available for use.

You are now familiar with dive time planning and should be capable of solving repetitive dives using either the NAUI Dive Tables or the NAUI Dive Time Calculator to avoid required decompression. It is important to note that decompression sickness cannot be entirely prevented, no matter what device you use to plan dives, due to individual factors and susceptibility. For this reason, conservative usage of all diving planning devices is strongly recommended.

10.8 Risk-reducing Recommendations

Some experts recommend the following practices, which you may wish to consider:

1. Limit diving to three dives per day.

2. Avoid multiple-day, multiple depth dives. After three days of repetitive diving, wait 24 hours before diving again.

3. Avoid multiple complete ascents (surfacing) during dives. Also avoid repetitive dives of short duration—called "yo-yo" dives—following a surface interval of less than one hour. The minimum time between dives specified by the dive tables is ten minutes, but a minimum surface interval of one hour between dives is recommended.

4. No dive tables, dive calculators, or dive computers will absolutely ensure against decompression sickness. They merely provide time limits based on statistical conclusions, so you must use them properly, conservatively, and with common sense to prevent injury.

Chapter 10 Review

The instructor should correct the student's answers, record the results, and return them to the student. Both teacher and student should sign after the last question.

REVIEW QUESTIONS	ANSWERS
1. What organization developed the no decompression tables now used by sport divers in the United States?	1. _____
2. Provide the no-decompression time limits for the following depths: 40 feet, 60 feet, 70 feet, 90 feet, and 100 feet.	2. _____ _____ _____ _____ _____
3. Define the following terms: actual dive time (ADT), repetitive dive, residual nitrogen (RNT), and adjusted maximum dive time (AMDT).	3. _____ _____ _____ _____ _____
4. What two pieces of equipment are required in order to make the no-decompression tables accurate and reliable predictors of diving safety?	4. _____ _____
5. When performing two dives at two different depths, should the deeper or more shallow dive be performed first?	5. _____
6. What is a precautionary decompression stop?	6. _____

REVIEW QUESTIONS	ANSWERS
7. For particularly cold and arduous dives, how should the tables be adapted?	7. _____
8. After scuba diving, how long should one abstain from flying in a plane?	8. _____
9. "PLAN YOUR DIVE AND _____ _____ _____!	9. _____

I have graded, recorded, and returned this student's responses.	Instructor's Signature: _____ Date: _____
I have seen my corrected review questions and now know the appropriate answers. Note: The answer sheet may either be taken out or retained with this book.	Student's Signature: _____ Date: _____

Chapter 11

~~~~~~

Dive Computers

by Karl E. Huggins

Dive computers (DC) are relatively new devices in recreational diving. While monitoring many variables underwater, the primary purpose of the dive computer is to assist the diver in avoiding decompression sickness. Although expensive, the diving community is clearly demonstrating that diving by computer is here to stay.

The beauty of the dive computer is that it monitors depth, time, residual nitrogen, surface interval times, and many other factors and displays this information clearly on a small screen. Thus it eliminates the need for several different gauges while manipulating the no-decompression tables to avoid the bends. And these computers are extremely accurate. Additionally, they keep track of nitrogen absorption more realistically as dictated by the actual dive and defined by the device's decompression model. Dive tables provide the diver with information based on the assumption that a "square" dive profile was performed.

Since the introduction of scuba in the 1950s many attempts have been made to create devices that determine a diver's decompression status in real time. These devices, which met with various levels of success, included mechanical and electrical analog computers and more recently microprocessor-based digital computers. Most of the technological and economic problems that hindered early devices were overcome in the early 1980s. Today, with the availability of inexpensive microprocessor technology, we have the largest variety of dive computers ever available to divers. Several units are available from various

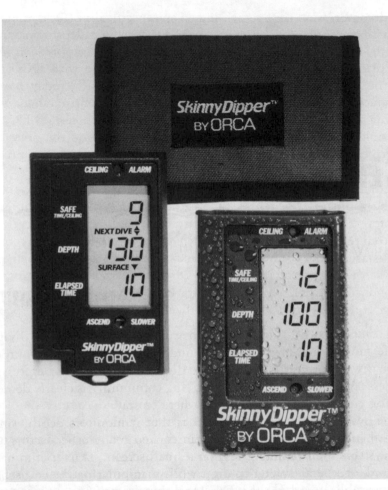

Figure 11-1. *Dive computers. (Courtesy Orca Industries)*

manufacturers. However, even though DCs have been around for more than five years, there is a lack of knowledge in the diving community on how they work and the concepts behind their operation. Too many divers are simply willing to turn their thinking over to an electronic box and let it guide them. When used properly the dive computer can be a very powerful, safe, and beneficial tool that the operator needs to learn how to use.

11.1 Dive Computers on Decompression Status

The major piece of information provided by a DC is the diver's decompression status, which is normally displayed as the amount of no-decompression time remaining on any specific dive. Other information that is provided by most of the DCs include depth, maximum depth, dive time, surface interval time, and no-decompression limits for planning subsequent dives. A major advantage with DCs comes in the accuracy of their depth readings. Most DCs today have an accuracy of $+/-2$ feet of seawater (fsw) over their entire range, which is much better than most mechanical gauges. With certain DCs it is possible to recall dive profile information that shows the diver their depth/time profile. Some DCs also provide the diver with tank pressure information.

There are two basic types of dive computers. One type is programmed with established dive tables, such as the U.S. Navy Air Decompression Tables. This type of DC will determine the maximum depth and bottom time during the dive and then determine the diver's decompression status from a set of tables that has been stored in its memory.

The other type of DC uses a decompression model and every few seconds computes the diver's decompression status based on that model. Most of the DCs available today utilize this technique. It is important that a diver using a DC understand the method the DC uses to compute decompression status.

11.1.1 HOW DECOMPRESSION STATUS IS DETERMINED

The general method used by DCs to compute decompression status is relatively simple. All DCs have a pressure transducer that is exposed to ambient pressure. This transducer converts the ambient pressure to an analog signal (voltage, resistance, capasitance, etc.). This in turn is converted by an analog-to-digital converter into a digital signal that can be understood by the DC's microprocessor. Once the ambient pressure (depth) is read by the microprocessor, the DC's program can use that information to compute decompression status.

For DCs that are programmed to read a set of tables, the maximum depth reading achieved during the dive and the total dive time are compared against the tables. If there is no-decompression time remaining the DC will display that time to the diver. If the diver ascends to a shallower depth he or she will not receive any credit since the maximum depth rule applies. If the diver descends to a deeper depth range, the DC will adjust the no-decompression time remaining down to the time appropriate for that depth range, just as would be done with proper use of a set of plastic tables.

For DCs that use a decompression model the method of determining decompression status is much different. To understand how these DCs work one must first have a rudimentary knowledge of decompression models.

All of the model-based DCs at this time use the concept that the body can be approximated as a group of compartments that absorb and eliminate nitrogen at different rates based on their assigned half-time. The half-time of a compartment is the time it will take to reach one half the pressure difference between the nitrogen pressure it initially holds and the ambient nitrogen pressure. For example, if a compartment initially held a nitrogen pressure of 20 psi and the ambient nitrogen pressure was at 40 psi, then after one half-time the pressure in the compartment would be at 30 psi. After another half-time the pressure would increase to 35 psi, and so on. After six half-times the compartment is, for all intents and purposes, considered saturated (the nitrogen pressure in the compartment is equal to the ambient nitrogen pressure).

The other part of the model states that these compartments have the ability to hold a certain amount of excess nitrogen in solution even when the ambient pressure is less than the compartment nitrogen pressure. If a compartment is in this state it is said to be supersaturated. The maximum amount of excess nitrogen that a compartment is allowed to have at sea level is called the Mo value for that compartment. For example, in the U.S. Navy model used to create their Air Decompression Tables, the Mo value for the five-minute half-time compartment is equal to 104 fsw (46.3 psi) of nitrogen and for the 120-minute compartment the Mo value is 51 fsw (22.7 psi). Since the air pressure at sea level is equal to 33 fsw (14.7 psi), the 120-minute compartment would require a total nitrogen pressure of 84 fsw (37.4 psi) [Surface pressure + Mo Value] or less in order to safely be brought to the surface. If the nitrogen pressure were greater then, according to the model, the nitrogen would come out of solution in the form of bubbles, causing decompression sickness.

The model-based DC uses the concepts of compartment half-times and Mo values by computing, every few seconds, the nitrogen pressure buildup release in the compartments of the decompression model that is used. If the nitrogen pressures in all the compartments are less than their corresponding Mo values the DC will indicate that the diver is within the no-decompression realm of the model. Most DCs will compute and display the amount of no-decompression time remaining if the diver stays at the present depth. If the diver moves to a shallower depth the remaining no-decompression time will increase since the compartments building up nitrogen pressure at a slower rate and, in some cases, may be off-gassing nitrogen from some compartments. If the diver were to descend the remaining no-decompression time would decrease due to more rapid nitrogen build-up in the compartments. If at any time the nitrogen pressure any of the compartments exceeds its Mo value the DC will provide the diver with information on decompression requirements that will allow the compartment(s) to off-gas to a point where no Mo is violated upon surfacing.

The model-based DC is a much more flexible machine than the tables-based DC, which is why the majority of the DCs that are available are model-based. However, due to greater flexibility, a computer programmed with a model and a set of tables based on the same model can vary widely.

11.2 Variations Between Tables and Computers

Much concern has been expressed about what seems to be a disparity between DCs and tables that are based on the same model. The reason for this disparity is that the tables by necessity have some built-in assumptions and rules to allow a simple table presentation that do not exist in model-based DCs.

The first rule is that the depth of the dive is either the exact or next greater depth. If the diver spent the entire dive at 51 fsw then the rule states that the 60 fsw entry on the table needs to be used and will assume a nitrogen pressure build-up that is greater than what would compute at 51 fsw. On the other hand, the DCs would compute nitrogen pressure based on the exact depth, which would result in more no-decompression time at 51 fsw than at 60 fsw.

The second assumption/rule is that the diver spends the entire dive at the deepest depth. In reality sport divers rarely stay at the deepest depth for the entire dive. For example, on the first dive of the day where the maximum depth is 60 fsw the U.S. Navy Tables allow 60 minutes of no-decompression time no matter if the diver only spent a few minutes at 60 fsw and the rest of the time at 40 fsw. A DC programmed with the U.S. Navy model would allow only 60 minutes of no-decompression time if the diver descended to 60 fsw and stayed at that depth. However, if the diver ascended to 40 fsw the remaining no-decompression time displayed by the DC would be adjusted to represent the slower nitrogen build-up. Thus it is possible to perform a dive to a maximum depth of 60 fsw for longer than 60 minutes and still remain within the confines of the U.S. Navy model.

The final assumption is a little more complex. It deals with how repetitive dives are calculated using the tables and DCs.

11.3 Summary and Recommendations for Dive Computers

The major disadvantage of a dive computer is that the device tends to eliminate the safety factors which are associated with table use. Since the computer considers the exact dive profile in computing the diver's decompression status, the safety factor obtained by the next greater depth/next longest time rule is lost. Additional safety is obtained by the fact that most divers do not spend their entire bottom time at the maximum depth, although their table entry must assume it was.

Also, as with all mechanical or electrical equipment, there is always the possibility the device will fail. It is recommended that divers carry a set of tables and back-up gauges in case of computer failure. If a dive computer fails during a dive deeper than 30 feet the dive must be terminated immediately.

It must be emphasized that water temperature, physical conditioning, diver hydration, exertion level, etc., are not measured or considered in the computations. Two exact depth/time profiles, one in warm water under low exercise conditions, and the other in a heavy-exertion, cold-water environment will produce the same decompression status. Divers must be aware, as in the use of tables, to modify dive profiles based on environmental factors and their physical condition.

One potential problem area with dive computers lies in the diver. In order for the computer information to be of any use to the diver, it must be read and acted upon. If a diver does not monitor or ignores the information presented, the device becomes useless. If the device is not used in the way it was designed, such as turning off the device between dives or being used by more than one diver, the information will not be accurate.

Divers should not use dive computers without proper knowledge and training. They should be used for no-decompression diving only. A dive computer used by one diver may not be used by another diver for another dive within the time period required for off-gassing for the initial diver as specified from the manufacturer. Ascent rates are recommended by the manufacturer and must be strictly followed.

The following are recommendations for use of dive computers as formulated by the American Academy of Underwater Sciences:

1. Each diver relying on a dive computer must wear his/her own unit.

2. On any given dive, both divers in the buddy pair must follow the most conservative dive computer.

3. If the dive computer fails at any time during the dive, the dive must be terminated and appropriate surfacing procedures should be initiated immediately.

4. A diver should not dive for 18 hours (the authors recommend 24 hours) before activating a dive computer to use it to control his/her diving.

5. Once a dive computer is in use, it must *not* be switched off until it indicates complete outgassing has occurred or 18 hours (the authors recommend 24 hours) have elapsed, or whichever comes first.

6. When using a dive computer, non-emergency ascents are to be at the rate(s) specified for the make and model of the dive computer being used.

7. Ascent rates shall not exceed 40 fsw/min. in the last 60 fsw.

8. Whenever practical, divers using a dive computer should make a stop between 10–30 fsw for 5 minutes, especially for dives below 60 fsw.

9. Repetitive and multi-level diving procedures should start at the maximum planned depth, followed by subsequent dives of shallower exposures.

10. Multiple deep dives should be avoided.

In summary, dive computers are only tools that can be used in diving. They should not be used as crutches or excuses to not teach, learn, or understand the use of decompression tables and the problems associated with decompression sickness.

Chapter 11 Review

The instructor should correct the student's answers, record the results, and return them to the student. Both teacher and student should sign after the last question.

REVIEW QUESTIONS	ANSWERS
1. What is the major piece of information provided by a dive computer (DC)?	1. _____
2. Discuss the accuracy of DCs.	2. _____
3. Describe the two basic types of dive computers.	3. _____
4. What is a Mo value?	4. _____
5. What are some disparities between the use of tables and computers?	5. _____
6. List three advantages of a DC.	6. _____

REVIEW QUESTIONS	ANSWERS
7. List three disadvantages of a DC.	7. _____ _____ _____
8. Who determines which ascent rate should be used with any particular DC?	8. _____ _____ _____
9. In a buddy pair when two DCs are used which one should both divers follow?	9. _____ _____ _____
10. What should a diver do if the DC fails below 30 feet under water?	10. _____ _____ _____
11. When not in use, should the DC be left on or off?	11. _____ _____

I have graded, recorded, and returned this student's responses.

Instructor's Signature:

_____

Date:

_____

I have seen my corrected review questions and now know the appropriate answers.
Note: The answer sheet may either be taken out or retained with this book.

Student's Signature:

_____

Date:

_____

Chapter 12

~~~~~~

Preventive
Maintenance of
Diving Equipment

Because scuba diving is an equipment-oriented sport, your diving will be more efficient and enjoyable if you know how to take proper care of your gear. Not only does regularly scheduled maintenance increase the life of your equipment, but it also ensures the reliability of the equipment, thereby increasing your diving pleasure and safety.

12.1 Mask, Fins, and Snorkel

The basic skin diving equipment used for scuba diving activity is primarily made of neoprene rubber. Several conditions and substances can significantly deteriorate rubber and ruin masks, fins, and snorkels if they are not protected. These include prolonged sunlight, chlorine, ozone, and some suntan lotions. To prolong the life of the mask, fins, and snorkel, the diver should rinse them thoroughly in fresh water after each use. Warm, soapy water is advised for especially abused skin diving equipment. After allowing these items to drip-dry, silicone spray should be applied to prevent drying and cracking of the rubber. Dried-out straps should always be replaced immediately.

12.2 Wet Suits

Wet suits are also made of neoprene rubber and should be washed and rinsed after each dive. Baking soda helps to clean and disinfect the suit. The suit should be hung up to allow it to dry after washing. When the wet suit is dry, silicone spray should be applied to all zippers and snaps to protect the metal and promote maneuverability. The suit should not be rolled up or packed away after cleaning, but should remain on hangers, or else laid flat if stretching is feared.

When holes or tears appear in the wet suit material, it can be easily glued or patched with wet suit cement available in dive shops. This is a contact cement which requires several coats and must be allowed to dry before tears can be pressed together. However, the cement works quite well for the patient diver.

12.3 Regulators

Both chlorine and salt water are especially destructive to the longevity of regulators. Therefore, the regulator must be rinsed with warm,

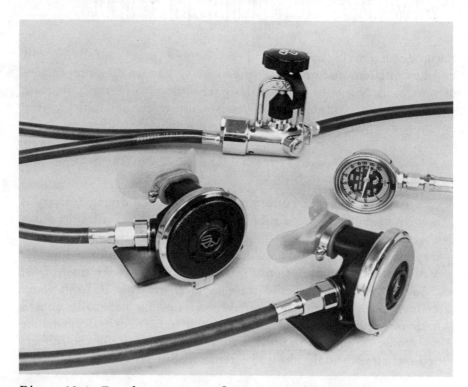

Figure 12-1. Regulator storage. (© Geri Murphy, 1981)

fresh water. During this rinse, the first stage of the regulator should remain higher than the second stage, and the purge button on the second stage *must not* be depressed, because this may allow water and other contaminants to enter the interior of the regulator.

The regulator should be laid flat during storage rather than being hung by the first stage (Figure 12-1). Hanging a regulator, while more convenient, may cause undue stress and kinking of the hose where it connects to the first stage. Whenever possible, the regulator should be rinsed while it is still on the tank and pressurized. The regulator must be overhauled and cleaned at least once a year, but only by a certified equipment repair specialist.

12.4 B.C.D.

A complete freshwater rinsing is also required for the B.C.D. Special attention should be devoted to all the inflators, including the oral, CO_2, and auto-tank inflators. These mechanisms must be rinsed with extra care and then lubricated with silicone spray. The overinflation valve also demands the same care. The B.C.D. should always be emptied of water and then partially inflated to keep the interior walls of the air bladder from sticking.

12.5 Tank, Valve, and Backpack

The tank, valve, and backpack may be rinsed as a unit. The O-ring should be replaced when it dries out or loses its contour, and the backpack cam should be lubricated and adjusted.

The tank should be stored with a little air pressure in it (100–300 psi). The tank should be secured in place in a vertical position. The tank must be visually inspected at least once a year and hydrostatically tested once every 5 years.

12.6 Gauges and Accessories

All remaining scuba apparatus should be rinsed in warm, fresh water and stored away from excessive temperatures. Gauges should preferably be stored in a protective carry bag.

Whenever possible, all scuba gear should be stored together in one room or one closet in an orderly fashion. Using a large pegboard to hang certain items is especially convenient. If scuba items are located in two or more rooms, failure to pack at least one scuba item for a dive trip becomes almost inevitable.

Selected References

Farley, M.B., and Royer, C. *Scuba Equipment Care and Maintenance*. Port Hueneme, Calif.: Marcor Publishing, 1980.

Gravers, D., and Wohlers, R. *PADI Advanced Dive Manual*. Santa Ana, Calif.: Professional Association of Diving Instructors, 1980.

Chapter 13

~~~~~~

Underwater Communications

One of the greatest benefits derived from scuba diving is the peace and tranquility it offers you. Being underwater is relaxing; you won't hear any talking or yelling and, what's more, there are no telephones ringing! However, there is a disadvantage to the silence of the underwater world: the difficulty in underwater communication. This important diving skill may cause you some frustration because the language you'll be using is limited, and little or no time is spent in your basic classes developing this skill.

If you master a specific means of underwater communication, you must be certain that your diving partner also knows your system; otherwise poor communication will result. You'll learn that just as on land, underwater communications is a two-way street.

The two most popular methods of communicating underwater are hand signals and an underwater writing slate. Other methods use a whistle, buddy-line pulls, hand squeezes, and lights.

13.1 Hand Signals

The first rule of efficient hand signaling underwater is to remember that after the sender transmits a message, the receiver must return an appropriate hand signal. Simply nodding the head as an acknowledgment of the signal does not provide sufficient information for good underwater communication. When employing hand signals, the diver

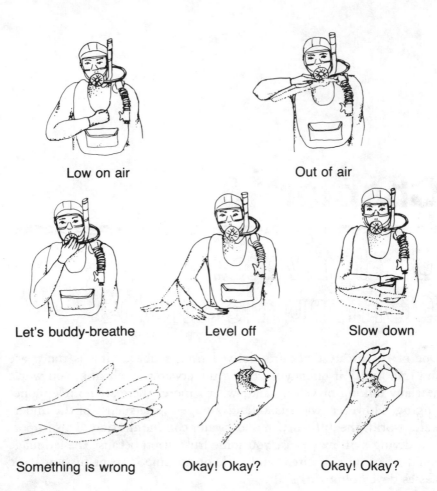

Low on air

Out of air

Let's buddy-breathe

Level off

Slow down

Something is wrong

Okay! Okay?

Okay! Okay?

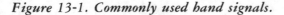

Figure 13-1. Commonly used hand signals.

should use deliberate and exaggerated movements of the hands for effective communication. It should be remembered that many of the standard hand signals are difficult to transmit while wet suit mitts are worn; five-fingered wet suit gloves are better for this purpose. Figure 13-1 illustrates the most commonly used hand signals in sport diving. To be effective, both divers must understand and agree upon all hand signals to be used.

In addition to these standard signals, other hand signals are developed within a buddy team. When these particular signals are added to the standard underwater language, they should be reviewed by both divers prior to the dive. A few such signals are illustrated in Figure 13-2.

Stop Down Up

Which way? Buddy-up

Boat Repeat

Figure 13-1. (continued)

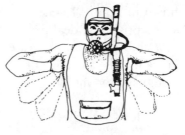

I could shoot myself! Turkey!

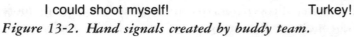

Figure 13-2. Hand signals created by buddy team.

What?

Okay! Okay?   Okay! Okay?

Distress

Figure 13-3. Surface hand signals.

Surface hand signals are mostly reserved for emergency situations, and the entire arm in addition to the hand is used. The surface signals are shown in Figure 13-3.

Not surprisingly, deaf people make excellent divers because of their superior ability to communicate underwater by means of hand signals. If you want to be a proficient communicator underwater, try studying sign language for the deaf.

13.2 Underwater Slate

Writing underwater allows divers to communicate information more elaborately and concisely. If writing slates are to be the major mode

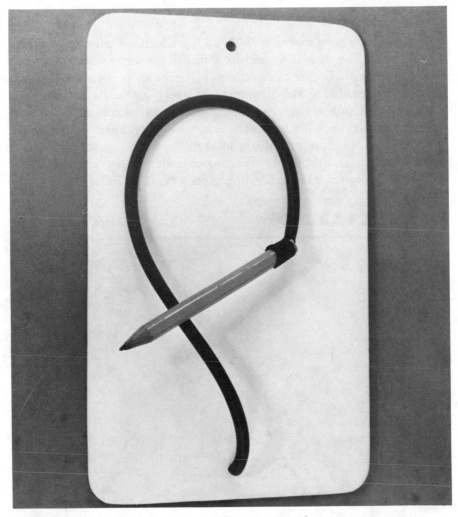

Figure 13-4. Underwater slate. (© Geri Murphy, 1981)

of underwater communication, both divers must have their own slates. Two divers sharing one writing slate consumes too much time.

The writing slate may be located in a variety of places. Mounting the slate on the back of the equipment console provides ideal positioning. It may also be attached to the diver's B.C.D. or placed in the B.C.D. pocket. To prevent loss, the slate should always be secured to the diver along with the writing utensil which is attached to the slate. Nylon cord or surgical tubing may be used in both cases. A grease pencil or soft lead pencil serves well as writing instrument (Figure 13-4).

13.3 Other Communication Methods

The most effective means of summoning assistance from the surface is by *whistle*. The whistle should be attached on the vest where it can be easily reached. In case of an emergency, five short, quick blasts are made on the whistle. The advantage of using a whistle to summon help is that it produces a maximum noise level with a minimum of effort. However, the whistle must only be used in emergency situations.

Buddy-lines are more commonly used in waters of limited visibility, but they make a valuable contribution to underwater communication even in clear water. The buddy-line should be short (3 feet) and must

THE FAR SIDE   By GARY LARSON

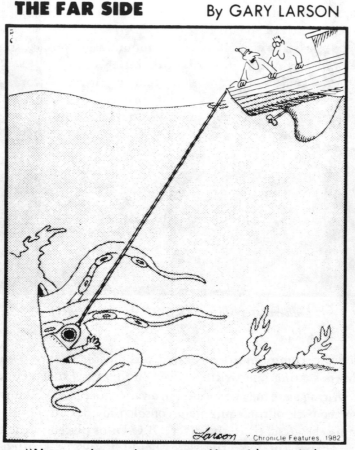

"Now wait a minute . . . He said two jerks means 'more slack' and three meant 'come up' . . . but he never said nothin' about one long, steady pull."

not be tied to either diver. Instead, loops are secured at both ends of the line where they may either be held by the divers or worn on the wrists.

Buddy-lines used in clear water usually serve as attention getters. When used in limited visibility, line-pulling signals may be developed and substituted for hand signals.

Hand-squeezing is another means of communicating quickly underwater. Line-pulling and hand-squeezing signals may be identical; the most basic signals are as follows: one pull or squeeze—stop; two pulls or squeezes—go; four pulls or squeezes—surface; and five pulls or squeezes—come together.

Line pulls and hand squeezes not only promote effective communication, they also encourage relaxation through tactile stimulation. Therefore, divers should be encouraged to use these techniques as supplements to the standard hand signals and the underwater slate.

Underwater lights also aid in the communication process, but they are almost always restricted to night diving.

To promote underwater communication and thereby encourage diving safety and pleasure, divers should master hand signals and use several underwater modes of communication. Unfortunately, this is one practical aspect of diving which is often neglected by diving

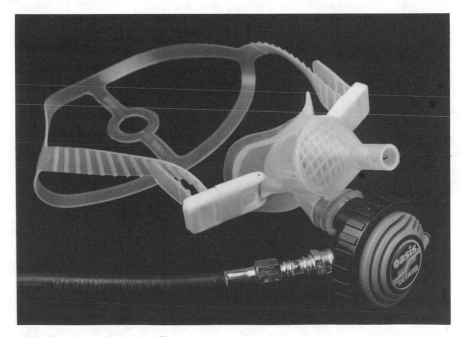

Figure 13-5. AquaVox.™ *(Courtesy AquaVoc, Inc.)*

instructors and students alike. Recently some underwater talking devices have been developed to aid underwater communication.

Selected References

Eastman, N. and Landrum, G. *Underwater Communication: Hand Signals for Scuba Divers*, 2nd ed. Princeton, N.J.: Princeton Book Company, Publishers, 1984.

Fead, L. *Easy Diver*. Crestline, Calif.: Deepstar Publications, 1977.

Riekehof, L.L. *The Joy of Signing*. Springfield, Mo.: Gospel Publishing House, 1978.

Chapter 14

~~~~~~

Continuing Underwater Education and Specialty Diving

Your certification card allows you to become acquainted with the wonders of sport diving. Although your open-water course may be comprehensive in content, it merely opens the door to numerous opportunities in scuba diving. The certification card you receive at the end of your course should be considered much like the learner's permit you received when learning how to drive an automobile. Additional underwater training can be gained through supervised underwater experiences. Underwater photography, night diving, underwater archaeology, wreck diving, ice diving, and cave diving are just a few underwater opportunites which your basic "C" card allows you to pursue.

14.1 Continuing Underwater Education

Before becoming involved in supplemental scuba training programs, basic divers should broaden their base of education by receiving training in lifesaving, cardiopulmonary resuscitation, first aid, and use of small craft. These supporting areas not only make divers more competent, but also instill confidence by training divers to respond appropriately in a crisis. The American Heart Association, the American Red Cross, the YMCA, and the U.S. Coast Guard are good sources for this training.

14.1.1 RESCUE DIVING TECHNIQUES COURSE

Perhaps the most valuable diving course one can participate in following the initial certification course is a Scuba diver rescue course. It not only teaches self-rescue techniques but instills confidence and prepares divers to rescue others. The rescue course is a prerequisite for many other advanced courses, including leadership courses. The course covers rescue, self-rescue, resuscitation, and defensive diving skills.

14.2 Advanced Scuba Diving Courses

Specific scuba diving courses are available to train sport divers beyond the basic or beginning diving level. These diving courses emphasize general diving skills and techniques which are applicable in a variety of underwater settings. Most divers refer to these courses as advanced open-water or sport diving courses. They include such skills as underwater navigation, search and recovery, scuba lifesaving and rescue techniques, deep diving, and night diving skills. The advantage of enrolling in advanced open-water courses is not only the added experience gained, but also the expert instruction offered and the extra safety provided by the instructor.

Upon mastering a repertoire of sport diving skills, divers may then enroll in advanced specialty diving courses in areas such as cave diving, ice diving, wreck diving, underwater photography, underwater archaeology, and others. The most popular organizations offering these courses in the United States are the YMCA, the National Association of Underwater Instructors, the Professional Association of Diving Instructors, and the National Association of Skin Diving Schools.

For divers who have considerable diving experience and who enjoy teaching, some organizations offer a progression of courses from teaching assistant to scuba instructor. Scuba instructor candidates must display expertise in three basic areas: diving skill, diving knowledge, and teaching methodology.

14.2.1 INDEPENDENT EXPERIENCE

Divers can gain considerable experience on their own by assisting in basic classes offered at local universities, dive shops, and YMCAs. These alternatives allow the diver to meet new diving partners and dive within the jurisdiction of the presiding instructor, again promoting safety. Joining dive clubs and dive shop groups encourages diving by offering planned, supervised dive trips along with providing dive partners.

Gaining diving experience independently of dive shops, universities, and dive clubs is another means of continuing the underwater education process but may not be so easy or safe. Diving with informal groups is often somewhat disorganized and at times can be unsafe if dive masters and safety teams are not established. Social diving, where six or so divers simply jump into the water to dive without proper planning, may be fun but can also be extremely dangerous. All newly certified divers would be wise to consider themselves as novice divers until they have successfully completed a dozen open-water scuba dives in a variety of environments. Novice divers are strongly urged to dive under the direct supervision of a certified scuba instructor or dive master.

The purpose of this chapter is *not* to teach divers how to perform scuba dives which require special skills, but to stress that these dives require unique training and supervision and probably differ significantly from the open-water environment experienced during the basic certification course. Of vital importance is the transition from basic scuba diver to specialty sport diver through supervised experience.

14.3 Surf Penetration

The decision to penetrate surf in scuba gear should be made only after careful inspection of wave action, currents, potential hazards, and consideration of diver's ability. Chapter 4 should be reviewed for the mechanics of wave and surf action. Because passing through surf requires skill and prudence, perhaps the best way to handle heavy surf is to avoid it. The awkward and cumbersome state imposed by scuba gear on divers is significantly augmented by the underestimated power of surf (Figure 14-1).

When the decision to enter the water through surf has been made, the following points should be remembered:

1. Establish a dive master, beach attendant, and safety team.
2. Have all gear on and working, including mask, fins, gloves, and accessories, before actually beginning the dive.
3. Passage through the surf should be made as quickly as possible; do not dally or hesitate in the surf.

Figure 14-1. Surf. (© Paul Tzimoulis, 1981)

4. Slightly inflate the B.C.D. before entering the water.

5. Place the regulator in the mouth to keep it free of sand.

6. Shuffle backward into the surf with the dive partner, holding hands whenever possible; look over the shoulder for oncoming breakers.

7. Time the sets of breaking waves and work with the water rather than fighting against it.

8. When addressing breaking waves from the rear, stop, crouch, tuck the chin, and allow the wave to pass overhead.

9. When addressing breaking waves from the front, deflate the B.C.D., dive under the wave, and stay close to the bottom.

10. When exiting from surf, crawl on hands and knees.

11. After exiting the water, do not remove any gear until well up on the beach above the high-water mark.

14.4 Boat Diving

Although many divers use boats exclusively for dive trips, some experienced divers have never even been on a boat. Boat diving generally makes diving easier and more enjoyable, but unfortunately is more

Figure 14-2. Dive boat. (Courtesy Hall's Diving Center)

expensive. Boat diving does require certain rules, techniques, and etiquette to ensure diver safety. In addition to the basic boat diving techniques, some techniques depend on the idiosyncrasies of different boats. The best way of learning the rules of a particular diving vessel is to speak to the captain prior to the boat's departure. Large, spacious, flat-bottomed boats with stable diving platforms attached to the stern are preferred by sport divers (Figure 14-2).

Before departure, divers should remember to

- arrive at least 15 minutes early;
- appoint a dive master, bottom-time keeper, and safety team;
- introduce themselves to the captain and acquaint themselves with the boat and its rules;
- secure all scuba tanks and keep all gear neatly in one location;
- locate life jackets, fire extinguishers, rescue equipment, and first-aid kit; and

- review emergency procedures with the boat captain and safety team.

While underway, divers should

- keep the entry point clear of divers and equipment;
- ask the captain for the recommended entry;
- check for currents prior to entering the water and set a trail-line (100–200 feet) with a surface float attached;
- display the diver's flag;
- inform the dive master of the dive plan and check the No-Decompression Tables;
- be certain that the anchor is set and secure;
- use the anchor line for descents and ascents—each dive should begin and end at the anchor line;
- when diving, stay close to the boat;
- allow only one diver at a time on the ladder; and
- have the dive master or boat captain take a visual roll call before and after each dive.

The following rules of etiquette should be observed:

- determine if tipping the captain and mates is expected.
- never place a loaded speargun on board a boat.
- keep all gear in a dive bag.
- help to tidy up the boat on return to the dock.
- use the leeside (downwind) rail when seasick, not the bathroom.
- do not throw trash overboard.
- do not linger at entry, exit, and anchoring points.

14.5 Night Diving

Diving at night is so fascinating that many scuba divers actually prefer night diving to day diving. Much of the marine life in the ocean is nocturnal, that is, they are more active at night. Conversely, the active life forms witnessed during the day often sleep at night, enabling night divers to approach these creatures easily and touch them. Perhaps the most stimulating attraction of night diving is the color. When bright lights are used underwater at night, all the colors of the spectrum are magnificently illuminated. This is especially true in tropical waters where many colorful corals and sponges become more exposed during their nocturnal feeding. Even the boat ride to the night dive site can be spectacular; the intensity of the stars shining at night is matched only by the phosphorescence in the water.

Sensory deprivation is a significant stressor, as indicated in Chapter 5. Because night diving drastically reduces the sense of sight through limited visibility, it is easy to understand why some divers become fearful of night diving. However, with the aid of proper lighting both on the surface and underwater, good dive planning, and recommended night diving techniques, this type of specialty diving can become most intriguing.

14.5.1 LIGHTING

Underwater diving lights: The safety and enjoyment of night diving are significantly augmented by powerful and reliable underwater lights. Dive lights must be waterproof and rugged. Three items must be checked routinely to increase the reliability of the underwater lights. These are the O-ring seals, the batteries, and the light bulbs. When an underwater light fails or provides poor illumination, usually one of these items is responsible; therefore they should be replaced frequently.

Before purchasing an underwater light, several varieties should be tested in a darkened room for brightness, width of the light beam, and handling ability. Many large, broad-beamed diving lights provide good illumination underwater, but they may be too cumbersome for a diver to control underwater.

A nice way of keeping track of each other while diving underwater is to attach a chemical glow stick to the top of each diver's tank. These light sticks are very inexpensive and add an interesting effect to the dive.

Shore lights: A major problem associated with night dives originating from shore is getting lost on the return to land after the dive. One way to circumvent this problem is to ensure adequate and reliable lighting on land. Night dives should not be conducted without shore personnel, in addition to the safety team, to maintain good lighting.

A campfire and directional lanterns are best for most night dives. At least two directional lanterns are required. These lights should be placed in a line perpendicular to the shoreline, with the lantern closest to the water sitting lower than the light in the rear. Several lights are also needed for suiting up prior to the dive. Kerosene lanterns and inexpensive "cold" light tubes are ideal for land purposes. Diving lights must be reserved for *underwater use only* to conserve the batteries. Good lighting must also be provided at the entry and exit points on land to avoid tripping.

Boat lighting: Diving from a boat during a night dive excursion offers many advantages. It eliminates long surface swims, enhances entries and exits, and prevents divers from getting lost by having the boat remain directly above the diving group. These benefits are only available, however, when the diving vessel is properly lighted, above and below the surface of the water.

The deck of the dive boat must be well lighted, particularly the entry and exit points, the suiting-up area, and the bottom-time recording station. Several strong lights must be mounted on the boat to accomplish this; moving these lights during the dive only creates confusion. Lights must also be secured on the boat under the surface of the water. Most importantly, a bright, flashing strobe light should be attached to the bottom of the boat and divers should never lose sight of this light while diving. It is helpful to have a light attached to the anchor line, enabling divers to find the line for a controlled ascent at the end of the dive.

14.5.2 PLANNING

When planning to conduct a night dive, several considerations must be taken into account:

- Select several competent nondivers to tend the land or boat lights; this is perhaps the most important consideration in night diving and must be taken seriously.
- Select a dive master, bottom-time keeper, and safety team.
- Dive only when environmental conditions are ideal; calm water is a must.
- Dive in a location that is familiar to the group, preferably an area that has been experienced underwater that same day, during daylight hours.

- Check all lights and carry spares; each diver must have a light because sharing one light between two divers is unsafe.

- Prepare all diving equipment *before dark* to eliminate confusion and to speed up the suiting-up process.

- Buddy-up novice night divers with experienced night divers.

14.5.3 TECHNIQUES

Underwater communication and relocating the exit points are the primary techniques which must be mastered for safe night diving. Although other considerations are important, these two are of the utmost concern. Safe night diving techniques are as follows:

- Use a compass to find the coordinates of the underwater site and return route before entering the water.

- Use buoyed lines for safe, controlled ascents and descents, whenever possible.

- Use a combination of hand signals and light signals for nocturnal underwater communication; the underwater light must never be flashed in the diving partner's face.

- Use the following signals with the light for underwater communication.

    1. *O.K., all is well*—Make slow, big circles with the light.

    2. *Attention*—Quickly shake the light from side to side.

    3. *Something is wrong*—Quickly shake the light up and down.

- Shine the light to the left or the right of the diver's chest when using hand signals so that the sender can transmit the desired hand signal.

- Do not use the underwater light as a toy rather than a tool; overusing the light will eventually lead to poor illumination.

- Constantly monitor air supply, depth, and direction, with particular attention devoted to land or boat orientation.

- Wear wrist lanyards with dive lights to prevent loss.

In summary, night diving can be a thrilling experience. Some divers perceive night diving as a puzzle, where the underwater light only reveals one piece at a time, and the total picture is not visualized until the end of the dive; hence the challenge of night diving.

14.6 Advanced Specialty Diving

Advanced forms of specialty diving require sophisticated equipment, planning, and skills surpassing those demanded by other types of diving. Perhaps the challenge to advanced specialty divers originates in the fact that most people would not even *think* of penetrating these exotic underwater environs. Cave diving, ice diving, and wreck diving are typical examples of advanced specialty diving. The common thread connecting these specialty dives is that they do not provide the luxury of a direct and unobstructed escape to the surface. Getting lost and running out of air or becoming positively buoyant and being pinned to an underwater ceiling are the two greatest menaces.

At first glance, advanced specialty dives would appear to be extremely dangerous. However, after listening to an expert cave, ice, or wreck diver, one quickly learns that these specialty dives are not only fascinating and rewarding but are also safe, *when properly planned*. However, exploring these unique environments without a licensed specialty instructor can be catastrophic. A certified course of instruction in an advanced specialty area is the *only* way through which a scuba diver should investigate these astonishing underwater worlds. In addition to the normal scuba diving gear, specialty divers require the use of alternate air systems and safety lines and reels which demand much practice to master. Other forms of advanced specialty diving, such as underwater photography, archaeology, and research, while not as dangerous, also require expert instruction.

Selected References

Fead, L. *Easy Diver*. Crestline, Calif.: Deepstar Publications, 1977.

Gravers, D., and Wohlers, R. *PADI Advanced Dive Manual*. Santa Ana, Calif.: Professional Association of Diving Instructors, 1980.

Chapters 12–14 Review

The instructor should correct the student's answers, record the results, and return them to the student. Both teacher and student should sign after the last question.

REVIEW QUESTIONS	ANSWERS
1. List three different forms of underwater communication.	1. _____ _____ _____
2. Demonstrate the hand signals for the following messages: • Level-off • Buddy-up • Slow down • Where is . . . ? • Repeat • Stop! • Low on air • O.K. • Buddy-breathe • Boat	2. _____ _____ _____ _____ _____ _____ _____ _____ _____ _____
3. Identify two advantages of using a buddy-line.	3. _____ _____
4. List three examples of boat diving etiquette.	4. _____ _____ _____
5. List three different types of lighting required for night diving.	5. _____ _____

REVIEW QUESTIONS	ANSWERS
6. List three types of specialty dives that require advanced training.	6. _____ _____ _____
7. List three substances that can deteriorate rubber masks, fins, and snorkels.	7. _____ _____ _____
8. What should be applied to all wet suit zippers?	8. _____
9. How should the regulator be stored when not being used?	9. _____
10. How many psi should remain in a stored scuba tank?	10. _____
11. After being used in salt water, all equipment should be rinsed in _____.	11. _____

I have graded, recorded, and returned this student's responses.

Instructor's Signature:

_____

Date:

_____

I have seen my corrected review questions and now know the appropriate answers.
Note: The answer sheet may either be taken out or retained with this book.

Student's Signature:

_____

Date:

_____

Chapter 15

Scuba Math

The following chapter includes two separate treatments of scuba diving calculations used for understanding underwater physics.

John Zumbado, a YMCA instructor and expert in this field of diving, explains diving physics through a series of formulas and calculations. Specifically, he teaches the reader to calculate changes in pressure, volume, breathing rate, buoyancy, heat loss, sound, and light which occur underwater at varying depths. John's excellent presentation is a formal one, being complete and comprehensive.

Sid Ragona, Ph.D., a NAUI instructor and Penn State researcher, presents pressure, air consumption, and bouyancy calculations in a less formal yet very practical way. Both treatments of this technical aspect of scuba diving will definitely assist the reader in better understanding of underwater physics.

Scuba Calculation by John Zumbado

15.1 Pressure

Definition: Force per unit area.

Gauge: Pressure that is measured with gauge that is referenced to zero on the surface.

Absolute: Pressure that is measured with a gauge that is referenced to zero 60 mi. above the surface. This gauge will read 14.7 psi on the surface.

Ambient: Pressure that is felt by the diver. Equals absolute pressure on the surface. Equals absolute pressure *plus* the pressure due to the water for the depth the diver is at.

Hydrostatic: Pressure due to the water alone for the depth the diver is at.

Units:

— 1   ATM

— 14.7 PSIA

— 33   FSWA

$$P = D + 33 \text{ (fswa)}$$ (Use 34 for fresh water)

Partial Pressure:

— Pressure due to the percentage of a gas present in a gas mixture.

— For example, pressure due to oxygen assuming 20% air mixture:

$$P_{02} = (P).20$$

EXAMPLES:

1. What is the partial pressure of 0_2 at 132 ft. of salt water?

   $P = (D + 33).2 = (132 + 33) = (165).2 = 33$ fswa

   $P = (33)\dfrac{\text{fswa}}{33} = 1$ atm

   $P = (33)$fswa $\times .445 = 14.7$ psia

   $33/14.7 = 0.445$ salt water, and $34/14.7 = 0.432$ fresh

2. The maximum limit for diving using a pure oxygen is 25 ft. in salt water, to prevent oxygen poisoning. Find the equivalent depth for diving with an air supply having 20% oxygen.

   $$P = (D + 33)x.2$$
   $$[100\% \ O_2 \text{ pres. @25 ft.}] = [\text{Equivalent pres. @ D ft.}]$$
   $$(25 + 33) = (D + 33)x.2$$
   $$D = \frac{(25 + 33)}{.2} - 33 = 257$$

15.2 Volumes (Boyle's Law)

On descent volumes get smaller.

On ascent volumes get bigger.

The deeper you go the more air you need to fill your lungs to the same volume at ambient pressure.

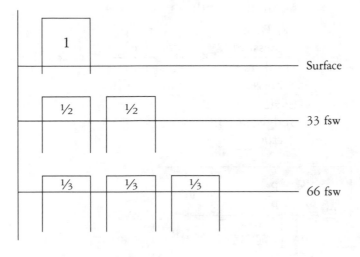

$$V = (\frac{D + 33}{D + 33}) \times V \qquad \text{(use 34 for fresh water)}$$

EXAMPLE:

How much will a 10 pint lung capacity have to expand to cause an air embolism if it is known that damage can happen in 4 ft. of water— shallow end of the pool.

$$V = (\frac{D = 34}{D = 34}) \times V \Rightarrow V = (\frac{\Box + 34}{\Box \mid + 34}) \times 10 \text{ pints} \rightarrow \begin{matrix} \text{vol. of} \\ \text{lungs} \end{matrix}$$

$$V = (\frac{4 + 34}{0 + 34}) \times 10 = (\frac{38}{34}) \times 10 = 11.52 \text{ pints}$$

15.3 Time Underwater

Less air available if gauge reading is low.

Less air available if tank is filled hot versus water temperature.

Less air available the deeper you go.

$$T = \frac{\text{Amount of available air}}{\begin{bmatrix} \text{Fudge factor due} \\ \text{to Boyle's law to} \\ \text{bring breathing} \\ \text{rate from surface} \\ \text{to dive depth} \end{bmatrix} \times \begin{bmatrix} \text{Breathing} \\ \text{Rate} \end{bmatrix}}$$

$$T = \frac{\dfrac{\text{Tank}}{\text{Tank rated}}_{\text{pressure}}^{\text{pressure}} \times \dfrac{\text{Abs. temp.}}{\text{Abs. tank}}_{\text{temp. at fill}}^{\text{of dive}} \times \text{tank volume}}{\begin{matrix}\text{Boyle's} \\ \text{fudge} \times \text{BR} \\ \text{factor}\end{matrix}}$$

$$T = \frac{\dfrac{P}{P} \times \dfrac{T}{T} \times V}{\left[\dfrac{D + 33}{D + 33}\right] \times BR}$$

EXAMPLES:

1. Find how long a scuba tank will last underwater at 99 ft. under the following conditions:

   a. steel tank of 71.2 cu. ft. volume at a rated pressure of 2250 psi + 10%.
   b. Tank filled to 2000 psi at 100 degrees F.
   c. Dive in fresh water at 50 degrees F.
   d. Your breathing rate is 2 cu. ft. per min.

$$T = \frac{\dfrac{P}{P} \times \dfrac{T}{T}}{\left[\dfrac{D + 33}{D + 33}\right] \times BR} = \frac{\dfrac{2000}{2475} \times \dfrac{(460 + 50)}{(460 + 100)} \times 71.2}{\left[\dfrac{99 + 34}{0 + 34}\right] \times 2}$$

$$T = \frac{.81 \times .91 \times 71.2}{3.91 \times 2} = \frac{52.40}{7.82} = 6.70 \text{ min.}$$

2. Find out how long an 80 cu. ft. aluminum tank will last under the same conditions.

$$T = \frac{\dfrac{P}{P} \times \dfrac{T}{T} \times V}{\left[\dfrac{D + 33}{D + 33}\right] \times BR} = \frac{\dfrac{2000}{3000} \times \dfrac{(460 + 50)}{(460 + 100)} \times 80}{\left[\dfrac{99 + 34}{0 + 34}\right] \times 2}$$

$$T = \frac{.67 \times .91 \times 80}{3.91 \times 2} = \frac{48.57}{7.82} = 6.21 \text{ min.}$$

NOTE: These calculations do not include any reserve psi you might elect to choose. If you want to return from the dive with 500 psi, you should use 2000 − 500 = 1500 for all the above calculations.

15.4 Breathing Rate (BR)

Easily determined from time underwater formula.

When calculating ignore temperature effects and for shallow depths use an average depth that represents the dive depth.

Units are cu. ft./min.

Units in psi/min., while seeming to simplify the time under water, are valid only for a given tank used.

$$BR = \frac{\dfrac{P - P}{P} \times V}{\left[\dfrac{D + 33}{D + 33}\right] \times T}$$ (Use 34 for fresh water)

EXAMPLE:

Calculate your breathing rate from a quarry dive *averaging* 10 ft. Length of dive is 48 min. Your starting tank pressure was 2200 psi and your exit pressure 700 psi. You were using a steel tank of 71.2 cu. ft.

$$BR = \frac{\dfrac{P - P}{P}}{\left[\dfrac{D + 33}{D + 33}\right] \times T} = \frac{\dfrac{2200 - 700}{2475} \times 71.2}{\left[\dfrac{10 + 34}{0 + 34}\right] \times 48}$$

$$= \frac{\frac{1500}{2475} \times 71.2}{\left[\frac{44}{34}\right] \times 48}$$

$$BR = \frac{.61 \times 71.2}{1.29 \times 48} = \frac{43.15}{62.12} = .69 \text{ cu. ft./min.}$$

Breathing rate (br) in *psi per minute,* only for one *particular tank,* simplifies the time underwater equation to:

$$T = \frac{\frac{T}{T} \times P}{\left[\frac{D+33}{D+33}\right] \times br} \qquad \text{(Use 34 for fresh water)}$$

since

$$BR = \frac{br}{\dfrac{P_{Rated}}{V}}$$

EXAMPLE:

Find how long will a tank last a diver using 50 psi per minute out of an 80 cu. ft. tank, filled with 1000 psi, while diving in 30 ft of salt water. Assume no temperature effects.

$$T = \frac{\frac{T}{T} \times P}{\left[\frac{D+33}{D+33}\right] \times br} = \frac{1000}{\left[\frac{30+33}{0+33}\right] \times 50} = \frac{1000}{\frac{66}{33} \times 50}$$

$$= 10 \text{ min.}$$

Note that if this diver uses a 71.2 cu. ft. tank, his *br* will be different, and he must know what his *br* for a 71.2 tank is.

15.5 Buoyancy

1 Cu. Ft. of Water Weighs:

64 lbs. (salt water)

62.4 lbs. (fresh water)

Archimedes' Principle: A body immersed in a liquid will be buoyed by a force equal to the weight of the liquid.

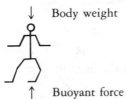

↓ Body weight

↑ Buoyant force

Buoyancy Considerations:

— If body weight more than water weight—body sinks

— If body weight less than water weight—body floats

— If body weight equal to water weight—body is neutrally buoyant

EXAMPLES:

1. A diver weighs 125 lbs. and displaces 2 cu ft. of salt water. How much weight, if any, does she need to be neutrally buoyant?

   ↓ Body weight = 125 lbs.

   ↑ Buoyant force = 2 × 64 = 128 lbs.

   Since 125 < 128 body will float, and diver will need 128 − 125 = 3 lbs. to achieve neutral buoyancy.

   Note that this diver will sink in fresh water since weight of fresh water is 2 × 62.4 = 124.8 lbs. Therefore, the diver will be 124.8 − 125 = − 0.2 lbs., considered 2.6 lbs. negative.

2. You want to lift a treasure chest weighing 320 lbs. when submerged in salt water. Find the minimum volume that you must expand a lifting bag to lift the chest. Neglect weight of ropes and bag, and assume you are diving in salt water.

   $$\text{Volume} = \frac{\text{body weight in water}}{\text{water weight of 1 cu. ft.}} = \frac{320}{64} = 5 \text{ cu. ft.}$$

3. You want to lift an outboard motor from 66 ft., in salt water. Using procedure of Example 2 you find that 4 cu. ft. of air must be put in the lifting bag at 66 ft. How much air (volume) must be available from the surface?

$$V = \left[\frac{D + 33}{D + 33}\right] \times V = \left[\frac{66 + 33}{0 + 33}\right] \times 4 = 3 \times 4 = 12 \text{ cu. ft.}$$

15.6 Heat Transfer

Diving texts say that water absorbs 25 times more heat than air. To prove this statement consider the heat absorption problem as follows:

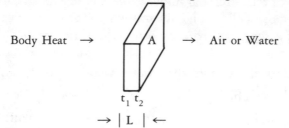

Body Heat $\rightarrow$ A $\rightarrow$ Air or Water

$t_1\ t_2$

$\rightarrow | L | \leftarrow$

For this condition:

Heat Loss $= \dfrac{K\ A\ (t_2 - t_1)}{L}$, where K is the coefficient of thermal conductivity.

Heat loss due to water $= X$ (Heat loss due to air)

Solving for X, $X = \dfrac{\text{Heat loss due to water}}{\text{Heat loss due to air}} = \dfrac{\dfrac{K_{water}\ A\ (t_2 - t_1)}{L}}{\dfrac{K_{air}\ A\ (t_2 - t_1)}{L}}$

but for small Ls $X = \dfrac{K_{water}}{K_{air}} = \dfrac{0.343}{0.014} = 24.500$

Units are $\dfrac{mW}{cm\ (\text{degrees K})}$

Conduction: Heat transfer from molecules at one temperature (t_1) to other molecules at another temperature (t_2), as noted in the heat transfer problem, and the flow is from higher temperatures (the body) to a lower temperatures (the water).

Convection: Heat transfer from one place to another due to motion of a hot material. A circulatory motion occurs in liquids (water), due to variation in liquid densities. This motion combines hot and cold liquid molecules, eventually warming the cold molecules.

Radiation: Is the continuous emission of energy from a body's surface. The sun's energy reaches us, and because we are not transparent to this energy, we absorb it and is converted to heat.

Sound and Hearing: Sound travels at 1090 ft./sec. in air and in water between 4800 and 5100 ft/sec, depending on water temperature.

Difficult to tell direction underwater, because our hearing depends on the slowness of the sound velocity in air. Our brain can detect the direction of a sound source by noting the time it takes the sound to reach each of our ears. This time is shorter because the sound velocity is higher in water.

The brain, however, can detect direction underwater, with difficulty due to reduced sound levels, by detecting pressure differences through the head tissue.

15.7 Optics and Light

Average Absorption of Colors in Water

Color	Absorption	
	Begin	End (ft)
Red	10	30
Orange	35	55
Yellow	60	85
Green	90	110
Blue	—	—
Violet	30	95

Vision Underwater:

Objects Appear	Ratio	Percent
CLOSER	$\frac{3}{4}$	25
BIGGER	$\frac{4}{3}$	33.33

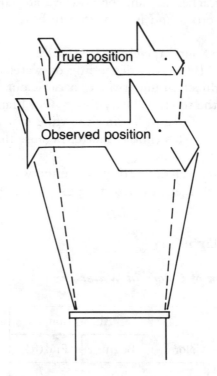

True position

Observed position

Scuba Math by Sid Ragona

For detailed dive planning, a sound knowledge of diving mathematics is extremely helpful. In this section, a series of diving calculations is presented along with examples and solutions. This section is divided into three categories: pressure calculations, air consumption calculations, and buoyancy calculations.

15.8 Pressure Calculations

The absolute pressure at sea level is 14.7 pounds per square inch (psi) This value of 14.7 psi is also referred to as one atmosphere (atm).

$$1 \text{ atm } = 14.7 \text{ psi}$$

As a diver descends, the pressure increases by one atmosphere with every 33 feet of sea water (34 feet in fresh water). This is summarized in the following table:

Depth	atms	psi
sea level	1	14.7
33	2	29.4
66	3	44.1
99	4	58.8

To calculate the absolute pressure in psi at depths other than increments of one atm, we use FORMULA 1:

$$\text{psi at depth} = 14.7 \text{ psi} + \frac{14.7 \text{ psi} \times \text{depth in feet}}{33 \text{ feet}}$$

EXAMPLE 1:

Calculate the psi at depths of 10, 26, and 44 feet.

Solutions:

1. 10 feet: $14.7 \text{ psi} + \dfrac{14.7 \text{ psi} \times 10 \text{ft.}}{33 \text{ ft.}} = 19.2 \text{ psi}$

2. 26 feet: $14.7 \text{ psi} + \dfrac{14.7 \text{ psi} \times 26 \text{ft.}}{33 \text{ ft.}} = 26.3 \text{ psi}$

3. 44 feet: $14.7 \text{ psi} + \dfrac{14.7 \text{ psi} \times 44 \text{ft.}}{33 \text{ ft.}} = 34.3 \text{ psi}$

In order to calculate the absolute pressure in atmospheres at different depths we use FORMULA 2:

$$\text{Absolute pressure (atm)} = 1.0 \text{ atm} + \frac{\text{depth in feet}}{33 \text{ feet}}$$

EXAMPLE 2:

Calculate the absolute pressure in atmospheres at depths of 10, 33, and 87 feet.

Solutions:

1. 10 feet: $1.0 + \dfrac{10 \text{ ft.}}{33 \text{ ft.}} = 1.3 \text{ atm}$

2. 33 feet: $1.0 + \dfrac{33 \text{ ft.}}{33 \text{ ft.}} = 2.0 \text{ atm}$

3. 87 feet: $1.0 + \dfrac{87 \text{ ft.}}{33 \text{ ft.}} = 3.6 \text{ atm}$

15.9 Air Consumption Calculations

Air consumption rate can be calculated by dividing the psi used in the scuba tank by the time it took to use it as expressed in FORMULA 3:

$$\text{air consumed} = \frac{\text{psi used}}{\text{time in mins.}}$$

Air consumption is directly proportional to absolute pressure, thus the deeper a diver descends, the greater the air consumed. The commonly used yard stick in air consumption calculations is the Surface Air Consumption rate or SAC rate. This is the amount of air used at sea level. Knowing the average depth of the dive and the psi used during a given period of time, the SAC rate can be calculated by using FORMULA 4:

$$\text{SAC Rate} = \frac{\text{psi used} / \text{time (mins.)} \times 33 \text{ ft.}}{\text{average depth} + 33 \text{ ft.}}$$

EXAMPLE 3:

A buddy team dives at 50 feet for 10 minutes. Diver A uses 400 psi and Diver B uses 500 psi. What are the SAC rates for Diver A and Diver B?

Solutions:

1. Diver A: $\dfrac{400 \text{ psi} / 10 \text{ mins.} \times 33 \text{ ft.}}{50 \text{ ft.} + 33 \text{ ft.}} = \dfrac{40 \text{ psi} / \text{min.} \times 33 \text{ ft.}}{83 \text{ ft.}}$

   $= 15.9 \text{ psi/min.}$

2. Diver B: $\dfrac{500 \text{ psi} / 10 \text{ mins.} \times 33 \text{ ft.}}{50 \text{ ft.} + 33 \text{ ft.}} = \dfrac{50 \text{ psi} / \text{min.} \times 33 \text{ ft.}}{83 \text{ ft.}}$

   $= 19.9 \text{ psi/min.}$

On the other hand if a diver's SAC rate is already known, the air consumption rate at depth can be calculated by using FORMULA 5:

$$\text{psi/min. consumed} = \text{SAC rate} \times \frac{33 \text{ ft.} + \text{depth in ft.}}{33 \text{ ft.}}$$

EXAMPLE 4:

A diver has a SAC rate of 11 psi/min. What will the diver's air consumption rate be at 25 feet and how much will be used in 30 minutes?

Solution:

$$\text{psi/min. consumed} = 11 \text{ psi/min.} \times \frac{33 \text{ ft.} + 25 \text{ ft.}}{33 \text{ ft.}} = \frac{11 \times 58}{33 \text{ ft.}}$$

$$= 19.3 \text{ psi/min.}$$

in 30 minutes the diver would use 30 min. × 19.3 psi/min. = 580 psi

EXAMPLE 5:

If a diver uses 2000 psi in 30 minutes at a depth of 50 feet, what is the diver's SAC rate and how much air would the diver consume per minute at 30 feet, and 20 feet.

Solution:

First determine SAC rate using Formula 4:

$$\text{SAC rate} = \frac{2000 \text{ psi/30 min.} \times 33 \text{ ft.}}{50 \text{ ft.} + 33 \text{ ft.}} = \frac{66.7 \text{ psi/min.} \times 33 \text{ ft.}}{83 \text{ ft.}}$$

$$= 26.5 \text{ psi/min.}$$

Then using Formula 5:

1. 30 feet: psi/min. = $26.5 \text{ psi/min.} \times \dfrac{33 \text{ ft.} + 30 \text{ ft.}}{33 \text{ ft.}}$ = 50.6 psi/min.

2. 20 feet: psi/min. = $26.5 \text{ psi/min.} \times \dfrac{33 \text{ ft.} + 20 \text{ ft.}}{33 \text{ ft.}}$ = 42.6 psi/min.

EXAMPLE 6:

If a diver in cold water uses 2500 psi in 15 minutes at 60 feet, how long would the same amount of air last at 25 feet?

Solution:

First determine the SAC rate using Formula 4:

$$\text{SAC rate} = \frac{2500 \text{ psi/15 min.} \times 33 \text{ ft.}}{60 \text{ ft.} + 33 \text{ ft.}} = 59.1 \text{ psi/min.}$$

Then using formula 5, determine consumption rate at 25 feet:

$$\text{psi/min. consumed} = 59.1 \text{ psi/min.} \times \frac{33 \text{ ft.} + 20 \text{ ft.}}{33 \text{ ft.}} \quad 94.9 \text{ psi/min.}$$

Therefore, if the diver uses 94.9 psi/min at 20 feet, 2500 psi would last:

$$2500 \text{ psi}/94.9 \text{ psi/min.} = 26.3 \text{ minutes.}$$

15.10 Air Consumption Rate with Different Tank Sizes

A diver's air consumption rate when expressed in psi/min is dependent on the size of the scuba tank used. Using different sized tanks results in different air consumption rates. In order to convert air consumption rates from one tank size to another we use FORMULA 6:

$$\text{psi/min for Tank 2} = \text{psi/min for Tank 1} \times \frac{\text{vol. of Tank 1}}{\text{vol. of Tank 2}}$$

EXAMPLE 7:

A diver has an air consumption rate of 12 psi/min. when using a steel 72 cu. ft. tank. What would the diver's air consumption rate be using an aluminum 80 cu. ft. tank?

Solution:

$$\text{psi/min. for Tank 1} = 12 \text{ psi/min.}$$
$$\text{Volume of Tank 1} = 72 \text{ cu. ft.}$$
$$\text{Volume of Tank 2} = 80 \text{ cu. ft.}$$

$$\text{Therefore, psi/min for Tank 2} = 12 \text{ psi/min.} \times \frac{72 \text{ cu. ft.}}{80 \text{ cu. ft.}}$$

$$= 10.8 \text{ psi/min}$$

EXAMPLE 8:

A diver uses 1000 psi in 30 minutes at 20 feet when using a 80-cu ft tank. How many psi could the diver have consumed on the same dive using a 50-cu ft tank?

Solution:

Air consumed for Tank 1 = 1000 psi
        Volume of Tank 1 = 80 cu. ft.
        Volume of Tank 2 = 50 cu. ft.

$$\text{Air consumed for Tank 2} = 1000 \text{ psi} \times \frac{80 \text{ cu. ft.}}{50 \text{ cu. ft.}} = 1600 \text{ psi}$$

15.11 Buoyancy Calculations

The weight of an object and its volume are the two factors that determine whether the object will float, sink, or remain neutrally buoyant. The dry weight of an object exerts a downward force, while the weight of water displaced by an object provides an upward force. Therefore, if the weight of water displaced by an object is greater than the dry weight of the object, the object will float. Conversely, if the weight of water displaced is less than the weight of the object, the object will sink.

EXAMPLE 9:

An object with a volume of one cubic foot weighs 57 lbs. How much extra weight is needed to make the object neutrally buoyant in sea water and fresh water? (one cubic foot of sea water = 64 lbs.; one cubic foot of fresh water = 62.4 lbs.)

Solution:

In the case of sea water the upward force provided by the water displaced is 64.0 lbs. and the downward force provided by the weight of the object is 57 lbs. Therefore, 64.0 lbs. − 57.0 lbs. = 7.0 lbs. of upwards force, meaning an additional 7 lbs. of weight needs to be added to make the object neutral. In the case of fresh water, 62.4 lbs. − 57 lbs. = 5.4, therefore an additional 5.4 lbs. of weight needs to be added to obtain neutral buoyancy.

EXAMPLE 10:

What weight of sea water does a lift bag need to displace in order to lift an anchor with a dry weight of 67 pounds and a volume of 0.18 cubic feet?

Solution:

$$\text{upward force} = 0.18 \text{ cu.ft.} \times 64.0 \text{ lbs/cu.ft.} = 11.52 \text{ pounds}$$
$$\text{downward force} = 67 \text{ pounds}$$

Therefore, the weight in water equals the downward force minus the upward force.

Weight in water   = 67 lbs — 11.52 lbs. = 55.48 lbs.

EXAMPLE 11:

A propeller has a dry weight of 260 pounds, and a volume of 2.8 cubic feet. How many 50-pound lift bags are needed to lift the propeller from the bottom of a fresh water lake?

Solution:

upward force = 2.8 cu.ft. × 62.4 cu.ft. = 174.72 lbs.
downward force = 260 lbs.

Therefore, the weight in water equals 260 lbs. — 174.72 lbs. = 85.28 lbs. The upward force provided by lift bags needs to be greater than 85.28 lbs. so two 50-lb. lift bags are required.

EXAMPLE 12:

A diver with all his equipment weighs 188 lbs. when neutrally buoyant in fresh water. What is the volume of the diver and his equipment and how much additional weight is required to make this diver neutrally buoyant in the ocean?

Solution:

1. If the diver is neutral in fresh water then the upward force equals the downward force of 188 lbs. The volume of water that needs to be displaced to provide an upward force of 188 lbs. is 188.0 lbs/62.4 lbs/cu.ft. = 3 cu.ft.

2. In the ocean, the upward force on the diver is equal to the weight of ocean displaced; thus 3 cu.ft. × 64 lbs/cu.ft. = 192 lbs.

192 lbs. — 188 lbs. = 4 lbs.

Therefore, the diver needs 4 additional pounds of weight to be neutrally buoyant in the ocean.

Appendix A

"Bubbleography": A Checklist of In-print Books of Interest to Divers

by Bob Bridge

This is a short version of the "Bubbleography" list. It does not include out-of-print titles, and it is not annotated. Readers interested in receiving a longer version of this list are invited to contact Bob Bridge at 7740 S. Western Ave., Chicago, IL 60620-5867.

The compiler would like to express his gratitude to Helix, whose well-stocked underwater book department was made available to him. Helix sells many of the books listed here and publishes an Underwater Book List, which is available by calling 1-800-33-HELIX. Books are also available from the individual publishers.

Destinations

Blount, Steve. *Diving & Snorkeling Guide to the Bahamas: Nassau and New Providence Island.* Glen Cove, NY: PBC, 1985. 64 p. Paperback. ISBN 0-86636-030-1.

Bower, Stephen, and Bruce Nyden. *Diving and Snorkeling Guide to the Virgin Islands.* Glen Cove, NY: PBC, 1984. 96 p. Paperback. ISBN 0-86636-032-8.

Calhoun, Fred, and Chris Christensen. *Diver's Guide to Cape Ann.* Montclair, CA: NAUI, 1977. 36 p. Paperback. ISBN 0-916974-25-1.

Deacon, Christine. *Australia Down Under: Exploring Australia's Underwater World.* Sydney: Doubleday, 1986. ISBN 0-86824-241-1.

Dean, John. *Diver's Travel Guide to the Caribbean and the Bahamas.* San Francisco: Travel & Sports, 1987. 268 p. Paperback. ISBN 0-942427-00-9.

Farley, Michael, and Lauren Farley. *Baja California Diver's Guide.* Port Hueneme, CA: Marcor, 1984. 224 p. illus. Paperback. ISBN 0-923348-05-5.

Farley, Michael, and Lauren Farley. *Diver's Guide to Underwater Mexico.* Port Hueneme, CA: Marcor, 1986. 191 p. Paperback. ISBN 0-923348-06-3.

Fielding, Ann. *Underwater Guide to Hawai'i.* Honolulu: University of Hawaii, 1987. 144 p. ISBN 0-8248-1104-6.

Frame, Sandy, and Rick Baker. *Diver's Almanac Guide to the West Coast.* Costa Mesa, CA: HDL, 1988. 208 p. illus. Paperback. ISBN 0-937359-40-8.

Guettermann, Stephen F. *Diver's Almanac Guide to the Bahamas and Caribbean.* Costa Mesa, CA: HDL, 1986. 208 p. Paperback. ISBN 0-937359-17-3.

Halas, John. *Diving and Snorkeling Guide to the Florida Keys.* Glen Cove, NY: PBC, 1984. 96 p. Paperback. ISBN 0-86636-031-X.

Johnston, Greg. *Diving and Snorkeling Guide to Florida's East Coast.* Glen Cove, NY: PBC, 1987. 96 p. Paperback. ISBN 0-86636-077-8.

Lewbel, George S., and Larry R. Martin. *Diving and Snorkeling Guide to Bonaire and Curacao.* Glen Cove, NY: PBC, 1984. 96 p. Paperback. ISBN 0-86636-035-2.

Lewbel, George S., and Larry R. Martin. *Diving and Snorkeling Guide to Cozumel.* Glen Cove, NY: PBC, 1984. 96 p. Paperback. ISBN 0-86636-033-6.

Mount, Tom, and Patti Schaeffer. *Tom & Patti Mount's Dive & Travel Haiti.* Miami: Sea-Mount, 1989. 86 p. Paperback. ISBN 0-915539-03-9.

North, Wheeler. *Underwater California.* Berkeley: University of California, 1976. Paperback. ISBN 0-520-03039-7.

Pitcairn, Feodor, and Paul Humann. *Cayman; Underwater Paradise.* Bryn Athyn, PA: Reef Dwellers, 1979. Paperback. ISBN 0-9602530-0-9.

Roessler, Carl. *Diving and Snorkeling Guide to Grand Cayman Island.* Glen Cove, NY: PBC, 1984. 96 p. Paperback. ISBN 0-86636-034-4.

Rosenburg, Steve. *Diving and Snorkeling Guide to Northern California.* Glen Cove, NY: PBC, 1987. 96 p. illus. Paperback. ISBN 0-86636-075-1.

Scheckler, Dale. *Diving and Snorkeling Guide to Southern California.* Glen Cove, NY: PBC, 1987. 96 p. illus. Paperback. ISBN 0-86636-075-1.

Scheckler, Dale. *Diving and Snorkeling Guide to the Channel Islands.* Glen Cove, NY: PBC, 1987. 96 p. Paperback. ISBN 0-86636-076-X.

Shobe, John, and Kate Kelley. *Diver's Guide to Underwater America.* Durham, NC: Menasha Ridge, 1987. 288 p. ISBN 0-89732-059-X.

Stachowicz, Jim. *Diver's Guide to Florida and the Florida Keys.* Miami: Windward, 1976. 64 p. Paperback. ISBN 0-89317-007-0.

Thorne, Charles. *Diver's Guide to Maui.* Kihei, HI: Pacific Isle, 1985. Paperback. ISBN 0-9614775-0-4.

Trupp, Philip Z. *Diver's Almanac Guide to Florida and the Keys.* Costa Mesa, CA: HDL, 1988. 208 p. Paperback. ISBN 0-937359-36-X.

Wallin, Doug. *Diving and Snorkeling Guide to the Hawaiian Islands.* Glen Cove, NY: PBC, 1984. 96 p. Paperback. ISBN 0-86636-036-0.

Equipment

Cichy, Francis C., Hilbert Schenck, and John McAnniff. *Corrosion of Steel and Aluminum Scuba Tanks.* Narrangansett: University of Rhode Island Sea Grant Publications, 1978. 20 p. Paperback. ISBN 0-938412-05-1.

Cousteau, Jacques-Yves, and Alexis Sivirine. *Jacques Cousteau's Calypso.* New York: Abrams, 1983. 192 p. ISBN 0-8109-0788-7.

Farley, Michael B., and Charles Royer. *SCUBA Equipment Care and Maintenance.* Port Hueneme, CA: Marcor, 1980. 176 p. Paperback. ISBN 0-932248-01-2.

Gonsett, Bob. *Scuba Regulators; Air Pressure Reduction Valves for Diving.* Montclair, CA: NAUI, 1975. 65 p. Paperback. ISBN 0-916974-08-1.

Gonsett, Bob. *Scuba Tanks; High Pressure Cylinders for Diving*. Montclair, CA: NAUI, 1973. 46 p. Paperback. ISBN 0-916974-07-3.

Loyst, Ken, and Michael Steidley. *Diving with Dive Computers*. San Diego: Watersport, 1989. Paperback. ISBN 0-922769-08-7.

Miscavich, Ron. *Equipment Safety Program: Tanks*. Montclair, CA: NAUI, 1977. Paperback. ISBN 0-916974-27-8.

Taylor, Herb. *The Sport Diving Catalog: A Comprehensive Guide and Access Book*. New York: St. Martin, 1982. 320 p. Paperback. ISBN 0-312-75323-3.

Fiction

Clarke, Arthur C. *Dolphin Island; a Story of the People of the Sea*. New York, NY: Ace, 1987 (©1963). 192 p. Paperback. ISBN 0-441-15220-1.

Clarke, Arthur C. *The Deep Range*. New York: NAL, 1987 (©1958). 175 p. Paperback. ISBN 0-451-14753-7.

Fleming, Ian. *Thunderball*. New York: Berkley, 1985 (©1961). 240 p. Paperback. ISBN 0-425-08634-8.

Pohl, Frederick, and Jack Williamson. *Undersea City*. New York: Ballantine. Paperback. ISBN 0-345-30814-X.

Pohl, Frederick, and Jack Williamson. *Undersea Quest*. New York: Ballantine, 1982. Paperback. ISBN 0-345-30701-1.

Verne, Jules. *Twenty Thousand Leagues Under the Sea*. New York: Washington Square, 1966. 389 p. Paperback. ISBN 0-671-46557-0.

Flora and Fauna

The Audobon Society Field Guide to North American Fishes, Whales, and Dolphins. New York: Knopf, 1983. 848 p. ISBN 0-394-53405-0.

Bavendam, Fred. *Beneath Cold Waters: The Marine Life of New England*. Camden, MN: Down East, 1980. 128 p. Paperback. ISBN 0-89272-184-7.

Chaplin, Charles C.G. *Fishwatchers Guide to West Atlantic Coral Reefs*. Valley Forge, NY: Harrowood, 1989. 64 p. Paperback. ISBN 0-915180-09-X. Plastic. ISBN 0-915180-08-1.

Cousteau, Jacques-Yves, and Yves Paccalet. *Jacques Cousteau: Whales*. New York: Abrams, 1988. ISBN 0-8109-1813-7.

Cribb, James. *Marine Life of the Caribbean*. Toronto: Skyline, 1984. ISBN 0-19-540616-8.

Eddy, Samuel. *How to Know the Freshwater Fishes*. Dubuque, IA: W. C. Brown, 1978. 224 p. Spiralbound. ISBN 0-697-04750-4.

Ellis, Richard. *The Book of Sharks; A Complete Illustrated Natural History of the Sharks of the World.* San Diego, CA: Harcourt, Brace, 1983. 256 p. Paperback. ISBN 0-15-613552-3.

Ellis, Richard. *The Book of Whales.* New York: Knopf, 1985. Paperback. ISBN 0-394-73371-1.

Ellis, Richard. *Dolphins and Porpoises.* New York: Knopf, 1982. 270 p. ISBN 0-394-51800-4.

Greenberg, Idaz. *Field Guide to Marine Invertebrates.* Miami: Seahawk, 1980. Plastic. ISBN 0-913008-11-7.

Greenberg, Idaz. *Fishwatcher's Field Guide.* Miami: Seahawk, 1979. Plastic. ISBN 0-913008-10-9.

Greenberg, Idaz. *Great Barrier Reef Fishwatcher's Field Guide.* Miami: Seahawk, 1984. 1 card col. illus. Plastic. ISBN 0-913008-15-X.

Greenberg, Idaz. *Guide to Corals and Fishes.* Miami: Seahawk, 1977. 64 p. Paperback. ISBN 0-913008-08-7.

Greenberg, Idaz. *Hawaiian Fishwatcher's Field Guide.* Miami: Seahawk, 1983. Plastic. ISBN 0-913008-13-3.

Greenberg, Idaz. *Red Sea Fishwatcher's Field Guide.* Miami: Seahawk, 1982. Plastic. ISBN 0-913008-12-5.

Greenberg, Idaz. *Waterproof Guide to Corals and Fishes.* Miami: Seahawk, 1977. 64 p. Plastic. ISBN 0-913008-07-9.

Greenberg, Idaz, and Jerry Greenberg. *Sharks and Other Dangerous Sea Creatures.* Miami: Seahawk, 1981. 64 p. Paperback. ISBN 0-913008-09-5.

Greenberg, Jerry, and Idaz Greenberg. *Guide to Corals and Fishes of Florida, the Bahamas, the Caribbean.* Miami: Banyan, 64 p. Paperback.

Greenberg, Jerry, and Idaz Greenberg. *The Living Reef.* Miami: Seahawk, 1970. 128 p. Paperback. ISBN 0-913008-01-X.

Greenberg, Jerry, and Idaz Greenberg. *Waterproof Guide to Corals and Fishes of Florida, the Bahamas, the Caribbean.* Miami: Banyan, 64 p. Plastic.

Greenberg, Jerry. *Beneath Tropic Seas: The Fishes.* Miami: Seahawk, 1987. 64 p. Hardbound. ISBN 0-913008-18-4. Paperback. ISBN 0-913008-19-2.

Greenwood, P. H. *A History of Fishes.* New York: Halsted, 1975. 467 p. Paperback. ISBN 0-470-99012-0.

Halstead, Bruce W. *Dangerous Aquatic Animals of the World; A Color Guide.* Princeton, NJ: Darwin, 1988. 288 p. ISBN 87850-050-2.

Halstead, Bruce W. *Dangerous Marine Animals; That Bite, Sting, Shock, Are Non-Edible.* Cambridge, MD: Cornell Maritime, 1980. 220 p. ISBN 0-87033-264-3.

Humann, Paul. *Cayman Seascapes; Paul Humann's Portfolio of Marine Life.* Grand Cayman: Underwater Specialists, 1986. Clothbound. ISBN 0-936655-00-3. Paperback. ISBN 0-936655-01-1.

Iversen, Edwin S., and Renate H. Skinner. *How to Cope With Dangerous Sea Life.* Miami: Windward, 1977. 64 p. Paperback. ISBN 0-89317-017-8.

Jensen, Albert C. *Wildlife of the Oceans.* New York: Abrams, 1979. 231 p. ISBN 0-8109-1758-0.

Lilly, John Cunningham. *Communication Between Man and Dolphin.* New York: Crown, 1987. 288 p. Paperback. ISBN 0-517-56564-1.

McClane, A.J. *McClane's Field Guide to Freshwater Fishes of North America.* New York: Holt, Rinehart, 1978. 212 p. Paperback. ISBN 0-03-021116-6.

McClane, A. J. *McClane's Field Guide to Saltwater Fishes of North America.* New York: Holt, Rinehart, 1978. 283 p. Paperback. ISBN 0-03-021121-2.

McIntyre, Joan. *The Delicate Art of Whale Watching.* San Francisco: Sierra Club, 1982. 160 p. ISBN 0-87156-323-1.

McPeak, Ronald H., Dale A. Glunts, and Carole R. Shaw. *The Amber Forest; Beauty and Biology of California's Submarine Forests.* San Diego: Watersport, 1988. Clothbound. ISBN 0-922769-00-X. Paperback. ISBN 0-922769-00-1.

Pitcairn, Feodor, and Kirstin Pitcairn. *Hidden Seascapes.* Boston: Little, Brown, 1984. ISBN 0-8212-1577-9.

Randall, John E. *Caribbean Reef Fishes.* Neptune City, NJ: TFH, 1983. 352 p. ISBN 0-87666-498-2.

Randall, John E. *The Underwater Guide to Hawaiian Reef Fishes.* Newton Square, PA: Harrowood, 1980. Plastic. ISBN 0-915180-02-2.

Roessler, Carl. *Coral Kingdoms.* New York: Abrams, 1986. 244 p. ISBN 0-8109-0774-7.

Roessler, Carl. *The Underwater Wilderness; Life Around the Great Reefs.* New York: Chanticleer, 1977. 319 p. ISBN 0-918810-00-0.

Scheffer, Victor B. *A Natural History of Marine Mammals.* New York: Scribner's, 1976. 170 p. Paperback. ISBN 0-684-16952-5.

Scheffer, Victor B. *The Year of the Whale.* New York: Scribner's, 1969. 213 p. Paperback. ISBN 0-684-71886-3.

Shoemaker, Hurst, and Herbert S. Zim. *Fishes.* New York: Western, 1987 (©1955). 160 p. Paperback. ISBN 0-307-24059-2.

Snyderman, Marty. *California Marine Life.* Port Hueneme, CA: Marcor, 1987. 288 p. Paperback. ISBN 0-932248-07-1.

Spotte, Stephen. *Marine Aquarium Keeping; The Science, Animals, and Art*. New York: Wiley, 1973. 171 p. Clothbound. ISBN 0-471-81759-7. Paperback. ISBN 0-471-82591-3.

Stamm, Douglas R. *Underwater; The Northern Lakes*. Madison: University of Wisconsin, 1977. 116 p. Paperback. ISBN 0-299-07264-9.

Stokes, F. Joseph. *Diver's and Snorkeler's Guide to the Fishes and Sea Life of the Caribbean, Florida, Bahamas, and Bermuda*. Philadelphia: Academy of Natural Sciences, 1988 (©1984). 160 p. ISBN 0-910006-46-6.

Zeiller, Warren. *Tropical Marine Fishes of Southern Florida and the Bahama Islands*. Cranbury, NJ: Fairleigh Dickinson, 1975. 127 p. ISBN 0-8386-7914-5.

For Younger Readers

Briggs, Carole S. *Skin Diving Is for Me*. Minneapolis: Lerner, 1981. ISBN 0-8225-1132-0.

Briggs, Carole S. *Sport Diving*. Minneapolis: Lerner, 1982. ISBN 0-8225-0503-7.

Carrick, Carol. *Dark and Full of Secrets*. New York: Clarion, 1984. 32 p. Hardbound. ISBN 0-89919-271-8. Paperback. ISBN 0-317-56448-X.

Dive to the Coral Reefs. New York: Crown, 1986. ISBN 0-517-56311-8.

Ferrier, Lucy. *Diving the Great Barrier Reef*. Mahwah, NJ: Troll, 1976. 32 p. Hardbound. ISBN 0-89375-005-0. Paperback. ISBN 0-89375-021-2.

Fine, John Christopher. *Sunken Ships and Treasure*. New York: Macmillan, 1986. ISBN 0-689-31280-6.

Hackwell, John. *Diving to the Past; Recovering Ancient Wrecks*. New York: Macmillan, 1988. 64 p. ISBN 0-684-18918-6.

Halstead, Bruce W., and Bonnie L. Landa. *Tropical Fish*. New York: Western, 1975. 160 p. Paperback. ISBN 0-307-24361-3.

Hauser, Hilary. *Call to Adventure*. Longmont, CA: Bookmakers Guild, 1987. 240 p. Paperback. ISBN 0-917665-18-X.

Jennett, Judith. *Snorkel Diving for Young People*. Montclair, CA: NAUI, 1979. 84 p. Paperback. ISBN 0-916974-24-3.

Jensen, Antony, and Stephen Bolt. *Underwater Dive*. Milwaukee: Stevens, 1989. 32 p. ISBN 1-55532-918-7.

Lampton, Christopher F. *Undersea Archaeology*. New York: Watts, 1988. 96 p. ISBN 0-531-10492-3.

McGovern, Ann. *Night Dive.* New York: Macmillan, 1984. 64 p. ISBN 0-02-765710-8.

McGovern, Ann. *Shark Lady: True Adventures of Eugenie Clark.* New York: Scholastic, 1987 (©1979). 96 p. Paperback. ISBN 0-590-41178-0.

McGovern, Ann. *Sharks.* New York: Scholastic, 1977. 48 p. Paperback. ISBN 0-590-10234-6.

Morris, Dean. *Underwater Life.* Milwaukee: Raintree, 1987. 48 p. ISBN 0-8172-3214-1.

Roessler, Carl. *Mastering Underwater Photography.* New York: Morrow, 1984. 112 p. Clothbound. ISBN 0-688-03881-6. Paperback. ISBN 0-688-03882-4.

Sullivan, George. *Treasure Hunt: The Sixteen-Year Search for the Lost Treasure Ship Atocha.* New York: Holt, 1987. 128 p. ISBN 0-8050-0569-2.

History and Personal Narratives

Bascom, Willard. The Crest of the Wave: Adventures in Oceanography. New York: Harper & Row, 1988. 320 p. ISBN 0-06-015927-8.

Cousteau, Jacque-Yves, and Frederic Dumas. *The Silent World.* New York: N. Lyons, 1987 (©1965). 288 p. Paperback. ISBN 0-941130-73-8.

Earle, Sylvia, and Al Giddings. *Exploring the Deep Frontier: The Adventure of Man in the Sea.* Washington: National Geographic, 1980. 300 p. ISBN 0-87044-343-7.

Edwards, Hugh. *Sharks and Shipwrecks.* New York: Times Books, 1975. 127 p. ISBN 0-8129-0559-8.

Ellsberg, Edward. *Men Under the Sea.* Westport, CT: Greenwood, 1981 (©1939). 365 p. ISBN 0-313-23030-7.

Gordon, Bernard L. *Man and the Sea; Classic Accounts of Marine Explorations.* Chestnut Hill, MA: Book & Tackle, 1980. 497 p. Paperback. ISBN 0-910258-10-4.

Hugill, Stan. *Shanties from the Seven Seas.* New York: Routledge, Chapman, 1980 (©1961). 416 p. Hardbound. ISBN 0-7100-1573-9. Paperback. ISBN 0-7100-0412-4.

McKenney, Jack. *Sharks, Wrecks, and Movie Stars; The Adventures of an Underwater Photographer.* Durham, NC: Menasha Ridge, 1989. Paperback. ISBN 0-89732-082-4.

Madsen, Axel. *Cousteau; An Unauthorized Biography.* New York: Beaufort, 1986. 288 p. ISBN 0-2253-0386-9.

Instruction and Leadership

Boehler, Ted, Jeanne B. Sleeper, and John Hardy. *The NAUI Professional Resource Organizer.* Colton, CA: NAUI, 1977. 448 p. Looseleaf. ISBN 0-916974-26-X.

Graver, Dennis. *Open Water Instuctor Guide.* Montclair, CA: NAUI, 1987. 284 p. Loose-leaf. ISBN 0-916974-33-2.

Medical Stuff

Dueker, Christopher W. *Scuba Diving in Safety and Health.* Menlo Pk, CA: Diving Safety Digest, 1985. 224 p. Paperback. ISBN 0-9614638-0-5.

Dueker, Christopher W. *Scuba Diving Safety.* Mountain View, CA: Anderson World, 1978. 132 p. Paperback. ISBN 0-89037-135-0.

Eastman, Peter. F. *Advanced First Aid Afloat.* Centreville, MD: Cornell Maritime, 1987. 214 p. Paperback. ISBN 0-87033-169-8.

Emergency Care and Transportation of the Sick and Injured. Committee on Allied Health, American Academy of Orthopaedic Surgeons. Chicago: The Academy, 1986. 638 p. Paperback. ISBN 0-89203-012-7.

Fisher, Alexander A. *Atlas of Aquatic Dermatology.* New York: Grune & Stratton, 1978. 120 p. ISBN 0-8089-1139-2.

Lanoue, F. *Drownproofing; A New Technique for Water Safety.* New York: Prentice-Hall, 1978. 55 p. Paperback.

Lifesaving, Rescue, and Water Safety. Garden City, NY: Doubleday, 1974. 240 p. Paperback. ISBN 0-385-06349-0.

Lippmann, John, and Stan Blugg. *The DAN Emergency Handbook.* Glen Cove, NY: PBC, 1985. 54 p. Plastic. ISBN 0-9590306-1-1.

Mebane, G. Yancey, and Arthur P. Dick. *DAN Underwater Diving Accident Manual.* Durham, NC: Duke University, 1982. 24 p. Paperback.

Strauss, Richard H., ed. *Diving Medicine.* Orlando: Grune & Stratton, 1976. 432 p. ISBN 0-8089-0699-2.

The Oceans (and Other Wet Places)

Bascom, Willard. *Waves and Beaches; The Dynamics of the Ocean Surface.* New York: Doubleday, 1980. Paperback. ISBN 0-385-14844-5.

Carson, Rachel. *The Sea Around Us.* New York: Oxford, 1961. 221 p. Clothbound. ISBN 0-19-500500-7.·New York: NAL, 1954. 221 p. Paperback. ISBN 0-451-62483-1.

Cousteau, Jacques-Yves, and Mose Richards. *Jacques Cousteau's Amazon Journey*. New York: Abrams, 1984. 236 p. ISBN 0-8109-1813-7.

Cousteau, Jacques-Yves. *Jacques Coustea: The Ocean World*. New York: Abrams, 1985 (©1979). 446 p. ISBN 0-8109-8068-1.

Fine, John Christopher. *Exploring the Sea*. Medford, NJ: Plexus, 1982. 160 p. ISBN 0-937548-03-0.

Greenberg, Jerry, and Idaz Greenberg. *The Coral Reef*. Miami: Banyan, 1976. 64 p. Paperback. ISBN 0-686-75254-6.

Ingmanson, Dale E., and William J. Wallace. *Oceanology; An Introduction*. Belmont, CA: Wadsworth, 1989. illus. ISBN 0-534-09552-6.

Parker, Henry S. *Exploring the Oceans; an Introduction for the Traveler and Amateur Naturalist*. Englewood Cliffs, NJ: Prentice-Hall, 1986. 386 p. Clothbound. ISBN 0-13-297714-1. Paperback. ISBN 0-13-297706-0.

Stowe, Keith. *Essentials of Ocean Science*. New York: Wiley, 1987. 353 p. Clothbound. ISBN 0-471-80973-X. Paperback. ISBN 0-471-63547-2.

Thurman, Harold V. *Introductory Oceanography*. Columbus, OH: C. Merrill, 1975. 544 p. ISBN 0-675-20855-6.

Reference Books

Anderson, Frank J. *Submarines, Diving, and the Underwater World; A Bibliography*. Hamden, CT: Archon, 1975. 238 p. ISBN 0-208-01508-6.

Calhoun, Fred. *Physics for Divers*. Colton, CA: NAUI, 1978. 94 p. Paperback. ISBN 0-916974-28-6.

Collins, Stephen W., II. *Down to the Sea with Books*. Grand Terrace, CA: NAUI, 1973. 41 p. Paperback. ISBN 0-916974-04-9.

Corbett, S. E. *Diver's Reference Dictionary*. San Pedro, CA: Best Publishing, 1986. ISBN 0-941332-03-9.

Diving with Undercurrent. Vol. II. New York: Atcom, 1987. 108 p. Paperback. ISBN 0-915260-37-9.

The Underwater Handbook; A Guide to Physiology and Performance for the Engineer. New York: Plenum, 1976. 912 p. ISBN 0-306-3084-6.

Skills and Specialties

Cayford, John E., and Ronald E. Scott. *Underwater Logging*. Centreville, MD: Cornell Maritime, 1964. 92 p. Paperback. ISBN 0-87033-128-0.

Church, Jim, and Cathy Church. *Beginning Underwater Photography.* Gilroy, CA: J. & C. Church, 1987. 96 p. Paperback. ISBN 0-9616093-1-1.

Church, Jim, and Cathy Church. *The Nikonos Handbook.* Gilroy, CA: J. & C. Church, 1986. 167 p. ISBN 0-9616093-0-3.

Eastman, Norris, and Gerald Landrum. *Underwater Communication; Hand Signals for Scuba Diving.* Pennington, NJ: Princeton Book Company, 1984. 48 p. Paperback. ISBN 0-916622-30-4.

Fine, John Christopher. *Exploring Underwater Photography.* Medford, NJ: Plexus, 1986. 174 p. ISBN 0-937548-07-3.

Giguere, Jon-Paul. *Make Money in Diving.* Milwaukee: Rowe, 1981. Paperback. ISBN 0-933832-07-9.

Hall, Howard. *Howard Hall's Guide to Successful Underwater Photography.* Port Hueneme, CA: Marcor, 1982. 189 p. Paperback. ISBN 0-932248-03-9.

Lewbel, George S. *The Decompression Workbook; A Simplified Guide to Understanding Decompression Problems.* New York: Pisces, 1984. Paperback. ISBN 0-86636-023-9.

Maloney, E. S. *Chapman; Piloting, Seamanship, and Small-Boat Handling.* New York: Morrow, 1987. 656 p. ISBN 0-688-07246-1.

Meuninck, Jim. *Diving Opportunities for Fun and Profit; Over 100 Ways to Make Money Diving.* Edwardsburg, MI: Media Methods, 1986. 216 p. Paperback. ISBN 0-939865-00-9.

Mount, Tom, and Patti Schaeffer. *The Complete Guide to Underwater Modeling.* Miami: Sea-Mount, 1989. 80 p. Paperback. ISBN 0-915539-00-4.

Seaborn, Charles. *Underwater Photography.* New York: Amphoto, 1988. 143 p. Clothbound. ISBN 0-8174-6336-6. Paperback. ISBN 0-8174-6336-4.

Snyder, Paul, and Arthur Snyder. *Knots and Lines Illustrated.* Tuckahoe, NY: J. DeGraff, 1967. 104 p. ISBN 0-8286-0046-5.

Sohn, William. *Underwater Photographer's Market.* Milwaukee: Rowe, 1982. Paperback. ISBN 0-933832-17-6.

Somers, Lee H. *Cold Weather and Under-Ice Scuba Diving.* Montclair, CA: NAUI, 1974. 37 p. Paperback. ISBN 0-916974-03-0.

Tackett, Eric. *Underwater Crime Scene Investigation.* Fountain Vly, CA: Lasertech, 1987. 144 p. Paperback. ISBN 0-318-22519-0.

Tucker, Wayne C. *Diver's Handbook of Underwater Calculations.* Centreville, MD: Cornell Maritime, 1980. 191 p. Paperback. ISBN 0-87033-254-5.

Underwater Prospecting Techniques; The Gold Diver's Handbook. San Bruno, CA: Merlin Engine Works, 1983. Paperback. ISBN 0-686-38066-5.

Textbooks and Handbooks

Ascher, Scott M., and William L. Shadburne. *Scuba Handbook for Humans.* Dubuque, IA: Kendall/Hunt, 1978. 95 p. Paperback. ISBN 0-8403-1126-5.

The British Sub-Aqua Club Diving Manual. Toronto: Scribner's, 1979 (1977). 571 p. Paperback.

Culliney, John L., and Edward S. Crockett. *Exploring Underwater; the Sierra Club Guide to Scuba and Snorkeling.* San Francisco: Sierra, 1980. 352 p. Paperback. ISBN 0-87156-270-7.

Fead, Lou. *Easy Diver.* Crestline, CA: Deepstar, 1977. 177 p. Paperback. ISBN 0-918888-02-6.

Lee, Owen. *The Skin Diver's Bible.* New York: Doubleday, 1986. 192 p. Paperback. ISBN 0-385-13543-2.

Mount, Tom, and Akira J. Ikehara. *The New Pratical Diving; A Complete Manual for Compressed Air Divers.* Miami: University of Miami, 1980. 200 p. Paperback. ISBN 0-87024-300-4.

The New Science of Skin and Scuba Diving. Piscataway, NJ: New Century, 1985. 320 p. Paperback. ISBN 0-8329-0399-X.

Pazos, Baltasar. *Tecnicas de buceo deportivo.* Mexico, DF: Editorial Diana, 1978. 212 p. Paperback.

Reseck, John, Jr. *Scuba Safe and Simple.* Englewood Cliffs, NJ: Prentice-Hall, 1975. 240 p. Paperback. ISBN 0-13-796680-6.

Sport diver manual. Englewood, CO: Jeppesen Sanderson, 1984. 290 p. Paperback. ISBN 0-88487-104-5.

U. S. Navy diving manual; Air Diving. Vol. 1. U. S. Navy. Washington: GPO, 1985. 357 p. ISBN 0-318-19917-3.

Treasure Hunting and Underwater Archaelogy

Bass, George F. *Ships and Shipwrecks of the Americas; A History Based on Underwater Archaeology.* New York: Thames & Hudson, 1988. ISBN 0-500-05049-X.

Boyer, Dwight. *Ghost Ships of the Great Lakes.* New York: Dodd, Mead, 1984. 320 p. Paperback. ISBN 0-396-08346-3.

Burgess, Robert F. *Sunken Treasure: Six Who Found Fortunes.* New York: Dodd, Mead, 1988. 224 p. ISBN 0-396-08848-1.

Burgess, Robert F., and Carl J. Clausen. *Florida's Golden Galleons.* Port Salerno: Florida Classics Library, 1982. 195 p. Paperback. ISBN 0-912451-07-6.

Daley, Robert. *Treasure*. New York: Pocket Books, 1986 (©1977). Paperback. ISBN 0-671-61895-4.

Frederick, James. *Diver's Guide to River Wrecks*. Milwaukee: Rowe, 1982. Paperback. ISBN 0-933832-17-6.

Geyer, Dick. *Wreck Diving: A Guide for Sport Divers*. Piscataway, NJ: New Century, 1982. 86 p. Paperback. ISBN 0-8329-0131-8.

Giguere, Jon-Paul. *Salvage Laws for Weekend Divers*. Milwaukee: Rowe, 1981. Paperback. ISBN 0-933832-09-5.

Greene, Vaughn. *Diving for Gold*. Bend, OR: Maverick, 1985. 120 p. Paperback. ISBN 0-89288-040-6.

MacInnis, Joe. *The Breadalbane Adventure*. Montreal: Optimum, 1982. ISBN 0-8890-159-3.

Marx, Robert F. *Shipwrecks in Florida Waters: A Billion-Dollar Graveyard*. Chuluota, FL: Mickler, 1986 (©1978). 147 p. Paperback. ISBN 0-913122-55-6.

Marx, Robert F. *Shipwrecks in the Americas*. New York: Dover, 1987. 544 p. Paperback. ISBN 0-486-25514-X.

Muckelroy, Keith. *Maritime Archaeology*. New York: Cambridge University Press, 1979. 270 p. Clothbound. ISBN 0-521-22079-3. Paperback. ISBN 0-521-29384-0.

Potter, John S., Jr. *The Treasure Diver's Guide*. Port Salerno, FL: Florida Classics, 1988 (©1972). 590 p. Paperback. ISBN 0-912451-22-X.

Rowe, Alan R. *Relics, Water, and the Kitchen Sink: A Diver's Handbook to Underwater Archaeology*. Norwalk, CT: Sea Sports, 1988. 56 p. Paperback. ISBN 0-9616399-1-1.

Rowe, Alan. *Dive into Yesterday; Underwater History in Your Own Backyard*. Milwaukee: Rowe, 1980. Paperback. ISBN 0-933832-02-8.

Throckmorton, Peter. *The Sea Remembers; Shipwrecks and Archaeology*. New York: Weidenfield, 1987. 240 p. ISBN 1-55584-093-0.

Undersea Treasures. Washington: National Geographic, 1974. 198 p. ISBN 0-87044-147-7.

White, James S. *Diving for Northwest Relics*. Portland, OR: Binford-Metropolitan, 1979. Clothbound. ISBN 0-8323-0335-6. Paperback. ISBN 0-8323-0336-4.

Appendix B

Emergency Procedures

B.1 Diving Accident Network

DAN

919-684-8111

Help with the treatment of scuba diving injuries—primarily arterial gas embolisms and decompression sickness—is available through the Diving Accident Network (DAN) by dialing (919) 684-8111. DAN consists of seven regional recompression facilities with physicians trained in diving medicine and is administered by Duke University in North Carolina. There are at least 4 million divers in the United States.

B.2 Cardiopulmonary Resuscitation

5:1 ratio = chest compressions: 1 lung inflation
Compression rate = 60 per min.
Lung inflations = interposed after each 5 compressions with no pause in compressions

A-B-C
STEPS OF CPR

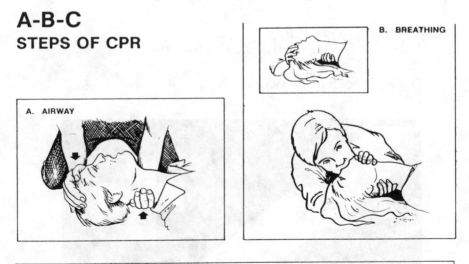

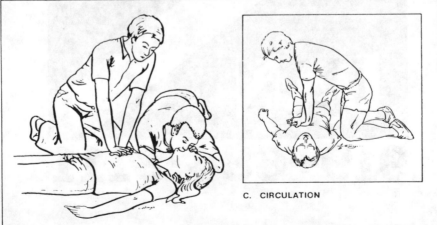

If no pulse is present, cardiac massage should be started after artificial respiration has begun to restore breathing. (© Brent Q. Hafen and Keith J. Karren, *First Aid and Emergency Care Workbook* [2nd ed.]. Denver: Morton Publishing Co., p. 72.)

Index

JUN 4 1992